THE MEDIUM TERM
Models of the British Economy

Also published on behalf of the Social
Science Research Council and the
National Institute of Economic and Social
Research:

An Incomes Policy for Britain,
edited by Frank Blackaby

The Medium Term
Models of the British Economy

Edited by

G. D. N. WORSWICK

and

F. T. BLACKABY

for

THE NATIONAL INSTITUTE OF ECONOMIC
AND SOCIAL RESEARCH

and

THE SOCIAL SCIENCE RESEARCH COUNCIL

Distributed in the United States by
CRANE, RUSSAK & COMPANY, INC.
347 Madison Avenue
New York, New York 10017

Heinemann Educational Books Ltd

LONDON EDINBURGH MELBOURNE TORONTO
AUCKLAND JOHANNESBURG SINGAPORE
IBADAN NAIROBI HONG KONG NEW DELHI

ISBN 0 435 84960 3

© SSRC/NIESR 1974
First published 1974

Published by Heinemann Educational Books Ltd
48 Charles Street, London W1X 8AH
Printed in Great Britain by
Butler & Tanner Ltd
Frome and London

Foreword

The Conference, of which this book is a report, was held on 10 and 11 April, 1973, in London; its origins are described in the introduction. The agenda was drawn up in consultation with contributors from the Treasury, the Department of Applied Economics at Cambridge, and the National Economic Development Office. The same group helped us in making a list of officials, experts from both sides of industry and academics who were known to be interested. The conference, like that on incomes policy which we held in January 1972, received sponsorship as well as financial assistance from the Social Science Research Council. We were grateful too to have once more the facilities of the Royal Society.

This book consists essentially of the papers prepared for this Conference, with an account of the discussion which took place. We have given the protagonists a fair amount of latitude in preparing their papers for publication. In some cases this has simply amounted to the revision at leisure of what was originally written rather hurriedly. We are grateful to them for being prepared to put forward their ideas and submit to cross-examination. We are grateful too to Professor Sir Bryan Hopkin and Mr. C. T. Saunders, both previous Directors of the National Institute, who have seen much of the development of medium term modelling in this country, for opening the discussion on the first day and taking the chair at the two sessions on the second day.

We thank Mrs. Jones, Miss Meadows, Mr. Mottershead, and Mrs. McInulty, all of the National Institute, for help in preparing the Conference.

The three models which are presented in Part I of the book, and discussed in Part II, are referred to, for convenience, as the Treasury model, the 'Stone' model (the Cambridge Economic Growth Project model) and the 'Par' model (the Cambridge Economic Policy Group model).

J. Mitchell, *Secretary,*
Social Science Research Council

G. D. N. Worswick, *Director,*
National Institute of Economic and
Social Research

March, 1974

v

Contents

PART III INDUSTRY MODELS

Notes on Contributors

T. S. Barker is a Research Officer at the Department of Applied Economics, University of Cambridge.

M. J. Bramson is an Operational Research Adviser at the National Economic Development Office.

A. Budd is a Senior Economic Adviser at H.M. Treasury

T. F. Cripps is a Research Officer at the Department of Applied Economics, University of Cambridge.

W. A. H. Godley is Director of the Department of Applied Economics, University of Cambridge.

S. F. Hampson is an Economist at the National Economic Development Office.

J. R. S. Homan is an Assistant Industrial Director at the National Economic Development Office.

F. W. Hutber is a Chief Statistician at the Department of Trade and Industry.

A. A. McLean is an Economic Adviser at H.M. Treasury.

Mrs. Caroline Miles is a Consultant to the National Economic Development Office.

P. Mottershead is a Research Officer at the National Institute of Economic and Social Research.

C. T. Taylor is Assistant Director of the Department of Applied Economics, University of Cambridge.

V. H. Woodward is a Research Officer at the Department of Applied Economics, University of Cambridge.

Editors:

G. D. N. Worswick is Director of the National Institute of Economic and Social Research.

F. T. Blackaby is Deputy Director of the National Institute of Economic and Social Research.

Introduction

Short-term forecasts of the course of the British economy—for twelve to eighteen months ahead—are by now a well-established feature of the economic policy system. They have been prepared both within and outside the Government for some thirty years now. The regular publication of some details of the official forecast, however, is of much more recent origin. The post-war Labour Government published targets in the first two of the annual Economic Surveys begun in 1947. In the second of these it also published a post mortem showing how far the outcome coincided with the original targets. When the differences were thrown back across the floor of the House of Commons by Opposition spokesmen they hurt, and publication of both targets and appraisals was dropped. It was nearly twenty years before another Labour Chancellor took the risk of publishing a few key aggregates to indicate the impact which he believed his budget decisions would have upon the economy as a whole. This time the practice stuck.

Official medium-term projections—for up to five years ahead—have a much shorter history; indeed they can hardly be said to be established as yet. There was a temporary excursus into this field at the time of the Marshall Plan. All potential beneficiaries had to submit to O.E.E.C., as it then was, economic programmes or plans to show how they proposed to achieve balance in their international accounts by 1952. In the event Britain worked clear of Marshall Plan obligations by 1950, and no more was heard of medium-term projections for a decade.

Official interest in medium-term programmes re-emerged in the late 1950s, with the coming together of a number of different lines of thought. First of all, many people were becoming increasingly concerned with Britain's slow rate of growth, and consequently critical of 'stop-go' policies which they considered to be at least partly responsible for it. This was the time when international league tables of growth-rates came into vogue, and when it was becoming less and less plausible to explain the high French and German figures as simply results of delayed post-war reconstruction. The French success in particular drew people's attention to their form of 'indicative planning'; the French, it was said, had found the magic formula for dynamizing the economy without the need for a vast apparatus of control. The trend of ideas at the time is shown by two conferences held in the early sixties. One

1

was the Federation of British Industries' conference on 'The Next Five Years' in November 1960. One of the groups at this Conference, which discussed Economic Growth in Britain, was critical of the rapid switches in Government policy for the lack of confidence they created, and suggested that 'Government and industry might see if it would be possible to agree on an assessment of expectations and intentions to be placed before the country as a framework for economic effort during the next five years'.[1] The second conference was specifically on French planning, in Spring 1961; it was organized by N.I.E.S.R. in association with the Institut de Science Economique Appliquée. The discussion was summed up by Sir Robert Shone of the Iron and Steel Board whose planning methods had been commended at the F.B.I. Conference: 'The French procedure of stating what the growth objective is, and what are the consequences for the various sectors of the economy, provides an opportunity for really confronting industrialists, trade unionists, politicians and many other interests with the adjustments, often difficult, which have to be faced if the objectives are to be secured.'[2] And—in surveying the forces which brought the idea of planning to the fore—there is also the fact that the then Prime Minister had written enthusiastically about indicative planning in a book published as long ago as 1939. 'The next step forward . . . in our social thinking is to move from "piecemeal planning" to national planning—from the consideration of each industry or service separately to a consideration of them all collectively.' The 'keystone of the structure of a planned economy' would be a National Economic Council consisting of representatives of the Government, Unions, employers and economic experts under the Chairmanship of the Minister of Economics.[3]

Another line of thought came from within the government machine itself, with a desire to bring about a more effective system of control over public expenditure. Programmes were started which implicitly contained commitments for many years ahead, but this could be neither appreciated nor subjected to control if the budget looked only twelve months ahead. The Plowden Committee[4] recommended longer looks, which have in the event become surveys of public expenditure up to five years ahead, and recommended also that public expenditure programmes should be scrutinized in the context of the expected developments of the economy as a whole.

[1] *The Next Five Years*, London, F.B.I., 1960, p 18.
[2] 'Economic Planning in France', P.E.P., *Planning*, 1961, **XXVII**, 454, pp. 233–4.
[3] H. Macmillan, *The Middle Way*, London, Macmillan, 1939, p. 176.
[4] *The control of public expenditure*, Cmnd. 1432, H.M.S.O., 1961, para. 12

These were the forces that generated the intense activity, both official and unofficial, in the preparation of medium-term projections, programmes or plans in the first half of the 1960s.

The Department of Applied Economics at Cambridge was first off the mark. In 1960 Professor Richard Stone began the project 'A Programme for Growth', a computable model of the British economy specifically intended to identify the obstacles in the way of faster growth. (The successor to these early models is one of the three considered at the Conference reported here.) The first semi-official exercise was the 1963 publication of the National Economic Development Council, *Growth in the United Kingdom Economy to 1966*,[1] a series of projections of production possibilities, investment requirements and so forth. Two years later came the National Plan[2] containing figures up to 1970 implying an average growth rate of output for 1964 to 1970 of 3·8 per cent per year. And, at about the same time as the National Plan, the National Institute presented rather longer-term projections for the economy in The British Economy in 1975.[3]

All this work, both official and academic, was inspired by the search for faster growth and all the studies contained fairly detailed projections of output, investment, consumption, exports and imports. There was ambiguity concerning the figures: were they forecasts or targets, hopes or intentions? But it is not true that all the authors shared the belief that faster growth would follow merely from putting on paper larger numbers for the future than the average of the recent past. The N.E.D.C. projections were supplemented by another paper, *Conditions Favourable to Faster Growth*,[4] which examined the range of alternative policies. The National Plan had its check list for action. But if the authors of the plans and programmes were less naive than they were later made out to be, they did not succeed in establishing the case for giving priority to economic growth, and their efforts were swamped by the deflationary policies pursued in the attempt to correct the balance of payments while retaining a fixed exchange rate.

The planning period, to all intents and purposes, came to an end at the time of the July deflationary measures of 1966—only eight months after the National Plan had passed through the House of Commons without a division. After the July measures nothing remotely approaching the 25 per cent target was regarded as feasible any longer. As

---

[1] *Growth of the United Kingdom Economy to 1966*, N.E.D.C., H.M.S.O., 1963.
[2] *The National Plan*, Cmnd. 2764, H.M.S.O., 1965.
[3] *The British Economy in 1975*, W. Beckerman and associates, C.U.P., 1965.
[4] *Conditions Favourable to Faster Growth*, N.E.D.C., H.M.S.O., 1963.

Mr. George Brown told the House of Commons: 'It means that the rate of growth we intended to get, and were set to get, and on the basis of which we predicted all other things for 1970, is no longer available.'[1]

Official work on medium projections virtually went underground. The Department of Economic Affairs did publish at the end of 1969 *The Task Ahead*,[2] which began with the words 'This is a planning document not a plan', and which was a lengthy essay, with a fair amount of quantitative detail, about the problems and prospects of the economy in the next few years, with some figures more fully worked out on alternative assumptions about the average rate of growth. Not long after its publication the Department of Economic Affairs itself was wound up. Official medium-term analysis continued, but was split between the Treasury and the then Ministry of Technology; and when the Ministry of Technology disappeared it was taken over entirely by the Treasury.

The Report of the Plowden Committee had led to the establishment of the Public Expenditure Survey, conducted annually for the whole of Government expenditure and including estimates for each of the next five years. The results of these Surveys are now embodied in an annual series of White Papers. The first of these, published in December 1969, referred to the range of national output increases from just under 3 per cent to about 4 per cent envisaged in *The Task Ahead* and adopted the lower of these figures as the basis of the expenditure programme. But from then on nothing was seen in public of any medium-term work until, as a result of pressure from the Select Committee on Expenditure, the Public Expenditure White Paper published in 1972 included a table —discussed elsewhere in this volume—to show that the expected trend of expenditure from 1971 to 1977 was compatible both with an average growth-rate between those years of $3\frac{1}{2}$ per cent, and also one of 5 per cent.[3]

By this time the function of official medium-term assessments had clearly reverted to the limited role suggested by the Plowden Committee: 'regular surveys should be made of public expenditure as a whole over a period of years in relation to prospective resources.' Their purpose was to answer such questions as—do the separate programmes of expenditure add up to an intolerable burden of taxation? Do they square with the expected movements of investment and the balance of payments?

[1] House of Commons Debates, 27 July 1966.
[2] *The Task Ahead—Economic Assessment to 1972*, Department of Economic Affairs, H.M.S.O., 1969.
[3] *Public expenditure to 1976–77*, Cmnd. 5178, H.M.S.O., 1972.

The Institute's interest in medium-term forecasting in recent years has had rather different origins. Many of those institutions and companies who are customers for short-term economic forecasts are also concerned to have some kind of medium-term assessment as well. Further, the time-horizon of 12 to 18 months has become increasingly confining, in that a good deal of research into the behaviour of the British economy, of others as well as ourselves, suggests that many lags may be longer than was previously supposed. Perhaps the best example of this is the long lag before the effects of devaluation had worked themselves out. In the absence of official projections or programmes we have, since 1967, usually accompanied our annual Review with a forward look of our own for at least three years ahead. With limited resources this has been inevitably somewhat of a back-of-envelope exercise, and when for the annual Review of 1972 we were offered the latest version of the Stone model the idea seemed attractive of trying to place our short-term forecasts in the context of the Stone medium-term assessment. In practice this proved much more difficult than we had anticipated. It was not simply that some of the empirical relationships appeared to differ but that a variety of conceptual differences emerged. We noticed also that some of the projections, notably for the balance of payments, appeared to differ substantially from those coming out of another medium-term model being developed by the Cambridge Economic Policy Group under the direction of Mr. Wynne Godley.

This was the origin of the conference held in April 1973 which is reported in this volume. We were sure that it would help us, and we thought it likely that it would help others as well, if we could bring together the three principal sets of model builders and ask them to expound their models, explaining the purposes for which they were designed, the economic characteristics of the model, and the methods used for estimating its coefficients. The first morning of the conference was devoted to this exposition and to detailed questioning. The plan for the afternoon session was to bring about a confrontation at different levels so that one could discover whether a difference in a particular projection for, say, 1975 arose simply because of a difference of the coefficients in essentially similar equations, or because the item being projected rested on quite different assumptions of how the rest of the economy was behaving or how a particular policy variable such as the rate of exchange, or the level of taxation, had been adjusted. We could hardly expect to resolve all differences in one afternoon but we ourselves learnt a great deal and used the opportunity of the conference and subsequent correspondence to develop the table originally prepared by Mr. Mottershead, which compared the different treatment of variables in the three models and is printed here on pages 126–9.

We also set ourselves two other objectives at the conference. The first was to discover more about the current successor to the 1963 N.E.D.C. study of the Growth of the Economy and the 1965 National Plan—the N.E.D.C. medium-term exercise which was to be published in the autumn of 1973.[1] We wanted to know what use it made of medium-term models, and how it differed from previous exercises. The second was to find out something more about some of the industry models which existed, to see what relationships they had to macro-models, and to what extent their general techniques were the same.

In view of the range of models and plans being developed in the countries of Western and Eastern Europe the limitation of our agenda to three macro-models of the United Kingdom might be criticized as unduly insular. However, we took the view that a conference to compare and contrast medium-term plans and projections in Western countries would be another sort of conference altogether; there was more than enough to do, in a single two-day conference, to explore the status of medium-term models in the United Kingdom.

[1] *Industrial Review to 1977*, 1973, N.E.D.O., £1.00.

Part I
The Three Macro-models

This part presents the basic papers on the three medium-term models with which the conference opened; at the end there is a brief tabular comparison. First, there is an account of the model used in the Treasury. Secondly, there are two papers on the Stone model. The first presents the basic structure of the model; the second applies it to the period 1972–75. This second paper replaces the one which was before the conference—which was a reprint of an article published in the *National Institute Economic Review*.[1] The new paper revises the figures in the light of later information.

There are also two papers on the 'Par' model. The first explains the concept. The second is an abridged version of the second in a series of annual studies by the Cambridge Economic Policy Group; it was prepared at the end of 1972 shortly after the annual Public Expenditure White Paper. It shows the Par concept being used for economic policy analysis. The authors comment: 'The statistical work contained in the report does not constitute a piece of basic research into how the economy works; it is grounded partly in specific pieces of research carried out at the Department of Applied Economics and partly in "folklore". While the report gives the detailed figuring which we found essential for the policy analysis[2] and for various documents submitted to the Select Committee on Public Expenditure, very little formal justification has been provided here for the choice of parameter values or for the structure of the assumed relationships.' The Appendix to this second paper reproduces the full set of tables on which the study was based and provides lists of sources and definitions of the variables used.

Finally, there is at the end of this part a tabular comparison of the three models, prepared by Mr. P. Mottershead of the National Institute and revised in the light of the model-builders' comments. Attached to this table there is an account of the more technical parts of the discussion which concerned the treatment of the more important variables.

[1] T. S. Barker and V. H. Woodward, 'Inflation, growth, and economic policy in the medium-term', *National Institute Economic Review*, No. 60, May 1972.
[2] London and Cambridge Economic Service, *The Times Business News*, 8 and 9 January, 1973.

1: The Treasury Model[1]

A. A. McLean

Medium-Term Projections in the Treasury

1. Although the Government has had a system for producing medium-term projections since the early 1960s, it was not until the end of 1968 that this was first formulated as an equation system. The multi-equation fully-computerized econometric model developed from this system is central to present-day medium-term assessment in the Treasury. It is this system in its present form and the way it is used that will be discussed here.

2. There were two main reasons for the development of the medium-term model. The first, connected with the early days of the National Economic Development Council, related to the wish to achieve a higher rate of economic growth. In this context a need was felt for a system which would permit formalized consideration of the implications of higher growth for investment, the balance of payments and the general availability of resources.

3. The second reason related to public expenditure. The Plowden Report of 1961 said that Government decisions about public expenditure should be taken in the light of the prospective resource position over a period of years. At its simplest this could mean that the size and growth of public expenditure should be considered in their relation to G.D.P.; but it was clearly better to have a full-scale model of the economy which would show, among other things, the amount of resources needed for a satisfactory balance of payments and for private investment, and thus relate public expenditure and private consumption to the remaining resources available. In the latest issue of the annual series of White Papers on public expenditure which began in 1969 a table was included for the first time showing on various assumptions possible patterns of resource use in the medium-term, given the public expenditure programmes set out in the White Paper.

---

[1] The author would like to acknowledge the helpful comments and criticisms on this paper received from his colleagues in the Treasury although he remains responsible for any errors it contains.

4. From the beginning, the development and use of the model has been directed towards economic growth questions and an evaluation of public expenditure plans in a national resource context. It is this second objective that has priority at present. Interest in the question of available resources relative to likely demands on these resources means that in addition to a normal Keynesian approach on the demand side it is possible to determine the available supply of resources and use this as an overall constraint.

5. In practice, however, the model is not used as a forecasting mechanism, but as an aid in exploring the implications of different policy assumptions, policy objectives and policy instruments. It may be used to simulate the effects of a variety of contingencies such as different exogenous values for key variables and different parameter values in equations. It can thus be used to calculate the approximate trade-offs between potentially conflicting policy objectives such as faster growth and an improved balance of payments position and in estimating the relative efficacy of various policies in overcoming these conflicts.

6. An important feature of the model which has been developed over its lifetime is its flexibility in terms of the constraints a user is able to impose by, for example, suppressing a relationship in the model. Thus targets can be imposed on key variables such as the current balance, unemployment, prices, etc., in order to work out their implications for the economy as a whole and to test the various policy changes that might be used to bring them about. Further, provision exists for building in to most of the equations an allowance for the effects of new policies and other events which are not already allowed for in an equation's formulation.

7. Although the model actually produces a projected path for developments from the latest year to some target or trend year in the future the main emphasis is on the implications of the final year trend position itself. By trend position is meant the longer-run, underlying position of the economy that will result from the policy and other assumptions made, abstracting from cyclical influences (discussed more fully later). The path to this trend position is regarded as less important as long as it does not involve severely unrealistic intermediate positions. Checks are also made to see how sensitive the final trend position is to the path by which it is achieved. A problem here is the way in which the effects from lagged relationships may not be fully worked out by the final year.

8. The pressure for a continuously operational aid to policy choices

meant that some of the eventual model was developed in what, in other circumstances, might be considered a sub-optimal, ad hoc way. No overall econometric strategy was followed and simultaneous estimation is not used. Originally quite a number of equations were quantitative formulations of the more intuitive and qualitative procedures that had been used before. Now, however, all equations are econometrically estimated except where this is felt to be inappropriate or where no statistically satisfactory relationship has been found. An example of this is in the tax sector where the various taxes are represented by formulations derived from the tax regulations.

9. Initially the solution system employed was recursive. However, certain blocks of the model are now solved simultaneously—the price circuit is one example—so that the whole system is best described as block recursive rather than fully recursive. Further, as part of the solution process, the whole solution sequence of the model may be iterated through several times so that as far as the user is concerned the solution is simultaneously obtained. The present solution system is a consequence of the development history of the model and the move to a fully interdependent system has not yet been undertaken because of the lack of time for the necessary changes to be developed and programmed and because the present system allows the full range of operations required from the model to be carried out satisfactorily.

Details of the Model

1. Given the way in which individual relationships in the model can be used or suppressed depending on the purpose for which it is being used, it is difficult to isolate something which can be meaningfully described as *the* structure of the model. Therefore, this section will concentrate on describing the individual relationships or groups of relationships used. The way in which these various sub-sectors of the model are fitted together for different purposes will be described in the next section.

2. The form of the equations discussed below is correct at the time of writing. However, reformulations to improve the relationships and to take into account changing circumstances are brought in from time to time so the model is subject to a continuous process of development.

3. The sequence of the discussion is somewhat arbitrary, though an attempt has been made to minimize the number of occasions a variable is mentioned in an explanation before it itself is discussed.

The Supply of Resources—Output and Employment[1]

4. This subsector consists of two equations. The first relates to employment and is of the form:

$$\log E_t = 0\cdot6219 \log Q_t + 0\cdot3818 \log E_{t-1} - 0\cdot1491 \log NH_t$$
$$\quad\quad (4\cdot7) \quad\quad\quad\quad (1\cdot9) \quad\quad\quad\quad (0\cdot5)$$
$$\quad\quad -0\cdot0131 t_1 - 0\cdot007 t_2 + 0\cdot6226$$
$$\quad\quad\quad (2\cdot6) \quad\quad (3\cdot1) \quad\quad\quad\quad\quad\quad\quad\quad \bar{R}^2 = 0\cdot96$$

where E = employment t_1 and t_2 are timetrends,
       Q = output t_1 starting in 1958
       NH = normal hours t_2 starting in 1963
       all logs are natural logs t and $t-1$ are time subscripts

i.e. employment is related to output, itself lagged (to allow for the lagged reaction of employment to output), normal hours (as a proxy for hours worked) and two time trends to represent the change over time of labour productivity. No explicit allowance is made for the effect of investment and other factors on productivity growth. This is not because they are believed to be unimportant but because of difficulties in finding usable relationships involving them.

5. The second relates unemployment to the full employment working population and employment—and is of the form:

$$T_t = 0\cdot4036 AWP_t - 0\cdot3855 E_t - 897\cdot693$$
$$\quad\quad (52\cdot3) \quad\quad\quad (10\cdot6) \quad\quad\quad\quad\quad \bar{R}^2 = 0\cdot998 \ DW = 1\cdot71$$

where T = unemployment
       AWP = full employment working population

i.e. unemployment is related to a supply of labour factor—working population—and the demand for labour—employment.

6. Recent data on productivity, employment and unemployment have raised questions as to whether or not relationships, such as those given above, which are based on fairly long runs of past data, are appropriate for projection purposes. Interpretation of the recent data is difficult and considerable work has been put into studying the problems raised. The present conclusions are that, whereas the employment/unemployment relationship has remained fairly stable, projections of productivity growth are surrounded by much greater uncertainty. Although for any given run of the model a definite growth rate for productivity has to be taken, no firm, central view is held at present.

[1] Since this paper was presented this sector has been modified to distinguish between government employment and output and that of the rest of the economy.

Demands on Resources

7. Once the total supply of resources is determined the interest is in the pattern of demand on these resources. The *Balance of Payments* components are considered as a whole as the main interest is their net impact on the supply of resources.

8. *Exports of goods* and *exports of private services* are estimated using demand equations, linking exports to world trade volume and the relevant relative price term. The coefficients and lag patterns imposed for the relative price terms are derived from Treasury research into exports. The other coefficients are freely estimated. The equations used are:

$$\log x_t^g = 6 \cdot 230 + 0 \cdot 457 \log WT_t - 0 \cdot 376 \log \left(\frac{p_{gt}^x}{p_t^{xw}} \right)$$

$$- 0 \cdot 750 \log \left(\frac{p_{gt-1}^x}{p_{t-1}^{xw}} \right) - 0 \cdot 375 \log \left(\frac{p_{gt-2}^x}{p_{t-2}^{xw}} \right)$$

$$\bar{R}^2 = 0 \cdot 985 \quad DW = 1 \cdot 58$$

$$\log x_t^{ps} = 4 \cdot 538 + 0 \cdot 605 \log WT_t - 0 \cdot 25 \log \left(\frac{p_{st}^{px}}{p_t^{xw}} \right)$$
$$\quad (20 \cdot 4)$$

$$- 0 \cdot 50 \log \left(\frac{p_{st-1}^{px}}{p_{t-1}^{xw}} \right) - 0 \cdot 25 \log \left(\frac{p_{st-2}^{px}}{p_{t-2}^{xw}} \right)$$

$$\bar{R}^2 = 0 \cdot 97 \quad DW = 0 \cdot 56$$

where x^g = volume of exports of goods (1963 prices)

x^{ps} = volume of private exports of services (1963 prices)

WT = index (1963=100) of exports of manufactures of main industrial countries (determined exogenously, proxy for volume of world trade)

p_g^x = price index for exports of goods (1963=100)

p^{xw} = index of competitors' export prices for manufactures (1963=100) (determined exogenously)

p_s^{px} = price index for exports of private services (1963=100)

Exports of government services are exogenously determined.

9. *Imports of goods* and *imports of private services* are both obtained from demand equations. For goods, imports are related to total final expenditure and a relative price term, the coefficient of which is imposed on the basis of Treasury research into disaggregated import equations. The rest of the equation is freely determined. Imports of private services are a function of G.D.P. (with a freely determined

coefficient). No relative price term is used at present owing to difficulty in identifying its effect in aggregate. The equations used are:

$$\log m_t^g = -4 \cdot 752 + 1 \cdot 254 \log TFE_t - 0 \cdot 5885 \log \left(\frac{p_{gt}^m}{p_t^{gdp}}\right)$$
(15·2)

$$\bar{R}^2 = 0 \cdot 95 \qquad DW = 1 \cdot 00$$

$$\log m_t^{ps} = -7 \cdot 525 + 1 \cdot 445 \log GDP_t \qquad \bar{R}^2 = 0 \cdot 92 \qquad DW = 0 \cdot 58$$
(12·6)

where m^g = volume of imports of goods (1963 prices)

m^{ps} = volume of imports of private services (1963 prices)

TFE = total final expenditure (1963 market prices)

p_g^m = index of imports of goods prices (1963 = 100)

p^{gdp} = G.D.P. (factor cost) price index (1963 = 100)

GDP = G.D.P. at 1963 factor cost prices

As with exports, *imports of government services* are exogenously determined.

10. Export price indices for both goods and private services are estimated using equations in which export prices are related to G.D.P. prices and competitors' export prices—thus allowing for both supply and demand factors. The sum of the coefficients on the two independent variables is constrained to equal one in both cases in order to eliminate money illusion. The constants (which are freely estimated) are intended to reflect the differences in productivity between the export-producing and the domestic-goods-producing sectors of the economy. The actual equations are:

$$\phi p_{gt}^x = -0 \cdot 0045 + 0 \cdot 418 \phi p_t^{xw} + 0 \cdot 582 \phi p_t^{gdp} \qquad \bar{R}^2 = 0 \cdot 81 \quad DW = 2 \cdot 40$$

$$\phi p_{st}^x = -0 \cdot 0043 + 0 \cdot 543 \phi p_t^{xw} + 0 \cdot 457 \phi p_t^{gdp} \qquad \bar{R}^2 = 0 \cdot 50 \quad DW = 2 \cdot 06$$

where ϕ is an operator such that $\phi X_t = \dfrac{X_t - X_{t-1}}{X_{t-1}}$

The price index used for exports of government services is exogenously determined.

11. Import price indices for both goods and private services are constrained at present to grow at the same rate as competitors' export prices for manufactures over the forecast period (i.e. they are, in effect, exogenous). For goods, this represents a departure from past behaviour because prices for non-manufactured imports have risen more slowly than for manufactured imports but it seems unreasonable to assume this will continue. Prices for non-manufactured imports are therefore assumed to rise in the future as fast as those for manufactured imports. For private services, prices have risen in the past at about the same rate as the index used for competitors' export prices for manufactures.

The prices for imports of government services are exogenous in terms of foreign currencies.

12. Both *private and Government transfers*, debits and credits are determined exogenously in value terms. *Net interest, profits and dividends* (I.P.D.)—*credits* are determined in two stages. I.P.D. before tax in value terms is derived as a function of current price world trade (determined exogenously), taken as a proxy for world income. A proportion of the resulting figure is deducted as tax to give I.P.D. after tax. *Net I.P.D.*—*debits* are calculated in value terms. The three components—interest paid overseas, profits paid overseas and dividends paid overseas—are estimated separately as proportions of their equivalent national item. Net I.P.D. debits are then obtained by deducting taxes (estimated separately) from the sum of these components.

13. External capital flows are determined exogenously at present. However, work is in progress towards developing forecasting relationships for this sector. The direction this work is taking involves relating inward direct investment to domestic company profits, outward direct investment to world trade, and import and export credits to the totals for imports and exports.

14. *Fixed investment* is considered in two parts—public and private. Public investment, including that by the nationalized industries, is exogenously determined as part of the broader process of the determination of public expenditure in general. The level and composition of public investment is normally assumed unchanged as different variants of the model are run, including those which involve changes in the rate of growth of output. However, alternative exogenous estimates can be used if information is wanted on the implications of varying this aggregate.

15. Private investment, apart from private dwellings and land transfer costs which are exogenously determined, is projected by using econometrically estimated equations. The major determinants used are G.D.P. or manufacturing output (related to G.D.P.). Some attempts have been made to bring in other variables but so far these have been unsuccessful. Five sectors are used—manufacturing, divided into plant and machinery, vehicles, and other new building and works; distribution; and other non-manufacturing.

16. The actual equations used for manufacturing investment are as follows:

$$\Delta Im_t^{P\&M} = 5 \cdot 58 \Delta Gm_t + 8 \cdot 46 \Delta Gm_{t-1}$$

$$(2 \cdot 0) \qquad\qquad (2 \cdot 8) \qquad\qquad\qquad \bar{R}^2 = 0 \cdot 56 \quad DW = 1 \cdot 57$$

$$+ 2 \cdot 23 \Delta Gm_{t-2} - 5 \cdot 97 \Delta Gm_{t-3}$$

$$(0 \cdot 8) \qquad\qquad (-2 \cdot 2)$$

$$\Delta Im_t^v = 1 \cdot 19 \ (\Delta Gm_t - 0 \cdot 8 \Delta Gm_{t-1}) + 1 \cdot 25 \ (\Delta Gm_{t-1} - 0 \cdot 8 \Delta Gm_{t-2})$$
$$\quad\quad (3 \cdot 7) \quad\quad\quad\quad\quad\quad\quad\quad (4 \cdot 0)$$
$$\bar{R}^2 = 0 \cdot 53 \quad DW = 1 \cdot 86$$

$$\Delta Im_t^{ONB} = 6 \cdot 42 \ (\Delta Gm_{t-1} - 0 \cdot 96 \Delta Gm_{t-2})$$
$$\quad\quad\quad (5 \cdot 5)$$
$$\quad\quad + 3 \cdot 58 \ (\Delta Gm_{t-2} - 0 \cdot 96 \Delta Gm_{t-3})$$
$$\quad\quad\quad (3 \cdot 2) \quad\quad\quad\quad\quad\quad \bar{R}^2 = 0 \cdot 70 \quad DW = 1 \cdot 74$$

where $Im^{P\&M}$ = investment by manufacturing in plant and machinery (1963 prices)

Im^v = investment by manufacturing in vehicles (1963 prices)

Im_t^{ONB} = investment by manufacturing in other new buildings and work (1963 prices)

Gm = manufacturing output index (1963 = 100)

Δ = the difference operator

These formulations which relate ΔI to ΔGm may seem contrary to one's expectations in terms of accelerator models but can be shown to arise from the use of gross investment as the dependent variable and the treatment of replacement investment (see Appendix). Abstracting from the problems of estimating, the lag structures seem to be in accordance with *a priori* expectations; the bulk of the explanation of investment in vehicles comes from the immediate past change in manufacturing output: on the other hand for buildings, where the gap between decision and execution is likely to be longer, it is the lagged change in output that is more important.

17.   The equations for the two remaining sectors are:

$$I_t^D = 0 \cdot 078 G_{t-1} - 0 \cdot 121 G_{t-2} + 0 \cdot 128 G_{t-3} - 1157$$
$$\quad\quad (1 \cdot 31) \quad\quad (-1 \cdot 34) \quad (2 \cdot 07)$$
$$\bar{R}^2 = 0 \cdot 93 \quad DW = 1 \cdot 33$$

$$I_t^{ONM} = 0 \cdot 018 G_t - 122$$
$$\quad\quad\quad (9 \cdot 23) \quad\quad\quad\quad\quad\quad \bar{R}^2 = 0 \cdot 92 \quad DW = 1 \cdot 22$$

where I^D = investment by distribution (1963 prices)

I^{ONM} = investment by other non-manufacturing (1963 prices)

G = G.D.P. expenditure base (1963 prices)

The use of output in terms of levels rather than changes is because the statistical fits obtained with changes were very poor. As with most other forecasting models the investment sector has proved very difficult in terms of obtaining satisfactory equations.

18.   As might be expected, *public consumption* is exogenously deter-

mined on the basis of the public expenditure programmes, together with an allowance for imputed rent.

19. With *stockbuilding* as with private fixed investment, considerable difficulty has been experienced in obtaining a really satisfactory equation. The equation used is derived from one in which the relationship of the level of stocks to output is estimated.

20. For certain purposes *personal consumption* is simply derived as a residual, being the difference between total supply and demand from the investment, balance of payments and public sectors. However the model is able to calculate desired consumption using a consumption function of the form

$$C_t = 0.7813RPDI_t + 0.1526C_{t-1}$$

where C is consumption at 1963 prices

$RPDI$ is real personal disposable income

These estimated coefficients imply a long-run savings ratio of 8·2 per cent, consistent with past experience.

21. The equation was freely estimated on quarterly data and then converted to an annual basis by specifying that the average lag and the long-run coefficient should be the same for the annual equation as for the quarterly version. The series for real personal disposable income is built up, on the assumption of constant tax rates or a constant tax burden, from separate projections of personal incomes, taxes on persons and consumer prices. Each of these items is discussed in turn.

22. With regard to *personal incomes* the most important single figure is per capita earnings. At present, and in common with most other forecasters, we can do no better than impose this exogenously. But the failure to project earnings does not matter all that much in a medium-term model which is primarily concerned with the allocation of real resources. For it can be assumed, over a 6-year period, that prices always react fully to any change in wages, so that real income— and hence consumption—is unaffected. (This assumption is reflected in the constant-profit-share version of the model, which has the property that a 1 per cent increase in wages results, *ceteris paribus*, in a 1 per cent increase in current price G.D.P. and hence in G.D.P. prices). Similarly any change in domestic wages and prices can be counterbalanced by exchange rate changes in such a way that the allocation of resources to the balance of trade is invariant.

23. The exogenously determined level of earnings per head, together with the level of employment predicted by the output employment equation, gives the wages and salaries bill. Total income from

employment is then derived by adding in exogenous estimates of forces pay and employers' national insurance and related contributions plus an estimate (based on a simple relationship with wages and salaries) of 'employers' other contributions' (mainly private pension schemes).

24. Income from employment is the largest component of total personal income but there are a number of other smaller components which have to be added to it. Income from self-employment is estimated as a proportion of total domestic income. Current grants from public authorities to the private sector are based on the public expenditure programmes adjusted for any difference in the level of unemployment assumed in the programmes on the one hand and in the economic projection on the other. Net receipts by persons of rent, dividends and interest income are calculated as part of a system of intersectoral income flows.

25. Given total personal income (in current prices) projections of prices and income taxes are needed to get to real personal disposable income (R.P.D.I.). The view taken on *prices* is guided in some circumstances by its implications for the share of profits in total domestic income. From the identity of income and expenditure we have

$$Y = TDY - SA + RE$$
where $\quad TDY = W + S + R + PC + OPE + \pi$
and
$\qquad Y \quad$ =current price G.D.P.
$\qquad TDY$=total domestic incomes
$\qquad SA \quad$ =stock appreciation
$\qquad RE \quad$ =residual error
$\qquad W \quad$ =wages and salaries
$\qquad S \quad$ =self-employment income
$\qquad R \quad$ =rent
$\qquad PC \quad$ =gross trading surplus of public corporations
$\qquad OPE$ =gross trading surplus of other public enterprises
$\qquad \pi \quad$ =gross trading profits of companies

Given an independent forecast of TDY we can use the identity to derive current price G.D.P. which (since constant price G.D.P. is determined separately) effectively determines the overall level of prices.

26. All the components of TDY except earnings and company profits are in fact obtained by fairly simple behavioural relationships; the proportion of TDY allocated to rent is projected to rise in line with past trends, while the share of self-employment incomes is assumed to be relatively stable; the gross trading surpluses of the public corporations and other public enterprises are also expressed as propor-

tions of *TDY*, but can be modified in line with government policy towards the nationalized industries. The income expenditure identity can thus be used in either of two ways. If prices are projected separately, *Y* is fixed and the identity is used to obtain company profits as a residual. Alternatively, if a view about company profits is imposed, this determines *TDY*, which in turn fixes current price G.D.P. and hence the level of prices, as described above.

27.   Whether or not a view about profits and hence the overall price level is imposed, the model begins by calculating a factor cost price index for each component of demand. The equation for consumer prices at factor cost, which is based on a constant mark-up hypothesis, is estimated as:

$$\Delta p_{c_t} = 0.823 \Delta WC_t + 0.692 \Delta WC_{t-1} + 0.777 \Delta MC_t + 0.348 \Delta MC_{t-1}$$
$$\quad (5.61) \qquad\quad (4.60) \qquad\qquad (6.52) \qquad\qquad (2.47)$$
$$\bar{R}^2 = 0.96 \quad DW = 1.99$$

where Δ is the difference operator

p_c =consumer price index

WC=wage and salary bill divided by total final output, at 1963 prices

MC=imports divided by total final output at 1963 prices

The equations for investment and stockbuilding prices are of exactly the same form. The price indices for central government and local authority consumption are constructed as a weighted average of the indices for consumer prices and average earnings, where the weights reflect the proportion of Government spending on goods and services and wages and salaries respectively.

28.   Although the price equations for the domestic components of demand embody a constant mark-up, the unconstrained operation of these equations does not result in a constant share of profits in total domestic incomes. There are a number of reasons for this. The constant mark-up hypothesis does not apply in the export sector. Any divergence between the movements of wages and those of import costs will, *ceteris paribus*, change the implicit profit share. Further the mark-up is different in each sector, so that total profits change if the final demand mix alters. Nevertheless the share of profits in total domestic incomes is a ratio which has behaved in an orderly fashion in the past, fluctuating according to the pressure of demand about a steady downward trend. The profit share is also affected by policies towards wages and prices. For both these reasons it may, on occasion, be sensible to over-ride the price equations in order to impose a view about profits. In this

case the regular price equations are used to establish the pattern of prices (i.e. the ratio of the indices to each other) but the overall level of prices is fixed by the constraint on the profit share as described above. In practice this is achieved by adding an equal percentage residual to each price index until G.D.P. prices reach the required level.

29. Personal *income taxes* can be projected in one of two ways. For some purposes it is convenient to assume that the ratio of personal taxes to personal income is held constant, in which case tax projections present no difficulty. Alternatively it is sometimes useful to know roughly what present taxes at announced rates would yield given the income projections though it cannot be claimed that the estimates obtained are very accurate projections of the yields of the taxes involved. The same caveat must be entered for the estimates for taxes on expenditure (discussed later).

30. For this second procedure use is made of Inland Revenue expertise embodied in a set of equations for taxes on employment incomes, on incomes of the self-employed, on unearned incomes, and for surtax and repayment of taxes to persons. These are not econometrically estimated behavioural equations in the normal sense. They are fitted equations produced by the Inland Revenue to simulate their projections of medium-term tax yields. The equations are designed to reflect the way taxes respond to marginal changes in income, but since their parameters do not in general correspond to recognizable tax parameters (like the standard rate of tax, or personal allowances) the effect of changes in tax policy has to be estimated by the Inland Revenue and fed into the model by residuals. When, in due course, a new equation is fitted to the revised tax projections resulting from the new policy, this is put into the model in place of the old equations and residuals.

31. Total *taxes on expenditure* at current prices are derived as the sum of individual taxes, each of which has its own forecasting relationship. These are in general either pure extrapolations of trends or simple relationships with the expenditure item on which the tax falls. The sophistication that can be achieved in this sector is limited by the fact that the independent variables used, such as consumers' expenditure, are projected only in aggregate. The total yield of each tax is split between the major components of demand by a set of ratios which reflect the proportions of each tax which fall in each demand component in each year. By totalling the projection for each tax a current price factor cost adjustment is arrived at for each expenditure item.

32. The constant price estimate of taxes and subsidies on expenditure

(the constant price factor cost adjustment) is a simple proportion of each of the major expenditure estimates (in constant prices). The proportions used are basically those which applied in 1963. However, an adjustment has had to be made, principally to the largest of them, that for consumers' expenditure, to allow for the fact that using the 1963 proportions does not give an exact estimate of the factor cost adjustment for subsequent years.

33. Given the constant market price expenditure estimates, the current and constant price factor cost adjustments, and the factor cost price indices, it is a straightforward process using the accounting identities to derive the market price indices for each expenditure aggregate.

Uses of the Model

1. The preceding section has given a description of the various parts of the model and some idea of how they are inter-related. The model is used for various purposes and to achieve these certain assumptions or restrictions have to be fed into it. These may involve bypassing or suppressing a set of relationships in the model.

2. A major use to which the model is put is the development of a *'central case'*. In this the level of available resources together with a feasible pattern of resource use are explored in the context of some overall constraints on the economy. The main interest is in whether, within the constraints, the various projected demands on resources are consistent with the likely supply.

3. A typical example might involve a target current balance surplus by a given year, a target rate of unemployment and a given total of government current expenditure. The unemployment target working through the unemployment/employment relationship and the employment/output relationship would give the projected level of available resources. Since no firm view is held on the likely future growth of productivity a given unemployment rate could be viewed as generating a range of possible resource totals corresponding to the likely range of productivity growth rates. However, for the sake of the discussion it will be assumed a single rate of growth of resources emerges. A balance of payments target could be seen as applying equally to the current and capital accounts. However, because the capital items are all assumed exogenous, at present, the target is effectively on the current account.

4. In order to ensure that the supply of resources is available and the

rate of productivity growth is sustained some investment is required. According to the model this is dependent on output and its rate of growth. Similarly an endogenous required level of stockbuilding is generated.

5. Taken with the predetermined level of Government current expenditure all the demands on resources except personal consumption have been determined. The residual between this demand and the available supply can be regarded as the resources available for allocation to consumption and as an indication of the amount of freedom in the economy to adjust one's view of the level of other demands. The equation derived for consumers' expenditure can be used to provide a rough estimate of the level of demand from this source that is likely to develop. Comparison of this with the resources available for consumption can in principle provide a rough check of the feasibility of the projected pattern of demand on resources though in practice the margin of error involved robs the result of much of its significance. As the level of consumers' expenditure is amenable to policy action an alternative criterion is the political acceptability of the implicit growth in consumers' expenditure.

6. The view taken of the likely values for the various demands on resources or of the likely level of available resources can be varied. This provides a test of the sensitivity of the results to errors in the initial estimates or to the range of possibilities where no strong central view is held.

7. An example of this kind of exercise was given in the White Paper on Public Expenditure published in December 1972. The intention in this case was to test the compatibility of the public expenditure totals given with different rates of growth of output. The rates of growth of G.D.P. were made exogenous (at 3·5 per cent and 5·0 per cent per annum) and the expenditure implications of these rates calculated with public sector expenditure as given in the White Paper, and personal consumption a residual. As an additional check two investment cases, imposed on either side of the model's unadjusted view, were run for each output growth path to reflect the uncertainty surrounding any investment projection. The results showed how, even given the wide range of cases used, the public expenditure figures do not lead to a serious squeeze on the resources available for private consumption.

8. The final year of the central case is seen as being on 'trend', i.e. as reflecting the underlying path of the economy once the cyclical influences arising from the point in the cycle of the starting year have worked themselves out. This leads to a further exercise within the framework

of the central case of developing a *'trend case'* where the economy is seen as being on its underlying path throughout the projection period, a concept paralleling that of the 'par economy' developed by the Cambridge Economic Policy Group.

9. To construct the trend case the model is constrained to have the central case final year growth rate throughout the projection period, with adjustments for institutional factors such as the change in the school-leaving age. The equations used are those used in the central case except that they are adjusted to eliminate the cyclical effects caused by their use of lagged variables. From this process a trend pattern of demands on resources emerges which can be checked for consistency and to see if the implied growth rates for sectors seem reasonable and acceptable.

10. A less important alternative to the central case is the so-called 'forecast' case. It does not involve a forecast in the sense of being the model-user's best judgment of the most likely future development path for the economy. It is the path the model forecasts that the economy will take if present trends in endogenous variables continue and no policy changes, particularly on taxes, take place. No attempt is made to project the likely cyclical pattern of the economy's development. Where exogenous variables are required the most reasonable values, based on recent past trends, tend to be used. No constraint or targets are set.

11. A possible result of a run of this sort is that the U.K.'s 'forecast' position becomes increasingly implausible as the projection proceeds. The only corrective pressure that would develop against any deterioration shown would come from any built-in stabilizers which were operating on the economy at the beginning of the projection period. Although this case is not very meaningful by itself, it does provide an indication of any tendencies, inherent in the present situation, for future problems to emerge.

Appendix

Starting from a model based on partial stock adjustment:

$$I_t = \sum_{r=0}^{\infty} \mu_r(K^*_{t-r} - K^*_{t-r-1}) + \delta K_{t-1}$$

or Gross investment = Net investment + replacement investment

where I = gross investment

K^* = desired stock of capital at end of period

K = actual stock of capital

μ = proportion of investment desired in a period carried out in that period

δ = replacement rate

Assume $K_t^* = \alpha G_t$ and we get: $I_t = \alpha \sum\limits_{r=0}^{\infty} \mu_r (G_{t-r} - G_{t-r-1}) + \delta K_{t-1}$

$$= \beta_0 \Delta G_t + \beta_1 \Delta G_{t-1} + \dots + \delta K_{t-1}$$

This implies an infinite number of independent variables most of which will have very little effect. Therefore, assume effect of ΔG decays geometrically after one period at rate λ. Two or more periods are implicit in the equations quoted but the extension is fairly trivial.

$$\therefore \ I_t = \beta_0 \Delta G_t + \beta_0 \lambda \Delta G_{t-1} + \beta_0 \lambda^2 \Delta G_{t-2} + \dots + \delta K_{t-1}$$

By a Koyck transformation: $I_t = \beta_0 \Delta G_t + \lambda I_{t-1} + \delta K_{t-1} - \delta \lambda K_{t-2}$

However, $K_{t-1} = (1 - \delta) K_{t-2} + I_{t-1}$

$$\therefore \ I_t = \beta_0 \Delta G_t + (\lambda + \delta) I_{t-1} + \delta(1 - \delta - \lambda) K_{t-2}$$

and $K_{t-2} = I_{t-2} + (1-\delta) I_{t-3} + (1-\delta)^2 I_{t-4} + \dots$

$$\therefore \ I_t = \beta_0 \Delta G_t + (\lambda + \delta) I_{t-1} + \delta(1 - \delta - \lambda) \ [I_{t-2} + (1-\delta) I_{t-3}$$
$$+ (1-\delta)^2 I_{t-4} + \dots]$$

Also $I_{t-1} = \beta_0 \Delta G_{t-1} + (\lambda + \delta) I_{t-2} + \delta(1 - \delta - \lambda) \ [I_{t-3} + (1-\delta) I_{t-4}$
$$+ (1-\delta)^2 I_{t-5} \dots]$$

Multiplying the second equation by $(1 - \delta)$ and subtracting from the first simplifies to:

$$\Delta I_t = \beta_0 \Delta G_t - (1 - \delta) \beta_0 \Delta G_{t-1} + \lambda \Delta I_{t-1}$$

In practice the estimate of λ is not significantly different from 0 so that the equation becomes:

$$\Delta I = \beta_0 \Delta G_t - (1 - \delta) \beta_0 \Delta G_{t-1}$$

and can be estimated in this form or, if a depreciation rate (δ) is imposed, an estimating equation of the form:

$$\Delta I = \beta_0 (\Delta G_t - (1 - \delta) \Delta G_{t-1})$$

2: The Cambridge Economic Growth Project Model

T. S. Barker

A. AN INPUT-OUTPUT MODEL OF THE BRITISH ECONOMY

The Main Features of the Model

The economic system is a highly complex one and we are a long way from a full understanding of how it works. The problem is made even more difficult by the impossibility of controlled experiment and the inadequacies of the data by which we monitor the operation of the system. Nevertheless economists have attempted to model the economy as a whole, partly out of intellectual interest and partly because of the practical needs of economic policy.

This paper is about a medium-term input-output model[1] which abstracts from much of the actual complexity of the economy. This complexity has three facets: the economic system comprises a huge number of economic agents and a large number of economic relationships between them; the system is dynamic in that all actions depend to greater or less degree on what has happened before; and thirdly, it is constantly subject to exogenous shocks which have an appreciable effect on its operation. The Cambridge Growth Project model is highly disaggregated by comparison with most macro-economic models although it still involves a gross simplification of economic institutions and processes. However it almost entirely abstracts from the dynamics of the system and from the influences of random and exogenous shocks in its variables and parameters. The model is of course being developed all the time and eventually we would hope to relax these restrictions, making it dynamic and providing an indication of the effects of variations in the parameters and variables. But for the purpose of this paper the model will be described in its present operational form, together

[1] The model discussed in the paper is being developed by a team of research workers under the direction of Professor Richard Stone. The author wishes to thank other members of the project for their advice and help in the preparation of the paper.

with the modifications we aim at introducing in the near future. As such it is static and also non-stochastic in that its projections are fully determined by the values of its parameters and exogenous variables.

General models are differentiated not only by their treatment of dynamics and shocks but by the purposes for which they are constructed. Input-output models were first constructed to estimate the effects on industrial structure of alternative patterns of final demand [12]. They have developed in four directions, by increasing the size of the models as the number of industries distinguished has grown, by extending the models to cover social and environmental factors, by making them dynamic and finally by making the previously exogenous final demands (imports, exports, consumers' expenditure and investment) determined within the model [4, 6]. The input-output model in Cambridge has concentrated on the last set of developments with the purpose of simulating in depth the real flows between sectors in the economy.

Allied to these developments has been the realization that problems of management and control require the explicit introduction in the model of policy instruments as well as economic targets. We have changed the emphasis of our work from the examination of the implications for faster growth [5], where little was said about how such growth would be achieved, to the examination of alternative projections, fully specified in terms of tax rates, etc., but which rule out *ab initio* many possible futures, on the grounds that the policy instruments have to be set at unrealistic levels [3]. Naturally this does not rule out the possibilities of new policies being introduced if the available ones prove wanting or unacceptable. But it does place the policy options to the forefront of any economic strategy.

Static input-output models project the economy for one year at a time, each projection being independent of every other projection. At present the Cambridge model projects the economy in 1975 and 1980 under a set of given assumptions about wage inflation, exchange rates, taxes, subsidies and public expenditures as well as a large number of other exogenous variables. These views of the future are not only conditional upon the assumptions about the exogenous variables, but also upon the underlying premise that the economy is fully adjusted to that particular combination of assumptions. This is what is meant by saying that the model projects an economy in 'equilibrium' in 1975 or that the values of the variables are at their 'normal' values for 1975. It should be noted that many of these projections would indicate that the economy was, on most definitions, grossly out of equilibrium with huge deficits on the balance of payments or heavy unemployment. If, however, the projections indicated a satisfactory outcome for employment, foreign payments and other targets of government policy, the equilibrium would still be a partial one because although we might assume that institutions and persons were satisfied with the outcome in 1975 and would not wish to revise their decisions because of that outcome, underlying conditions may be such that they would not continue to be satisfied in subsequent years.

The Structure of the Model

On a count of equations and variables, the model is very large by comparison with quarterly forecasting models. It distinguishes nearly 700 behavioural and technical relationships (not including individual inter-industry flows or the elements of classification converters) and about 300 identities. Although the model is large, its size comes from the disaggregation of many of the economic flows and the structure of the model is relatively simple.

The structure can be described as two interacting sequences, a quantity sequence and a prices and incomes sequence. The quantity sequence begins with volumes of industrial outputs. These are needed to calculate the intermediate demand for commodities, the stock-building requirements (assuming given stock-output ratios) and the levels of private fixed investment. For a given level of real disposable income and a set of relative prices, consumers' expenditures are calculated from a consumption function and the linear expenditure system. Again with given prices, but making a further assumption about the volume of world trade, it is possible to estimate imports and exports for the British economy. Finally public expenditure, both current and capital, is added in to provide the total volume of commodities to be supplied by industry.

The prices and incomes sequence begins with an assumption about earnings per man-year. Using a given set of wage differentials and levels of industrial employment, the wage bill by industry can be calculated. Labour costs per unit of output are added to costs of material and service inputs plus profit margins to obtain industrial prices. In turn, the domestic prices are combined with import prices to give prices for domestic absorption of commodities as industrial inputs, consumers' expenditure and other categories of final demand.

The two sequences interact in several places, most notably as follows.

(i) Relative prices determine the pattern of consumers' expenditure.
(ii) Absolute prices determine the levels of imports and exports.

(Other countries' price levels are assumed to be independent of British prices.)

(iii) The price index for consumers' expenditure is used to deflate the money value of personal disposable income.

(iv) Imports and domestic outputs affect prices of domestic absorptions.

(v) Employments by industry partly determine industry prices.

This structure broadly corresponds with that of most macro-economic models which concentrate on real flows of goods and services, for example that of the National Institute [22]. The driving force is effective demand which determines on the one hand industrial output and the derived demand for labour, and on the other hand the demand for imports and the resultant balance of trade surplus or deficit. Differences between the models become more marked when we consider the determination of prices. No attempt is made in the Cambridge model to link wage inflation with unemployment: instead the average wage, the exchange rate and import prices are given by assumption and the implications for prices in different sectors of the economy are worked out using input-output coefficients. But the differences can only really be appreciated by comparing the specifications of the relationships. The specification of the main sets of relationships in the Cambridge model is described in the next section of this paper.

The Main Relationships[1]

(i) *Supplies and demands for commodities*

Volumes of goods and services enter the supply-demand identities

$$m + t_{mo} + q = A_1 y + A_2 v + \Delta^* s + A_3 g + A_4 c + x \tag{1}$$

where m is the import of commodities

    t_{mo} is constant rates of duty

    q is output of commodities

    y is output of industries

    v is investment in fixed capital

    $\Delta^* s$ is stockbuilding

    g is government current expenditure

---

[1] *A note on algebraic conventions.*

Matrices are denoted by capital letters, vectors by small Roman letters and scalars by small Greek letters. $\hat{x}$ is a matrix with the elements of x in the principal diagonal, zeros elsewhere. I is the unit matrix, i the unit vector. log is the logarithm to the base e. Vectors and matrices of parameters are represented by the letters a, b, A and B. Prime denotes transposition.

    c is consumers' expenditure
    x is export of commodities
and A_1 to A_4 are parameters.

Each of the variables in this equation is a vector; the matrices of parameters are necessary to convert the vectors from their own classification into that of commodities, except in the case of A_1 which is an input-output matrix. All imported commodities are classified as the principal products of industries rather than according to the industries which use them.[1] This identity is always satisfied in the projections of the model. The parameters are estimated from past observations, with heavy reliance placed on information from the periodic census of production to obtain base year input-output coefficients.

(ii) *Import and export functions*
Imports are determined from equations of the form

$$\log (\hat{d}^{-1}m)=a_0+\hat{a}_1 \log d+\hat{a}_2 \log (\hat{p}_q^{-1}p_m^*) \qquad (2)$$

where $d =m+t_{mo}+q$ is the total demand for commodities,
    p_m^* is the 'effective' price index of imports in the domestic currency, i.e., it includes customs duties and freight and insurance charges to the port of entry
    p_q is the price index of domestic output
and a_0 to a_2 are parameters.

These equations are estimated by ordinary least squares 1949–66 with the inclusion, where relevant, of lagged relative price terms, capacity variables and time trends. The impact of these other variables is incorporated in the constant term assuming that capacity is at 'normal' levels and that relative prices remain constant. It should be noted that this equation is not used for all imports: some agricultural imports are primarily determined by government policy, whilst price elasticities for many raw materials and foodstuffs cannot be measured because of specification bias.

    The level of exports for a given rate of domestic and world inflation, a given set of exchange rates and growth in world trade is determined exogenously.[2] However we take account of the effects of changes from

---

[1] The alternative is the one used by Leontief [12] and is perhaps the more usual approach. Our treatment means that extra commodities have to be distinguished to take proper account of supplies which are mainly imported such as butter or woodpulp.
[2] We have used estimates provided by the National Ports Council [8], whose study projects exports by S.I.T.C. commodity and world area.

these given levels according to the equations

$$\log x_d = b_0 + b_1 \log (\hat{p}_w^{-1}\theta p_x) + b_2 b_3 \log (\hat{p}_q^{-1}p_x) \qquad (3)$$
$$\log x_s = b_5 + b_4 \log p_x + b_2 \log (\hat{p}_q^{-1}p_x) \qquad (4)$$

where x_d and x_s are the demand and supply of exports

θ is the exchange rate

p_x and p_q are price indices of exports and domestic output

p_w are price indices of competing exports in the rest of the world

and b_0 to b_5 are parameters.

The elasticities b_1 to b_4 are imposed on these equations using preliminary results of our own research on exports as well as published work [11, 31]. Assuming that demands equal supplies, equations (3) and (4) determine exports and export prices; however exports are not only responsive to the relative price of British exports to those of other countries but to the relative price of exported goods to home-produced goods. The latter variable is intended to pick up the effect of changing profit-margins: the greater the relative profits on exports the more the demand curve is pushed up by advertising and the more exports the producer is prepared to supply.

(iii) *Consumption*

Public consumption
This category of consumption is divided into defence, national health service, education and other spending: projections given in the annual White Paper on public expenditure [23] are used to provide real demands in these groups.

The determinants of private consumption
Consumers' expenditure is divided into spending on durables and on non-durables. In this section, only the consumption of non-durables is considered. Consumption is first determined as a whole, using an aggregate consumption function, then the total is divided between spending in different categories using the linear expenditure system.

The aggregate consumption function at present in the model is

$$\varepsilon = \alpha_0 + \alpha_1 \Lambda^{-1}\varepsilon + \alpha_2 \mu \qquad (5)$$

where ε is real consumers' expenditure on non-durables

μ is real personal disposable income (Blue Book definition)

Λ^{-1} is a lag operator

and α_0 to α_2 are parameters.

However we propose to replace this function in the near future by a slightly more complex one developed by Stone [18, 19] where each variable is now on a *per capita* basis.

$$\varepsilon = \alpha_1 \omega_1 + \beta_1(\mu_1 - \delta_1) + \beta_2(\mu_2 - \delta_2) \tag{6}$$

where ω_1 is the permanent component of real wealth

μ_1 and μ_2 are the permanent and transient components of real personal disposable income

δ_1 and δ_2 are real depreciations of personal assets to be included with the permanent and transient components of

income and α_1, β_1 and β_2 are parameters.

The wealth term is in fact calculated as accumulated saving from a base year (1949) estimate of permanent wealth, i.e.

$$\omega_1 = \Lambda^{-1}(\omega_1 + \sigma) \tag{7}$$

where $\sigma \equiv \mu_1 + \mu_2 - \delta_1 - \delta_2 - \varepsilon$, σ being net savings.

Permanent income is related to total income by

$$(\mu_1 - \delta_1) = \lambda(\mu - \delta) + (1 - \lambda)\Lambda^{-1}(\mu_1 - \delta_1) \tag{8}$$

where $\mu = \mu_1 + \mu_2$, $\delta = \delta_1 + \delta_2$

and λ is a constant.

Equations 6 to 8 are solved and first differences taken to provide the estimating equation which is fitted to data 1949–70. Various alternative formulations are also given and estimated in [18] and we intend to experiment with these in the model. In the projections depreciation and the lag structure of expenditures are taken as exogenous.

Once the total of non-durable spending is given, it is divided into a vector of consumers' expenditures with the linear expenditure system

$$e_1 = a_3 + \hat{p}_{e1}^{-1} a_4(\varepsilon \pi_\varepsilon - p'_{e1} a_3) \tag{9}$$

where e_1 is a vector of real *per capita* expenditures on non-durables

p_{e1} is a vector of price indices of e_1

ε is total real *per capita* expenditure on non-durables

π_ε is the price index of consumers' expenditure on non-durables

and a_3 and a_4 are vectors of parameters.

This system has been extensively written up [16, 21] and has the desirable properties of conforming to the postulates of consumer demand theory whilst at the same time ensuring that the individual expenditures sum to total expenditure. It has been estimated by maximum likelihood on annual data 1954–70, with linear time trends in the a_4 parameters to take account of changing tastes [7].

(iv) *Investment*

Investment by consumers in durables
The second component of consumers' expenditure is spending on durables. We distinguish three types of durable good, motor cars and cycles, furniture and floor coverings and radio and electrical goods. Spending in each category is fitted to a stock adjustment model of the type proposed by Stone and Rowe [20].

$$e_2 = a_5 + \hat{a}_6 \Lambda^{-1} e_2 + \hat{a}_7 \mu + \hat{a}_8 (\mu - \Lambda^{-1}\mu)$$
$$+ \hat{a}_9 p_{e2} + \hat{a}_{10}(p_{e2} - \Lambda^{-1}p_{e2}) \tag{10}$$

where e_2 is real *per capita* spending on durables

   μ is real *per capita* personal disposable income

   p_{e2} is the price of durables relative to the overall price index of consumers' expenditures

and Λ^{-1} is, as before, a lag operator.

These equations have been estimated with hire purchase terms although they have not always proved to be significant. As we do not expect hire purchase credit to be used as an instrument of future policy, we have not included it in the model.

Fixed investment in the public sector
Again, as with public consumption, the real spending in this category is taken as exogenous, using the figures given in the annual White Paper [23]. This is a change in our practice, because previously fixed investment in nationalized industries was estimated in the model by incremental capital-output ratios. The change is important because this investment is now assumed to be unresponsive to growth in the industries' outputs and therefore any extra output has to come through an increase in the use of labour.[1]

Fixed investment by private industries
The present treatment of industrial investment is essentially unchanged since the last complete specification of the model [2] except for the change of base year valuation from 1960 prices to 1963 prices. Briefly gross investment, classified by the industry doing the investing and by three types of asset, comprises replacements and extensions. Replacements are determined by estimates of average life [15] whilst extensions are related to the changes in industrial output:

$$V = A_5 + A_6 \Delta^* \hat{y} \tag{11}$$

---

[1] The reason for this is discussed more fully in section IV below.

where V is the matrix of gross investment, industry by asset

A_5 is replacements

A_6 is the matrix of incremental capital-output ratios

$\hat{y}$ is industrial output

and Δ^* is the forward first difference.

This is essentially the accelerator approach to investment determination, the accelerators being estimated from a peak-to-peak analysis of past investments and the changes in output. The effects of changes in investment incentives are incorporated in the model as changes in the matrix of replacements.

Stockbuilding

The last category of investment is stockbuilding which is estimated on the basis of normal stock-output ratios calculated for stocks of raw materials, work in progress and finished goods held by industry groups. One of the major stock-holding industries is engineering, and developments in the engineering industry have a disproportionate effect on stockbuilding. The relationships can be expressed as

$$\Delta^*s = A_7 \Lambda q - A_8 q \tag{12}$$

where s is the level of real stocks by commodity

q is real commodity output

Δ^* is the forward difference operator and Λ is the forward lag

and A_7 and A_8 are matrices of normal stock-output ratios, stocks of commodities by industries holding stocks.

This treatment is fully described in [2].

(v) *Employment, investment and output*

We adopt the vintage approach to production functions, analysing only the effects of gross investment on labour employed and industrial output. In addition, we have attempted to abstract from short-term changes in output caused by changes in the utilization of capacity, developing a model which assumes that normal output changes only when new equipment is installed or old equipment is scrapped. This model of the production process has been proposed and estimated by Wigley [32] and it has since been estimated in a more disaggregated form with data on long-run growth rates of the industrial sectors of the main model 1954–68. The form of the equations in the model is

$$\hat{y}^{-1}\Delta^*y = \hat{a}_{11}\hat{y}_e^{-1}\Delta^*y_e + (I - \hat{a}_{11}\hat{a}_{12}^{-1})\hat{a}_{13}^{-1}\hat{y}^{-1}v \tag{13}$$

where y is the normal level of industrial output

y_e is industrial employment

v is fixed investment by industry in all assets

Δ^* is the forward difference operator

and a_{11}, a_{12} and a_{13} are vectors of parameters.

The assumptions lying behind this approach are discussed in more detail in the next section of the paper. The functions provide us with estimates of the overall labour requirement after investment and output have been determined; but no constraint is put on this requirement, instead it acts as a guide to the pressures in the labour market given the other assumptions of a projection.

(vi) *Prices and profits*

The theory of profit embodied in the model is that industries set their prices so that profits will remain a constant proportion of the wage and salary bill after all costs have been passed on. Thus

$$p_y = A_1'p_h + w + p_r + t_y + m_y \tag{14}$$

where p_y is a vector of industrial unit-value indices

p_h is a vector of unit-values of commodity inputs

w is the wage bill per unit of output (including all national insurance contributions)

p_r is profit per unit of output

t_y is net taxes and subsidies per unit of output

m_y is direct imports per unit of output (e.g. charter payments for shipping)

and A_1 is the input-output matrix;

$$w = \hat{a}_{14}\hat{y}^{-1}y_e\rho \tag{15}$$

where a_{14} is a vector of industrial wage differentials

and ρ is the average industrial wage imposed by assumption;

and

$$p_r = \hat{a}_{15}w \tag{16}$$

where a_{15} is projected from past trends in each industry.

This leaves unit-values of domestic absorptions, p_h, and the unit-values of the various categories of final demand to be determined:

$$p_h = \hat{a}_{16}p_q + (I - \hat{a}_{16})p_m^* \tag{17}$$

Absorption prices p_h are a weighted average of output prices and import prices, the weights a_{16} being the proportion of domestic absorptions which is domestically-produced. Prices for final demands, the most important of which are consumers' expenditure prices, are derived from prices of domestic absorptions p_h with allowance for direct payments of wages and rent as well as for various subsidies and indirect taxes.

(vii) Incomes and expenditures

The most important financial sector from the point of view of the model is the personal sector, which is divided into households, non-profit-making bodies and life assurance companies, since it is the only one in which real expenditure decisions are affected by income (equation 5 above). However five other financial sectors are also distinguished so that a complete account can be given of expenditure and income in the economy [33]. Income arises from three sources: first, direct payments are made by industries in the form of profits, income from self-employment, wages and salaries and tax payments; second, other direct payments are made quite independently of the first source, in the form of direct transfers, pensions, interest payments and rent; and third, various inter-sectoral payments and receipts are made depending on the level and composition of incomes. In the third category there is the distribution of dividends by the company sectors to other sectors, property income paid abroad by industrial and commercial companies, and the payment of tax by each sector to the government sector.

Dividend distribution by the corporate sectors

The present corporate distribution functions included in the model are of the form

$$d_i = a_{17} + a_{18}\Lambda^{-1}d_i + a_{19}y_i + a_{20}d_{ti} \qquad (18)$$

where d_i is the payments of dividends by sector i

y_i is the gross income of sector i

d_{ti} is a tax variable (the difference between distributed and undistributed profits tax rates).

However we have work in hand which will replace these functions by ones which are more sophisticated in their treatment of the tax effects:

$$\log d_i = a_{17} + a_{18}\Lambda^{-1}\log d_i + a_{19}\log y_i^* + a_{20}\log \tau_i \qquad (19)$$

where y_i^* is gross income adjusted for the tax liability on profits and the tax gain from depreciation allowances

and τ_i is the net dividends foregone by the shareholder, i.e. it reflects the growth in share values through retentions.

This model is an adaptation of the equations developed by King [9, 10] with dividends defined as gross of tax. It implies that companies look to the post-tax income and revaluations ultimately accruing to the shareholder in their dividend decisions. The estimating equation also takes account of takeover activity but this variable is not included in the main model.

Property income paid abroad by industrial and commercial companies

This is calculated as a function of the stock of foreign investment in industry and weighted together by the share of foreign investment in each industry in the total.

Tax payments by the company sectors

Depreciation allowances have first to be estimated on the basis of allowances for current investment by type of asset and allowances on the existing stock of capital. Corporation tax accrues on taxable income after deducting tax at the standard rate payable on distributed dividends. It is paid after allowing for a time lag between tax accruals and payments.

Tax payments by the household sector

Income to households is divided into eight types ranging from self-employed income to family allowances. These incomes are adjusted to obtain the Inland Revenue's definition of taxable incomes which are then divided between income groups for 'single persons' and 'married men' separately. The division enables us to build up tax payments with a fair degree of accuracy, whether on the old basis of earned income allowances etc. or on the new basis of tax credits. Total tax payments are deducted from household income and the net current income of life assurance and superannuation companies (which the Central Statistical Office includes in the personal sector) is added in to obtain the money value of personal disposable income. This total is deflated by the price index of consumers' expenditure and divided by the population to obtain real personal disposable income *per capita* which is needed in the consumption function (equation 5).

The Growth in Productivity and Employment

Average labour productivity for the economy as a whole does not enter the model described above, although it is of course implied in any projection. However the concept does enter the assumptions of the vintage production functions for each industry (equation 13): productivity on new equipment is assumed to be a constant proportion of productivity on all equipment in use in each industry and a similar assumption is made about scrapped equipment. These proportions are estimated from long-term trends in the past growth of output and employment, assuming that equipment is scrapped when it yields zero profit [32]. Changes in the normal levels of output in the model can only come about through the installation of new equipment (gross fixed investment) or through the scrapping of old equipment. Since productivity of the former is generally higher than average for all equipment in use and that of the latter is generally lower, both investment and scrapping will imply higher average labour productivities; indeed in many industries this is sufficient to reduce their labour requirements over time.

As we have seen, investment is determined by the acceleration principle, whilst the growth in output is determined by demands on the system. The production functions can now be solved to find labour requirements. This implies that if industries find that their investment is insufficient to support a normal level of output, they reduce the scrapping of old equipment and therefore require more labour to man the less productive equipment in use. On the other hand an increase in investment (brought about for example by investment incentives) will save on labour requirements by raising average productivities in the industries which do the investing.

Average productivity for the whole economy is therefore determined partly by employment and output of the government sector which is exogenous and partly by the industrial structure of the growth in output and the maintained level of gross investment which in turn determine labour requirements in each industry. In the recent past there have been substantial changes in the structure of investment; for example over the five-year period 1966 to 1971 gross fixed investment in distribution and services rose by 43 per cent, whilst that in engineering and vehicles fell by 8 per cent.[1] We would look to these changes, rather than a change in underlying trend, to explain the recent rise in the growth of productivity. In consequence, in any projection of the economy, continued growth in overall productivity is dependent on the type of demands made on the industrial system and how it reacts to these demands with its investment plans. As it happens, in our current projections we anticipate continued changes in favour of services so that for growth rates of output 1971–75 of about 5 per cent per annum the growth in productivity is about 3·2 per cent per annum.

[1] C.S.O., *Monthly Digest of Statistics*, January 1973, pp. 12–13

So far there has been scant mention of the feasibility of the growth in output in terms of the capacity of the capital goods industries or the working population. None of the various obstacles to growth associated with these factors is built into the model: if the capacity of a particular industry threatens to choke the growth in the supply of a product, *ad hoc* adjustments would have to be made to the wage differential resulting in higher prices, more imports and reduced demands; and if the total of employment *in all industries*, as well as in government and the personal sector, approaches the total working population then any projection becomes increasingly untenable because wage levels in the model are assumed to be unrelated to the pressure of demand for labour. Forecasts of the working population, adjusted for the level of unemployment, are regarded as checks on the feasibility of projections rather than supplying a base on which to calculate the growth in productive potential.

The area of productivity, investment and employment is one of great importance in medium-term models and we are continuing the development of the vintage approach [14]. In particular there are several features of our present treatment which we intend to revise. First, the incremental capital-output ratios used in the investment functions (equation 11) are not necessarily compatible with those estimated for new equipment in the production functions (equation 13). Second, it would be better to treat labour and capital demands together rather than independently; after all, the investment decision is not taken in isolation from the state of the labour market. Third, the present method of estimation only makes use of long-term growth rates and all the year-to-year information is lost. Fourth, we are investigating the effect of investment incentives and labour taxes on investment and employment, and this requires estimates of price effects on factor demands. However there are considerable problems to be solved, both in theory and measurement, before explicit factor demand equations, with an implicit production function, can be introduced into the model.

The Exchange Rate, Inflation and the Balance of Payments

Recent historical experience of trade and payments crises have been particularly traumatic for British economic policy so it is only natural that a great deal of attention should be paid to the foreign trade sectors in models of the economy. The exchange rate is used in our model as a key instrument of policy to be adjusted with other instruments so as to achieve employment and balance of payments targets. This is wholly appropriate because changes in the exchange rate take a long time to work themselves out and we are more interested in their eventual effects than in the immediate deficit or surplus which follows a devaluation or revaluation.

Exchange rate movements shift the sterling demand schedule for exports and the sterling supply schedule for imports. We assume that exports are not in perfectly elastic supply, so that the sterling price rises after a devaluation; in fact we assume that the greater part of a devaluation is absorbed in rising sterling prices, with the passing on of import price increases and the raising of profit margins on exports. However there is also a second effect on exports, purely as a result of higher profit margins, and this results in increased volumes of exports without any reduction in their relative price. Import prices, on the other hand, are assumed to rise by the full amount of any devaluation except when the import comes from an economy like Eire whose exchange rate tends to move with sterling. The reasons for this assumption are that most manufactured imports have a highly elastic supply with regard to changes in the British price whilst most raw material and food imports have a highly inelastic demand.

The initial effect of these price changes is on the volumes of trade, the elasticities being derived from the log-linear trade functions (equations 2, 3 and 4 above). Five features of these functions are worth describing in detail.

Firstly the price elasticities are assumed to be constant. This is a useful property in forecasting work, since if the more usual form of the relationship is used[1] the estimated price elasticities will be lower at the end of the period than at the beginning. This effect will probably be exacerbated in any future projection. It is due to the fact that proportionally more imports are required at higher levels of real expenditure in the economy.

Secondly the introduction of the level of demand as an explanatory variable is necessary to account for the increasing share of trade in world production and consumption. The theoretical reason for this is that a much greater variety and design of products is available on the international as opposed to the national market due to economies of scale in production and differences in national demand structures. As consumers become better off, it can be shown that they demand more varieties of products, partly because they can afford them. This

[1] Involving constant marginal propensities to import rather than constant elasticities of demand for imports.

naturally results in an increasing proportion of imports in consumption which is directly related to the level of demand.

Thirdly the effect of customs duties and any temporary charge on imports is felt directly on imports through the relative price term. Any announcement about changes in duties or the end of the surcharge may produce a reallocation of imports over time, but this effect can be included in the equation by means of a dummy variable, leaving the effect on consumption of imports as part of the relative price effect. However data problems have precluded the same treatment for exports.

Fourthly lagged responses are included for price changes but not demand changes. It is reasonable to expect greater delay in price response than in the demand response because part of any changes in demand is directly on imported goods, whereas the response to prices requires a readjustment of purchasing patterns. A lagged response to demand will only appear in the function if trade responds less quickly than domestic output. The assumption that there is no difference in the lag may distort the short-term reaction but not the long-term one.

Fifthly the disaggregation allows for a much more sophisticated relationship between total import and export demands and prices than is usual in econometric models. Empirical studies [1, 11] have shown that different imports differ considerably in their reactions to changes in demands and relative prices. Since these determinants themselves change in composition both in the short-term and the long-term it would seem essential to do some disaggregation in order to remove the most blatant bias. For example, the unit-value series for imports of manufactures into Britain has been seriously distorted by changes in the prices of copper and other non-ferrous metals which have taken place in the last few years. However these non-ferrous metals are essential raw materials with low price elasticities and the imports have not responded to the price changes. Any attempt to measure price elasticities for imports of manufactures using this unit-value series will fail to obtain significant estimates of the right sign [13].

The export functions have been fitted for data 1951–68, but we are re-estimating them to include a longer span of post-devaluation years before including them in the model. At present the average price elasticity for exports is estimated at -1.75. The import functions are estimated for 1949–66 and again work is in hand to include post-devaluation years. Here the average price elasticity is estimated at -0.65, whilst the elasticity in response to a change in total demands is 1.46 [1].

The effect of devaluation in the model is highly dependent on what is assumed about fiscal policy and inflation. If fiscal policy is used to maintain full employment, and if the assumption of the average wage is not affected by the devaluation, then it will increase export volumes, export unit-values and import unit-values (all in sterling) and reduce import volumes. An effective 10 per cent devaluation in 1972 is estimated to improve the balance of trade in 1975 at current prices by £1,500m. under these circumstances. If, however, there are unemployed resources in the economy and deflationary policies are unnecessary (but maintaining the fixed domestic wage rates) then the change in the balance of trade is much smaller, of the order of £500m., because the effects of increased incomes more than offset the effects of relative price changes, and the volume of imports rises.

The other side of the coin to devaluation is the domestic inflation which often makes it necessary. This too can have major effects on employment and the balance of trade, except that the effects are less sudden and less noticeable, being more akin to a continued appreciation of the currency. In the model, the domestic average wage is given by assumption simply because we do not believe that a relationship between unemployment and wage inflation at any level of unemployment above about $1\frac{1}{2}$ to 2 per cent has any meaning in the medium-term context. But we are aware that the assumption has a critical effect on the projections, especially when the exchange rate is fixed, because fairly small changes in the rate of inflation (by contemporary standards) have substantial effects on employment and the balance of trade. And if the policy is to peg the exchange rate *and* to maintain full employment, the model would predict trade deficits of £600m. in 1975 for an extra 1 per cent per annum increase in the average wage 1971–75, not much by comparison with the increases in 1972.

The preceding discussion has been in terms of effects on the balance of trade, yet long-term equilibrium is in terms of the balance of official settlements. In the model the balance of trade is treated analogously to employment, that is as a target for policy or as an indication of the feasibility of a projection bearing in mind the probable outcome for the capital account and the possibility of the official financing of deficits.

Developing a Dynamic Input-Output Model

It was stressed at the beginning of the paper that the model is continually being modified and revised on account of new data, theories and techniques of estimation. Several of these developments have already been noted, particularly in respect of the foreign trade and production relationships. However in this concluding section I should like to concentrate on the question of developing the model so that it tracks year by year from the past instead of projecting the economy for one target year in the future.

As noted in the introductory section the purpose of the model is to represent underlying relationships in the system, abstracting from short-term fluctuations, so as to provide a framework for analysing the economy in the medium-term. This is reflected in the structure of the model, for example in the absence of capacity terms in the foreign trade functions, as well as in the methods of estimating the parameters which are often non-stochastic (the input-output coefficients) or based on long-term time trends (the production coefficients). Short-term variables are sometimes included in the estimating equations, only to be excluded from the model in much the same way that the stochastic terms are excluded although it should be emphasized that the assumptions made about short-term behaviour and about the error structure have an important bearing on the long-term parameters.

There are powerful advantages to this approach because it encourages ruthless simplification of many relationships—most notably those concerning stockbuilding—which may be highly problematic, but which contribute little to a medium-term assessment. Indeed if we were not prepared to do this, it is doubtful whether we would have been able to build an operational model at all. Nevertheless there are also substantial advantages in making our assumptions about transient behaviour explicit within the model. The differences between underlying trends and actual observations can then be made unambiguous and explicit in the light of a particular set of assumptions about the specification of the model and the values given to its parameters and exogenous variables.

The development of a dynamic model will enable us to tackle four problems we have encountered in our work. First there is the fundamental concept of the medium-term projection appropriate to economic planning. What precisely do we mean by a 'trend' or a 'normal' year in our projections? The answer to this question depends on being able to specify in detail the conditions we would impose on a model of the actual economy in order to produce the trend economy we are projecting. We know many of the conditions we might impose already, for example, fixed stock-output ratios and constant utilization of industrial capacity; but even these may prove inappropriate in the medium-term context.

Second, we have become increasingly aware that transient effects, which have traditionally been excluded from input-output models, remain significant even in the medium-term. Recent work by Stone on the consumption function [18] indicates long lags in adjustment; in a system of equations such adjustments reverberate and the assumption that the economy has reached equilibrium after three or four years is patently wrong. We have already recognized the adjustment lag for private consumption in the model by postulating the temporal distribution of any increase in income between the recent past and the projection year, but it would be clearly more satisfactory to solve the system as a whole year-by-year.

Third, the problems of economic management and control are bound up with the phasing of policies and the time lags in their operation. This applies equally to problems involving macro-economic adjustment and those involving structural change, with which we are particularly concerned. For example it would be of great interest for us to be able to pick up the 'J curve' effect of devaluation on the balance of trade—an effect which is implicit in the parameters of our trade functions, but which is ignored in our target year projections.

Fourth, at present the projections can only be tested by making assumptions about short-term behaviour, which is not represented in the model. Although the usefulness of a model is not determined by whether it can be tested (indeed a valuable service of models is to predict situations which never materialize) it would be salutary if checks could readily be performed on projections after the event.

Where does all this leave the 'underlying trends' of the medium-term projection? We can begin by ruling out the steady-state growth path for the system as a whole because it does not appear to be remotely within the time horizon of the medium-term, if it exists at all. Otherwise there are two alternatives which relate to the treatment of government policies. In each alternative all the exogenous variables except policy instruments would be set at 'normal' values, defined as long-run trends averaging over the cycle. The first alternative would have policy instruments at actual past or present values, giving a view of the economy without the effects of shocks and cycles in the exogenous variables or the relationships except those introduced by government policy. The projections under this alternative would be the dynamic analogue of our current no-policy-change target view. The second alternative is to postulate stabilizing government policies which automatically guide the economy along a prescribed path. The policies need not necessarily be optimum by any criterion, but they do have to be explicit. For example a full employment policy would have different effects on the development of the economy depending on whether it involved income tax changes, public expenditure changes or exchange rate changes.

Both of these alternatives would probably mean that the 'underlying trends' were in fact compensating cycles; but this is probably an inescapable fact of economic life.

B. AN APPLICATION OF THE MODEL TO THE PERIOD 1972–75

The Problem

The British government, after eventually tackling with some success the unemployment problem of 1969–72, has embarked on a grand strategy of economic growth, full employment and the control of prices and incomes. The strategy emerged after the 1972 budget which was reflationary for the second year running. An incomes and prices policy, the government argued, would have much more chance of success in a climate of rising real incomes. Previous failures were due to the use of the policy to back up other deflationary measures, but now the exclusive aim was to moderate the rate of inflation and to improve the position of the low-paid. Growth, as opposed to full employment, now became the emblem of economic policy and the government committed itself to sustaining a higher rate of growth—put at 5 per cent per annum 1972–74.

However there are serious doubts whether the labour force available will be sufficient for a 5 per cent growth rate to be sustained. And there is also the perennial problem of the balance of payments, which remains even with a floating currency because any depreciation of sterling has immediate effects on domestic prices undermining the control of inflation. This paper considers these problems in the context of medium-term projections of the British economy using a large scale input-output model. The model is described above in a separate paper.[1] Here the emphasis is on the application of the model to the analysis of current developments in the economy.[2]

The plan of the paper is first to set down the main assumptions underlying the projections, then to assess the projections given by the

---

[1] 'An input-output model of the British economy', see pp. 25 *et seq.* above.

[2] An earlier application of the model, which sets out the methodology and assumptions in more detail than is possible here, was published in 1972 as 'Inflation, growth and economic policy in the medium-term', by T. S. Barker and V. H. Woodward, *National Institute Economic Review*, No. 60, May 1972, pp. 37–55.

competitors in world markets. The domestic inflation in these countries has spilt over on to their export prices which have been further raised by currency revaluation. The quantitative effects on British exports are extremely uncertain since they depend on divergencies in rates of inflation which themselves have been rather variable from year to year. Nevertheless, the effects should be substantial and, providing the British rate of inflation as measured by the rise in home unit costs is restrained to 7 per cent per annum 1972–75 (see below), then we expect the net advantage to British exports to be somewhere in the range of 2–3 per cent per annum.

The competitiveness of exports and the price of imports is bound up with the exchange rate for sterling. In the year 1972 sterling floated down in respect to other currencies by nearly 10 per cent. Since the beginning of 1973 the dollar has weakened whilst other European currencies (except the Italian lira) have strengthened against the pound. We have assumed that the *effective* depreciation of sterling (i.e. taking into account movements in other currencies and the composition of British foreign trade) is 10 per cent since the Smithsonian agreement of December 1971.

(iii) *Domestic inflation*

Phase Two of the government's pay and prices policy [26] comes to an end in the autumn of 1973. But the policy is continuing and it is reasonable to anticipate that there will be some form of control over prices, pay, dividends and rent over the next two years. We have assumed that the control broadly takes the form of Phase Two of the policy, i.e., limits on pay which favour the lower-paid (but which are not related to productivity increases), limits on profits so that only unavoidable costs are passed on to prices and continued limits on dividends and rent.

This target for wage-cost inflation amounts to the restraint of the rate of increase of average industrial wages to just over 9 per cent per annum 1971–75 compared to 6 per cent per annum 1960–69. The rapid increase in import prices might result in the relaxation of the pay policy in which case domestic inflation will accelerate accompanied by a reduction in employment and a deterioration of the balance of payments (provided that tax and expenditure policies are unchanged and that sterling does not depreciate). We shall consider this alternative later, but in the meantime we shall assume that inflation is controlled.

Other elements of the prices policy are incorporated into our model. Thus cost increases due to value-added tax and import price increases are all assumed to be passed on to industrial prices, and profits are held down to a fixed proportion of each industry's wages bill, a proportion which is calculated by reference to past shares of profits in value-added.

The Use of Resources, Employment and the Balance of Trade

For the purpose of the analysis we shall take the target growth rate desired by the government to be 5 per cent per annum growth in gross domestic product at factor cost 1972–75. This is illustrated in chart 1 which shows two measures of gross domestic product, the output and the expenditure measures, from 1955 to 1972 with target growth 1972–75. The divergence of the measures in 1972 is remarkable and is a reminder of the margin of error in past data let alone in the projections. We have assumed that the divergence will not increase after 1972.

In order to reach this target growth, a slight reduction in the standard rate of income tax (of 1p in the £) is needed to raise effective demand. The resultant division of gross domestic product between its main components is shown in table 1. The exceptional growth in consumers' expenditure 1971–72 is clearly the short-term effect of the reduction in taxes in the 1972 budget and the increase in government expenditure in late 1972. There are several reasons why it will slow down in the longer term. First, the increase in import prices will reduce real income; second, the introduction of V.A.T. represents a return to the higher levels of indirect taxation operating before the 1972 budget;[1] and third, the inflation in wages and incomes will increase the real burden of taxation on personal incomes.

However the reduction in growth of consumers' expenditure after 1973 should be compensated for by an increase in growth of investment spending and exports. Gross fixed capital formation has been depressed since 1970 but the upsurge in orders for capital goods and in output of the engineering and construction industries since mid-1972 confirms that higher growth in the economy will stimulate investment. The increase in exports we have projected is due to buoyant world trade and the substantial improvement in competitiveness of British exports since the depreciation of sterling in 1972. It is therefore dependent on the continued control of domestic inflation in Britain which is one of the crucial assumptions underlying this set of projections.

---

[1] In the 1972 budget S.E.T. was halved and P.T. rates were reduced so as to smooth the transition to V.A.T. However the standard rate of V.A.T. was set so as to raise the same revenue as S.E.T. and P.T. at their full rates.

The increase in imports 1970–75 is well above that in earlier five-year periods. This is partly because the overall growth rate is higher, but there is also a tendency for imports to grow faster as the share of finished goods and semi-manufactures rises in the total.

Chart 1. Output and Expenditure Measure of Gross Domestic Product (at 1963 factor cost) 1955–72

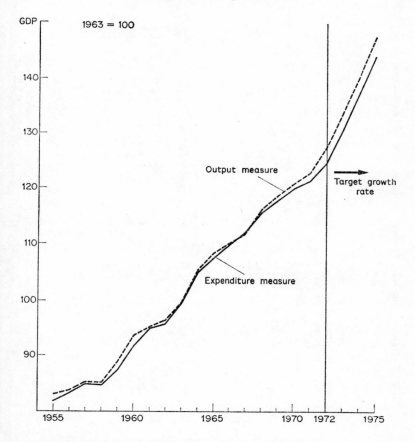

Table 2 shows the employment which is required to produce the output. It is broken down into employment by the goods and service industries separately, by government and by the personal sector. The projection of employment for target growth is compared with that for 'full employment' which is here defined as an unemployment rate of

Table 1. Gross Domestic Product and the Use of Resources, U.K., 1955–75

	Consumers' expenditure	Public authorities' current expenditure	Gross fixed capital formation	Stock building	Exports of goods and services	less imports of goods and services	Gross domestic product at market prices	less adjustment for factor cost	Gross domestic product at factor cost
				£ million 1963 prices					
1970	23447	5889	7152	266	8627	8356	37025	4406	32619
1972	25678	6340	7140	−331	9248	9543	38532	5015	33517
PROJECTIONS 1975 target growth	28277	6825	9355	363	11516	11726	44609	5502	39107
				growth rates per cent per annum					
1955–60	2·8	−0·1	5·6	15·8	2·7	4·4	2·5	4·0	2·4
1960–65	2·9	2·6	6·2	−9·8	3·6	3·0	3·3	2·6	3·3
1965–70	1·9	1·6	2·9	−6·8	6·2	4·9	2·5	3·3	2·4
1970–71	2·6	3·9	−0·6	..	5·1	4·6	1·7	4·0	1·4
1971–72	6·8	3·6	0·4	..	2·0	9·2	2·3	9·5	1·3
PROJECTIONS 1970–75 target growth	3·8	3·0	5·5	6·4	5·9	7·0	3·8	4·5	3·7

.. denotes not calculated

Source: *National Income and Expenditure, 1972; Preliminary Estimates of National and Balance of Payments 1967 to 1972*, Cmnd. 5261, H.M.S.O., March 1973.

2 per cent on a Department of Employment basis, using official projections of the working population. There is clearly going to be some pressure on the labour market if 5 per cent growth is maintained to 1975, but on these projections of the working population this pressure is not likely to be severe and is not going to halt the expansion. The

Table 2. Employment, U.K., 1955–75

(thousands)

	Industry goods	services	Govern- ment	Personal Sector	Total	Unemploy- ment	Working Population
1958	12035	8539	2944	760	24278	406	24684
1968	11876	9155	3517	735	25283	542	25825
PROJECTIONS 1975							
(1) target growth	11598	9445	3731	735	25509	..	..
(2) full employment	11526	9427	3731	735	25419	452	25871

.. denotes not calculated

reason for this is the continued rise in productivity which is sufficient to allow a reduction in the numbers employed in goods industries despite their much greater output. The projections imply a growth in productivity for the economy as a whole of 3·2 per cent per annum 1968–75 which is well above that achieved in the previous decade of 2·8 per cent per annum.

The projected change in the composition of employment shows a continuation of the changes which took place in the 1960s. Broadly speaking there is a shift out of goods-producing industries, particularly the primary industries like agriculture and coal, into the service industries and government.

Table 3 shows the balance of trade in goods and services for the target growth. This is derived from projections of volumes and unit values of exports and imports at a very detailed level; these are shown in total in the first two panels of the table, together with some past figures for comparison. The projected unit values show substantial increases over their 1972 levels. This is mainly because of the 1972 depreciation of sterling, although the rise in food, fuel and raw material import prices also influences the projections.[1] The terms of trade have fallen sharply from their 1971 levels; the projections show them as

[1] At the time of writing the unit values for exports and imports of *goods* had already risen to 160 and 159 respectively for the first quarter of 1973 (1963=100).

stabilizing at 101 with 1963 as 100. The net effect of the volume and unit value changes is a small deficit on the balance of trade.

It should be emphasized that the projected balance of trade is particularly uncertain and depends heavily on the containment of inflation. It only requires an extra 2 per cent per annum rate of wage increase 1972–75 to increase the balance of trade deficit from £139

Table 3. The Balance of Trade in Goods and Services, U.K., 1955–75

	Exports of goods and services			Imports of goods and services			Terms of	Balance of
	£m	£m 1963 prices	unit value 1963=100	£m	£m 1963 prices	unit value 1963=100	trade 1963=100	trade £m
1955	4177	4664	89·6	4481	4571	98·0	91·4	−304
1960	5147	5327	96·6	5554	5669	98·0	98·6	−407
1965	6561	6343	103·4	6861	6577	104·3	99·2	−300
1970	11344	8627	131·5	10844	8356	129·8	101·4	500
1971	12601	9065	139·2	11804	8738	135·1	103·1	797
1972	13229	9248	143·0	13430	9543	140·7	101·6	−201
PROJECTIONS 1975 target growth	20592	11516	178·8	20731	11726	176·8	101·1	−139

Source: *National Income and Expenditure, 1972 and preliminary Estimates of National Income and Balance of Payments 1967 to 1972, Cmnd. 5261, H.M.S.O., March 1973*

million to £1,800 million if the government fixes the exchange rate and tries to maintain full employment by domestic reflation.

All considered, this set of projections is very favourable to the government's plan for maintaining a 5 per cent growth rate over the 2–3 years from 1972. However there is little indication that the underlying, sustainable growth rate will be raised much above 3 to 3·5 per cent per annum which is the rate of growth of productivity in the economy as a whole. The 5 per cent growth is only possible because of the slack existing in the economy in 1972. In fact the projections indicate that total employment rises by 1 million between 1972 and 1975 as unemployment falls and participation rates rise. When the unemployment pool has been absorbed then there will not be enough labour to maintain faster growth without very large increases in investment. And on present evidence investment on the scale required will not be forthcoming in the immediate future. The government will eventually have to restrain growth in output within the capacity of the working population.

Inflation as a Threat to Full Employment

The main threat to employment in contemporary Britain is inflation. The projections given above presuppose that wages do not rise any faster than 9 per cent per annum 1972–75. If there is a tendency for them to rise much less than this, then the pressure of demand in the labour market will become intolerable as exports rise, whilst if they rise much more, then the volume of exports will suffer, bringing down effective demand in Britain. This knife-edge will exist at any rate of inflation which is taken as the basis for a particular policy stance.

Although the effect of extra inflation on foreign trade is the main reason for reduced employment it is not the only one. The fiscal system also depresses employment as inflation proceeds: the higher incomes of wage earners bring more of them into the higher personal tax brackets, whilst personal tax allowances become worth less in real terms as prices rise. It used to be assumed that this effect of inflation was compensated for by the reduction in real yields of specific duties. But these duties have been falling rather fast as a proportion of tax revenue because they have not been increased during recent years of high inflation and because a substantial part of the duties has been replaced by value-added tax, the revenue from which increases with prices.

The danger to employment is that the compensating adjustments to the exchange rate or to tax rates and government expenditures, which are necessary to prevent any extra inflation causing unemployment, do not take place quickly enough. It requires considerable political courage for a government, faced with a sudden upsurge of wages and prices, to counteract the depressing effects of the inflation by a devaluation *and* some reflation. Indeed a devaluation will worsen the inflation by raising import prices, but the alternative is the falling-away of exports and subsequent unemployment. If such unemployment is cured by domestic reflation the problem will re-emerge as a deficit in the balance of trade.

The policy of some reflation accompanying the devaluation is contrary to the orthodox prescription of deflation in order to release resources for the exporting and import-substituting industries. However if the initial position is one of full employment and balanced foreign trade, there is no question of releasing resources because none are needed: the problem is one of compensating for the internal inflation by manipulating the exchange rate. Clearly there is much more flexibility in doing this if the exchange rate is floating rather than fixed. When internal prices and incomes are rising, and the external position is safeguarded by a depreciating currency, some reflation is needed to offset the 'fiscal drag' of the tax system so as to maintain internal balance.

A crucial aspect of the policy is its timing. Since price effects take some time to work through (perhaps up to two or three years in the case of exports), the full effects of domestic inflation on trade will not be apparent at the time of the inflation. In fact the initial effects will be favourable to the trade balance because sterling export prices will rise in the short-term without much effect on export volumes. But if compensating action is not taken at the time of the domestic inflation, export growth will diminish, and unemployment will be created. At this point economic policy may well create what we might call a 'cycle of induced deficits'. The government will be tempted to cure the unemployment by domestic reflation because there is no obvious balance of payments crisis; but this in turn will eventually cause severe balance of payments problems because imports will increase in volume without any increase in exports to pay for them. Indeed, some exports may be diverted to the domestic market. The balance of payments problem will have to be solved by currency depreciation or control on imports; but this will now result in excessive demands on domestic resources which will have to be reduced by domestic deflation. If demand management is successful and wage inflation is contained then the devaluation will work and the cycle will come to an end. But if the deflation is insufficient or if wage or profit inflation emerges as competing groups try to maintain higher real incomes brought about by the earlier reflation, then the cycle will continue.

It is easy to see how policies may get out of phase like this so that the government generates a cycle of unemployment, inflation and real income by taking too short a view as to the outcome of its policies. The danger is particularly great when policy is geared to short-term demand management in an open economy. This strengthens the case for a floating exchange rate, but even if the rate were floating there is still a possibility of such a cycle being induced if speculators are very short-sighted.

The serious effects of inflation if exchange rate changes are mistimed make its control by a prices and incomes policy even more worthwhile. But too much can be expected of such a policy. As the pressure of demand for labour rises the incentives for collusion between employers and employees in breaking the spirit of the policy, if not the letter, also rise. And the policy cannot contend with inflation imported into the economy from abroad.

One of the more volatile elements in final demand is investment, particularly housebuilding. An extra 10 per cent increase in housebuilding increases employment by some 100,000 including all the indirect effects on the rest of the economy. To give an idea as to the deflation required to release this labour, the standard rate of personal tax would have to be raised by just over 1p in the £ if total employment was to be held constant. Clearly investment uncertainties represent a second threat to employment but only if investment is not enough to maintain full employment. If it is much greater than expected it will cause excess demand inflation and a deterioration of the balance of trade position if exchange rates are fixed. The inflation might go away, but only at the expense of a large balance of trade deficit because the extra demands for goods and services are being met by imports. In this event the correct policy is deflation rather than depreciation because the foreign exchange position is fundamentally in balance.

The problem of imported inflation is more serious, especially if the imports are unavoidable. If world prices change in favour of raw materials and foodstuffs and against manufactures, there will be a shift in the distribution of world real income against the more industrialized countries like Britain. There is no alternative in this situation: if external equilibrium is to be maintained, British real incomes must be lower than if the price change had not taken place. The rise in import prices poses three problems for policy. First, the balance of trade position will worsen sharply and will require correction by import controls or depreciation of sterling. However, one moderating factor here is the possibility that the higher food and raw material prices will raise incomes in producing countries and this in turn will raise their imports from Britain. Second, the price increase of basic foodstuffs will reduce real income but the reduction will be highly inequitable. Fiscal measures are required if the burden is to be spread more equitably over the population. Third, demand-management policies may be needed in order to reduce incomes still further because the reflationary effects of depreciation are not entirely compensated for by the deflationary effects of the import price increase. In these circumstances the prices and incomes policy is in difficulties because it has to combine control of wages and prices with some redistribution of income but now against the background of a slower growth in total real income. Furthermore, sterling depreciation is going to raise prices still further so that public confidence in the control of prices is liable to be seriously undermined.

A British prices and incomes policy cannot stop world inflation. It can however play a part, along with exchange rate policies and the management of demand, in isolating the domestic economy from the worst effects of world inflation. What is absolutely essential is that these policies work together in a coherent strategy for maintaining full employment. And this strategy has to be flexible: the threat to employment lies not only in an upsurge of inflation or a collapse of investment expectations but in the failure of policy to adjust to such changes.

C. REFERENCES

1. BARKER, T. S. *The Determinants of Britain's Visible Imports 1949–1966*. Vol. 10 in *A Programme for Growth*, ed. Richard Stone, Chapman and Hall, 1970.
2. BARKER, T. S. and LECOMBER, J. R. C. *Exploring 1972 with special reference to the Balance of Payments*. Vol. 9 in *A Programme for Growth*, ed. Richard Stone, Chapman and Hall, 1970.
3. BARKER, T. S. and WOODWARD, V. H. 'Inflation, growth and economic policy in the medium-term', *National Institute Economic Review*, No. 60, May 1972.
4. BRODY, A. and CARTER, A. P. (eds). *Input-Output Techniques*. Proceedings of the Fifth International Conference on Input-Output Techniques, North-Holland, 1972.
5. BROWN, Alan. *Exploring 1970. Some Numerical Results*. Vol. 6 in *A Programme for Growth*, ed. Richard Stone, Chapman and Hall, 1965.
6. CARTER, A. P. and BRODY, A (eds). *Contributions to Input-Output Analysis*. North-Holland, 1970.
7. DEATON, A. S. 'The estimation of the linear expenditure system.' Growth Project Paper 374, Department of Applied Economics, University of Cambridge, 1972.
8. ECONOMIC DIVISION, NATIONAL PORTS COUNCIL. *United Kingdom International Trade 1975*. National Ports Council, 1972.
9. KING, M. A. 'Dividend behaviour and theories of the firm.' Growth Project Paper 343, Department of Applied Economics, University of Cambridge, 1971.
10. KING, M. A. 'Corporate taxation and dividend behaviour—a comment'. *Review of Economic Studies*, XXXVIII(3), 115, 1971, pp. 377-80.
11. KREININ, M. E. 'Price elasticities in international trade.' *Review of Economics and Statistics*, 49, 1967, pp. 510–16.
12. LEONTIEF, W. W. *The Structure of the American Economy 1919–1939*. 2nd ed. Oxford University Press, 1951.
13. NATIONAL INSTITUTE OF ECONOMIC AND SOCIAL RESEARCH. 'The effects of the devaluation of 1967 on the current balance of payments.' *Economic Journal*, Supplement, March 1972.

14. PETERSON, A. W. A. 'Investment, employment and the theory of production.' Growth Project Paper 362, Department of Applied Economics, University of Cambridge, 1972.
15. PYATT, G. *Capital, Output and Employment 1948–1960*. Vol. 4 in *A Programme for Growth*, ed. Richard Stone, Chapman and Hall, 1964.
16. STONE, J. R. N. 'Linear expenditure systems and demand analysis: an application to the pattern of British demand.' *Economic Journal*, **64**, 1954.
17. STONE, J. R. N. 'Models for demand projections', in *Essays on Econometrics and Planning*, Pergamon Press; Statistical Publishing Company, Calcutta, 1965.
18. STONE, J. R. N. 'Personal spending and saving in postwar Britain', duplicated, Cambridge, January 1973.
19. STONE, J. R. N. 'Spending and saving in relation to income and wealth.' *L'industria*, **4**, 1966, pp. 471–99.
20. STONE, J. R. N. and ROWE, D. A. 'The durability of consumers' durable goods.' *Econometrica*, **28**, 1960.
21. STONE, J. R. N., BROWN, J. A. C. and ROWE, D. A. 'Demand analysis and projections for Britain 1900–1970: a study in method', in *Europe's Future Consumption*, ed. J. Sandee, North-Holland, 1964.
22. SURREY, M. J. *The Analysis and Forecasting of the British Economy*. National Institute of Economic and Social Research, Cambridge University Press, 1971.
23. U.K. CHANCELLOR OF THE EXCHEQUER. *Public Expenditure to 1976–77*. Cmnd. 5178, London, H.M.S.O., 1972.
24. U.K. CHANCELLOR OF THE EXCHEQUER. *Value-added Tax*. Cmd. 4621, London, H.M.S.O., March 1971
25. U.K. CHANCELLOR OF THE EXCHEQUER. *Value-added Tax*. Cmnd. 4929, London, H.M.S.O., March 1972.
26. U.K. CHANCELLOR OF THE EXCHEQUER. *The Programme for Controlling Inflation: The Second Stage*. Cmnd. 5205, London, H.M.S.O., January 1973.
27. U.K. CHANCELLOR OF THE EXCHEQUER. *The Price and Pay Code. A Consultative Document*. Cmnd. 5247, London, H.M.S.O., February 1973.
28. U.K. CHANCELLOR OF THE EXCHEQUER. *Financial Statement and Budget Report 1973–74*. London, H.M.S.O., March 1973.
29. U.K. CHANCELLOR OF THE EXCHEQUER. *The Operation of Stage Two*, Cmnd. 5267, London, H.M.S.O., March 1973.
30. U.K. CHANCELLOR OF THE EXCHEQUER and SECRETARY OF STATE FOR SOCIAL SERVICES, *Proposals for a Tax-Credit System*. Cmnd. 511, London, H.M.S.O., October, 1972.
31. WINTERS, L. A. 'A progress report on exports,' Growth Project Paper, Department of Applied Economics, University of Cambridge, 1972.
32. WIGLEY, K. J. 'Production models and time trends of input-output coefficients' in *Input-Output in the United Kingdom*, ed. W. F. Gossling, London, Cass, 1970.
33. WOODWARD, V. H. 'Linking incomes and expenditures in the model— a progress report,' Growth Project Paper 353. 1971, Department of Applied Economics, University of Cambridge, 1971.

3: The Par Model

A. THE CONCEPT OF A 'PAR ECONOMY'

W. A. H. Godley and T. F. Cripps

The Cambridge Economic Policy Group produced an analysis of medium-term prospects for the U.K. economy in February 1972, and again in January 1973,[1] using the concept of a 'Par economy' to link projections of future trends with the historical record of the actual past evolution of the economy. The first report contained a brief statement of the objectives and methodology of this analysis. Experience in using the concept of Par to provide a framework for analysis has convinced us that the method, although as yet not very precisely formulated, has practical value and may be capable of generalization.

The first section of this paper describes how the 'Par' system of analysis was conceived as a means of answering a specific policy question, and how it turned out to be a convenient way of handling the macro-economic statistics in relation to a wide range of issues. The second section gives a preliminary rationalization of the procedures we have so far evolved.

Analysis of Economic Management in the U.K.

The 'Par economy' was devised originally for one very specific purpose; to provide a system of information and prediction which would make it possible to assess the cost of alternative public expenditure programmes in relation to the total availability of resources.

Since the methods and objectives are sharply different from those associated with short-term forecasting and demand management, it may be useful briefly to rehearse these latter to bring out the contrast. For short-term demand management 'it is customary first to forecast what would actually happen over the next eighteen months, particularly

[1] *Problems in the Management of the Economy 1971–75*, Department of Applied Economics, Cambridge, February 1972, and *Prospects for Economic Management 1972–76*, D.A.E., January 1973. These reports and the present paper derive from research under a programme financed by the Social Science Research Council.

to output, unemployment and the balance of payments, on the assumption that there is no change in policy. Forecasts of the consequences of alternative policies can also then be made, and it is on the basis of these forecasts that Government decides what to do. Many aspects of policy, such as public expenditure, local authority rates, the exchange rate and trade policy, are assumed to be given; and so, broadly speaking, is the underlying structure and rate of growth of the economy. The short-term forecasting exercise is designed to guide the Government's decisions on changes in Central Government tax rates and on credit conditions, which are in practice the most flexible instruments for management of the economy which the Government possesses.'[1]

These procedures are clearly inappropriate as an aid to the taking of decisions which generate expenditure over many subsequent years and which cannot easily be reversed. Examples of this kind of decision are recruitment into the armed forces, civil service or teaching profession, or commitment to capital projects (e.g. motorways) with long lead times. Such decisions generate expenditure, sometimes on a rising scale, through several subsequent years and in many cases can be reversed, if at all, only at great cost in terms of waste, disruption and bad feeling. Furthermore, even where there are not logistical reasons which prevent flexible operation of an expenditure programme, there may be compelling political and humanitarian ones. There is no *technical* reason why national insurance benefits should not be changed either way at short notice, but their use as instruments of conjunctural policy is rather obviously out of the question for other reasons.

The point need not be laboured that the actual conjuncture of economic events—the quarter by quarter changes in output, the labour market, etc.—cannot be predicted at one point of time over a succeeding period of several years. Even if it were possible to make such predictions, it would almost certainly be wrong to regulate public expenditure[2] by reference to them. It would be ridiculous, for instance, to arrange now for a rise in the motorway construction programme two years hence, to be followed by a fall the following year, to counteract some contrary movement in private investment foreseen (*per impossibile*) at this stage.

It has, in fact, been generally accepted that in order to predict the total availability of resources against which prospective public expenditure can be measured, these have to be expressed in terms of 'trend' or

---

[1] *Problems in the Management of the Economy 1971–75*, para. 3.
[2] For convenience in this paper we ignore those kinds of public expenditure (which certainly exist) which can be raised or reduced quickly and flexibly.

'normal' values; i.e. ones which abstract from the short-term cyclical situation.

However, while 'trend' values for the future, particularly for the terminal year of the planning period are always used in medium-term planning exercises, it tends to be unclear what *precisely* 'trend' means. It is not always, for instance, clear how a projection of trends is to be verified in terms of actual events as these unfold. A point closely related to this is that while all medium-term plans enter trend values for the terminal year of the period under consideration, many (e.g., the National Plan of 1965) enter actual values, typically relating to a year in the recent past, for the beginning of the period, so that the exercise *looks* rather like a short-term forecast with the time period extended. In fact, however, time series are being shown with the figures in the left-hand columns of the table having a different logical status from those on the right: figures for intervening years (if there are any) tend to have a *shifting* logical status as the chalk changes progressively into cheese. It is particularly difficult to gauge the empirical content of such intermediate—part actual part trend—figures. In what terms could they possibly be verified subsequently even in principle? It would not, for instance, be legitimate to argue that they represent a forecast of the real path from the actual past to the trend future, simply because the trend future is something which no one expects will actually occur.

The suggestion we put forward is that the methodology and system of information and figuring used for the medium-term planning of public expenditure should explicitly be separated from that used for short-term demand management although there must be a way of relating the two systems with precision. Since the object of short-term management is (broadly speaking) to counteract the forces making for instability in the short term, the forecasting system must aim to capture these exogenous shocks and work out what their effect on the economy is going to be; starting from the actual past the time series moves to a (forecast) actual future. Since the object of medium-term planning, so far as this relates to public expenditure, is to reach a conscious and rational decision about how much of the nation's resources the public sector should preempt abstracting from short-run fluctuations, the forecasting system should also abstract from short-run fluctuations. The novelty[1] of our approach is to express not only the future but also the past in trend values thus giving all figures in every table the same

---

[1] So far as we know it is a new approach, though there has apparently been some parallel evolution in the O.E.C.D. and perhaps in the Treasury as well.

logical status. It is only in so far as we are able to turn the *actual* into the *trend* past and present—a manoeuvre requiring a precise set of rules—that projections of trend values can subsequently be verified and therefore acquire any empirical status.

The term 'Par' has been used as a term of art to define the particular set of trend values which, it is suggested, is the most appropriate for the purpose in hand.

(a) *The total availability of resources* is the level of G.D.P. as it would be in the future or could have been in the past had unemployment been kept at a constant rate. It is convenient though not strictly essential[1] to the logic and usefulness of the system if the unemployment rate chosen is a *target* rate—let us say the level at which, all things considered, it is prudent to aim on average over a period of several years. In making this definition of resource availability we are not begging any questions about the interaction between the structure of demand and its stability on the one hand and the growth of productive potential on the other; to the extent that these interrelationships are understood and can be measured they can be incorporated into the model. We would emphasize, however, that for the purpose for which the Par system is created it would be quite wrong to enter a productivity growth rate which was a target or desired growth rate, or even one different from what has occurred in the past, unless it can be shown what factors are going to bring about the change, how and why.

(b) So far as the *balance of payments* is concerned, the procedure is first to assess the surplus which will be (or would have been) necessary to maintain a satisfactory external balance sheet, and then predict the terms of trade which will be (or estimate the terms of trade which would have been) the counterpart of achieving this surplus at the target level of unemployment. The target surplus, in conjunction with the required terms of trade, implies a quantity of real resources which must be made available (i.e. not preempted by domestic demand) as a necessary but not sufficient condition for actually achieving the target. It is a *necessary* condition because unless it is met the pressure of domestic demand makes the surplus impossible; but it is *insufficient* because even if domestic demand is not excessive, there will be no surplus unless we are adequately competitive in world markets.

In sum, Par G.D.P. less the Par balance of trade (measured in

---

[1] Indeed in all our first attempts to construct a par system we chose a $2\frac{1}{2}$ per cent unemployment rate not because this was an objective, but because it seemed convenient to run par through the actuals of 1969 when unemployment was at roughly this level.

constant prices) equals the total availability of resources for domestic use. But it is important to emphasize, in accordance with the argument of the preceding paragraph, that the mere fact that domestic demand does not preempt an excessive share of total resources by no means guarantees that the target balance of payments will in fact be reached. Predictions of the Par economy are *conditional* predictions—the two conditions being that the full employment and balance of payments targets are continuously being met. At the risk of labouring the point— since it is very important and often misunderstood—the Par economy shows a healthy balance of payments but this is part of its *definition*; unspecified further measures (say incomes policy, devaluation or import controls) may well be necessary if the target surplus is in fact to be met.

(c) Par *private investment* is equal to the investment that would occur (or would have occurred) given Par output.

(d) In the Par system *public expenditure on goods and services* (both capital and current) is entered at expected (or observed) actual values so that

(e) the amount left over for *personal consumption* may finally be inferred as a residual.

The 'Par' system of concepts and (conditional) forecasts outlined above enables some judgement, admittedly of a very general kind, to be made about the character of the public expenditure programmes and whether or not they are acceptable. Starting from the total availability of resources defined to exclude short-term fluctuations, the amounts needed for the balance of payments and private investment are deducted, giving the total available for public and private expenditure; one of the Government's major decisions consists in determining how the division between these two should be made. The decision about how the Par economy is to be carved up is fully consistent with the use of flexible instruments of policy, mainly taxes but partly public expenditure (e.g. on minor building works) and possibly also changes in the exchange rate, to counteract forces which are destabilizing in the short term.

While our own system of figuring (so far as this relates to 'Par') has not yet gone beyond what is described above, it is rather uncouth and inadequate to reach conclusions simply in terms of total private consumption. It would be a more informative system if the implications were also drawn for taxation. This is particularly the case since in our present Par system Government transfers, which are, and have to be, part of its medium-term plan, have no place whatever. For this reason no valid inference can be drawn from the growth of total consumption about how the burden of taxation on an average household will change; for example, if national insurance benefits are going to rise particularly fast, less will be available for those who are not pensioners.

While no figures have yet been calculated or even mocked up it is clear in principle what would be the meaning of a 'Par' yield of the tax system; it would be the tax yield which would be the necessary counterpart of full employment, planned public expenditure (net of non-tax public sector receipts) and a satisfactory balance of payments[1] all being simultaneously obtained.

Similarly it will be quite an easy matter to calculate figures showing the past and prospective par public sector deficit. A small technical difficulty arises because both sides of the account have to be deflated by one price index if the balance between the two is to mean anything. One simple solution to this problem, adumbrated in the Green Paper *Public Expenditure: a new presentation* (Cmnd. 4017) is to measure public expenditure inclusive of the relative price effect and to deflate the tax yield by the G.D.P. deflator. (Neither this nor any other device will obviate the need to make a price forecast—or range of price forecasts—before the yield of the tax system measured 'at constant prices' can be inferred.)

Other uses of the Par system

While, as mentioned right at the beginning of this note, the Par economy was invented as a framework for planning public expenditure, we have found it an extremely useful adjunct to *conventional* short term forecasting methods in the analysis of the conjuncture.

One important point is that to the extent that the Par economy and its component elements exhibit stability, it becomes easier to diagnose various kinds of structural disequilibrium in the existing economic situation, the existence and importance of which might otherwise be ignored.

For instance, there appears, as a matter of observation, to be a rather high degree of stability in the 'Par' terms of trade.[2] If the actual

[1] Allowing of course for whatever change in the terms of trade is needed to achieve this. The terms of trade will affect both the real resources required for the balance of payments and, because of import prices, the level of real personal income (before tax) in relation to real output.

[2] The operations necessary to calculate the Par terms of trade for the past (implicit in the methodology set out in the early part of this paper) are as follows. First calculate what the balance of trade ($\hat{B}$) and terms of trade ($\widehat{TT}$) would have been if world trade, world industrial production and U.K. output had all been on trend. Then further modify $\widehat{TT}$ to an extent which is the counterpart of the change in U.K.'s relative costs needed to change $\hat{B}$ to the balance of trade required to maintain a satisfactory external balance sheet.

terms of trade are markedly different from Par—say the ratio of export to import prices is noticeably higher than Par—this gives a very simple and succinct warning that the balance of payments may be in fundamental disequilibrium, and even measures the degree of this disequilibrium. The reason of course is that the observed balance of trade is at any one point of time heavily influenced by a number of temporary factors—the condition of the world trade cycle, our own business cycle and short-term fluctuations in commodity prices—which may compound one another and totally obscure the underlying position. It is precisely the purpose of the 'Par' manoeuvres to correct for all these factors and summarize the results in one figure which can be readily inspected and understood.[1]

Another thing which can be readily detected by use of the Par system is whether or not the Government's fiscal 'posture' is out of balance. In the present state of the art, since we do not have an income side of the account nor a tax model we have to proceed by comparing Par personal consumption (which emerges from the existing system by residual) with observed consumption corrected for the difference between actual and 'Par' output. This comparison will give a rough indication of whether and to what extent the level of taxation is too high or low given the availability of resources and all the other (non personal consumption) claims which will sooner or later have to be met.

A superior way of judging the scale of any fiscal imbalance would, however, be to develop the income and taxation side of the system. The nature of the par fiscal balance has already been described; this should be compared with the 'full employment' fiscal balance at existing tax rates.

Par as a Framework of Analysis

The concept of a Par economy has so far been described in its specific application to the problems of macro-economic management in the U.K. The following section is a preliminary presentation of the logical structure implicit in the methodology which we are trying to develop.

Investigation of simple models

A quantitative model is intended to provide an approximate representation of relevant features of the economic system. The features which

---

[1] It was the fact that the Par terms of trade (measured by the ratio of two national income deflators) were so stable at about 100·0 between 1960 and 1970 whereas the actual terms of trade in 1971 were 103·7 that led us to forecast an extremely rapidly deteriorating position in January 1971 when the current account surplus was still running at £1000 million per annum and had shown no signs of dwindling.

must be captured are both conjunctural or short-term movements and the medium-term trend evolution of macro-economic variables. The purpose of our analysis of the U.K. was to see how well these features can be represented by a macro-economic model with very simple structure. The main lesson which can be learned from testing models against actual past data is that certain a priori conceptions lead to unacceptably large and systematic errors. Even in a very simple model most of the hypotheses which can be examined in this way are necessarily composite hypotheses. Fortunately the historical record itself often permits one to examine parts of a composite hypothesis independently. For example, in looking at foreign trade we can use periods of exchange rate stability to examine income effects, and, given hypotheses about the latter, we can use periods of substantial variation in exchange rates to examine price effects.

The historical evidence is often not very powerful even when applied to models with very simple structure. For the most part in the analysis of the U.K. we found that parameter values assigned a priori[1] looked reasonably satisfactory, and the lessons learned from an examination of past actual data were disappointingly few. The main points at which a priori expectations were significantly disturbed were assumptions about the terms of trade and about unemployment.

It is not clear what can be learned by fitting more complicated and flexible models to actual data. The chances are that the fit will be reasonably close, and even if it is not close the hypothesis which is discredited will be a complex composite hypothesis. The procedure of starting with very simple and conventional models may be more fruitful because there is a possibility that some primitive conventional notion may be discredited; and if in fact the simple model does yield a good approximate description, one has at least learned that the historical evidence has little to contribute to knowledge of economic structure at this level.

The Par system can be used to provide a simple framework which can accommodate both conjunctural and trend effects by operating

[1] Strictly speaking, the term 'a priori' should refer to assumptions adopted before scrutiny of the body of evidence under discussion. In practice the term can only be used loosely because evidence which influences the choice of assumptions can never be entirely independent of the evidence on which assumptions are tested. The more respectable evidence used to assign a priori structure and parameter values for the U.K. included theoretical preconceptions, knowledge of national income accounting conventions, and 1963 input-output tables. But the a priori assumptions must obviously have been influenced also by knowledge of econometric studies based on time-series data very closely related to that which was used to test the model.

with two distinct but precisely related models; a 'trend' model deals
with the underlying medium-term evolution of the economy and all
differences between actual and trend values of variables are handled
by a model of deviations from trend. Given assumed trend values, the
actual data can be used to test hypotheses about the interaction between
deviations from trend; and given an assumed model of deviations from
trend, the actual data can be used to test hypotheses about underlying
trends.

The practical value of this procedure depends on whether the decomposition of trends and deviations is reasonably unambiguous. This
in turn depends not only on the historical pattern of time-series but
also on the assumed degree of stability of par trends. If one is willing
to assert that the trend rate of growth of par values is constant over
periods of at least one cycle, the decomposition of trends and deviations
becomes reasonably well defined.

Historical evidence on trend phenomena

It is a matter of common observation that the trends of most macro-
economic variables are extraordinarily stable over rather long periods
of time in any one country. This point was brought out very neatly by
Professor Stone in his analysis of the principal components of time-
series in the U.S.A. in the inter-war period.[1] The stability of trends
makes it almost impossible to use historical evidence from one country
alone to test hypotheses about the structure of long-run interactions
between macro-economic variables. There are innumerable examples
of strong correlations between pairs of macro-economic time-series
which are attributable to the fact that both are dominated by trends
and most people are by now aware that an observed correlation of
trends is not a sound basis for causal inference.

The table on page 67 demonstrates this point for the basic macro-
economic series used in the analysis of the U.K. Seven out of the
sixteen variables show correlation coefficients of at least 0·95 with a
linear time trend and would therefore all show pairwise correlations
of at least 0·90 simply on account of the common trend. Ten out of
the sixteen variables would show pairwise correlations of at least
0·70 on account of the common trend.

At the first stage of development, the trend model is in all important
respects represented simply as a set of linear or exponential time
trends. Ultimately one might hope to develop a model of trend relation-

---

[1] Stone, J. R. N. 'On the interdependence of blocks of transactions.' *Supplement to
the Journal of the Royal Statistical Society*, **IX**, 1–2, 1947, pp 1–45.

ships with explicit causal structure based on the evidence of cross-sections of data from a number of industrial countries. Our estimates of trends in the U.K. have been checked informally for consistency with the experience of other countries.

The hypothesis of stability in underlying trends is perhaps not quite

Table 1. Correlations of macro-economic series 1960–72 with linear trends

Variable	Symbol	Correlations with trend	
		Level	Logarithm
G.D.P. at factor cost	Y	0·99	0·98
Consumers' expenditure	C	0·98	0·98
Volume of world trade	WX	0·97	0·99
Public current expenditure	CG	0·97	0·96
Imports of goods and services	M	0·96	0·98
Adjustment to factor cost	A	0·95	0·97
Exports of goods and services	X	0·95	0·97
Private fixed investment	IKP	0·94	0·94
Public fixed investment	IKG	0·90	0·89
Exchange rate	RX	0·80	0·80
Relative costs	UC	0·72	0·71
Public housebuilding	IDG	0·60	0·64
Unemployment	U	0·58	—
Private housebuilding	IDP	0·24	0·23
Stockbuilding	S	0·13	—
Employment	E	0·02	0·02

Note: Expenditure series are measured at constant prices. Full definitions of variables are given in *Prospects for Economic Management 1972–76, Statistical Appendix.*

so implausible as may at first appear. It is conditional on the assumption of stable trends for exogenous variables such as the volume of world trade and public expenditure on goods and services, and these variables have in practice shown rather steady trend growth rates.

Estimation of trends and deviation from trends
The first stage in estimating the Par model is to decompose actual series into trends and deviations from trend. Trend values are defined either by fitting time trends to actual series for exogenous variables (volume of world trade, exchange rate, unit costs) or by assigning values a priori to target endogenous variables (unemployment, public expenditure). Given deviations from trend of this subset of variables,

a model of deviations from trend which is fully specified a priori is used to predict deviations from trend of the remaining variables (G.D.P., investment, imports, exports, etc.). Subtracting the predicted deviations of these latter variables from their actual values, one hopes to find smooth trends left as residuals.

At this stage the model is tested on actual data by the criterion of whether the trends which are calculated as residuals are reasonably smooth and show plausible long-run movements. If the residual trends are not acceptable one can either adjust the parameters or structure of the model of deviations from trend, or redefine the trends of the first subset of variables used to specify the trend economy. The points at which residual trends were markedly irregular in the analysis of the U.K. were naturally enough those years which are already notorious for anomalous behaviour and where difficulties were therefore to be expected. When an anomaly is found in one variable one can quickly identify any other variables which show substantial deviations from trend at the same point of time, and this often provides the clue to the required modification of the model.

Once a firm set of values for the trend economy has been established, the individual trends are all extrapolated forwards to provide a base for conditional forecasts. In making this extrapolation the hypothesis of stability of trends which at present serves for a trend model is invoked. It is only possible to have any confidence in the extrapolation if the trend series estimated from past data themselves show sufficient stability over more than one cycle.

Projections can then be made using the model of deviations of trend, to produce alternative forecasts based on any desired set of exogenous conditions. The trend projections are therefore verifiable ex post when actual values of all the variables become available.

Par and targets of economic management
The procedure described above leads to estimates of trends which need not necessarily stand in any fixed relation to the norms or targets of economic policy. For example, the trend current balance of payments may show an accelerating improvement or deterioration because of differences in the trends of constituent items. It is therefore useful to make a distinction between the trend economy described above and the par economy as we have used the term in the analysis of the U.K.

The Par economy is defined primarily by norms of economic management. For the U.K. these were taken to be a constant rate of unemployment and maintenance of a satisfactory balance of net international liquid assets and liabilities. The reason for defining Par in terms of such norms is that Par was intended to represent in principle a sustainable path of evolution of the economy. The Par time-series are given a direct interpretation in terms of policy objectives and represent the changing pattern of economic structure required to achieve these objectives. Estimates of Par time-series are obtained simply by using the model of deviations from trend to adjust the trend economy to meet Par targets through alteration of the values of appropriate policy instruments.

A normative definition of Par has advantages for the presentation and interpretation of results in an analysis directed to policy issues. The Par series provide an initial guide to policies needed to hold target variables at values which are in an appropriate sense constant over time. Alternative projections can then be constructed to show how from any given starting point the values of target variables would change under the combined influence of initial deviations from Par and particular decisions about the values of policy instruments.

In medium-term analysis the presentation of results is a major problem in its own right because the investigation must cover the simultaneous operation of a number of policy instruments and therefore describes a set of policy options with several degrees of freedom. If particular projections are to appear interesting and relevant to policy-makers, they must be simply and clearly defined in relation to targets and instruments of economic management.

Appendix: Assessing the Accuracy and Reliability of the Par system

by T. F. Cripps

One of the key issues in the choice of method must inevitably be the judgement of accuracy and reliability. Where fully formulated stochastic models are used, it is generally possible to provide direct estimates of the expected accuracy of conditional predictions outside the estimation period. But these direct estimates are notoriously unreliable, and this must be a result of the unreality of the underlying assumptions.

The Par system, as described in the preceding paper, will not yield direct estimates of the accuracy of conditional projections—unless, of course, it were to be formulated in a well-defined stochastic framework and implemented by appropriate estimation procedures. But many other techniques for medium-term analysis which are in practical use also lack thorough-going statistical foundations. It does not seem necessary or convenient to insist that all quantitative analysis should be given such statistical foundations. However, the problem of devising a method for assessing accuracy and reliability must still be faced.

The fact that inferences about the standard error of conditional projections drawn from econometric estimation procedures are so unreliable has already led to the development of a considerable amount of research on the *ex post* evaluation of conditional projections. Such research generally follows Theil's[1] proposals in adopting the criterion of minimum ex post prediction error.

It seems reasonable to accept as a minimum requirement that any proposed analytic method should be capable of verification in the sense that prediction errors can be ascertained *ex post*. The preceding paper has already indicated how this can be done for the Par system. But even if *ex post* errors can be calculated, it will not often be possible to obtain a large sample of independent observations of such errors— and the criterion of minimum error does not look very convincing when only a few observations are available.

The real weakness of this criterion is that it ignores the question of whether, with hindsight, we feel that a particular error should or should not have been made. For example, imagine a comparison of two models with similar orders of magnitude of accuracy within estimation periods. Suppose that in a prediction outside the estimation period model I provides an estimate which is found *ex post* to have a smaller error than the estimate provided by model II. At first sight it is tempting to take this as evidence for preferring model I. But imagine that when the estimation period is extended to include this predicted observation, model I now agrees with model II that the appropriate error of approximation for this observation is after all rather large and near to the value originally found for model II. Which model do we now prefer? It seems plausible to argue that model II is preferable because it is more consistent or stable. One may suspect that model I originally achieved a better result for rather discreditable reasons.

The most appropriate criteria seem really to be *accuracy*, as indicated by the size of errors both within and outside the estimation period, and *stability* as indicated by the variability of the error attached to each observation as the estimation period itself is varied. We have not yet made a proper investigation of the stability of the Par system used for analysis of the U.K. But the following simple example may help to illustrate the kind of investigation which could in principle be carried out.

[1] Theil, H. *Economics and Information Theory.* North-Holland Publishing Co., 1967.

Defining C as consumers' expenditure at 1963 market prices and Y as personal disposable income, compare the following two models:

I *'Par model'* $C - C^* = \beta(Y - Y^*)$

   where Y^* is an exponential trend fitted by least squares on logarithms of Y, and C^* and β are estimated by iterating

   (a) C^* as an exponential trend fitted by logarithms on

   $$\hat{C} \equiv C - \beta(Y - Y^*)$$

   (b) β fitted by least-squares on $C - C^*$, $Y - Y^*$.[1]

II *'Linear model'* $C = \alpha + \beta Y + \gamma t$

   where t is a linear trend and α, β, γ are estimated by O.L.S.

To test stability, both models have been estimated on data for each of six estimation periods:

10-year periods	1952–61
	1957–66
	1962–71
15-year periods	1952–66
	1957–71
20-year period	1952–71

Prediction errors have then been calculated for the entire period 1952–71 (including the estimation period) so that for each year there are six observed errors for each model. Charts I and II show the maximum and minimum errors for each model, the range of errors within estimation periods being shaded in black.

The apparent accuracy of the two models, as indicated by R.M.S. errors within estimation periods, is almost exactly the same, at about £110 million. For predictions up to five years before the start or after the end of the estimation period, the Par model shows a slightly smaller R.M.S. error, at £190 million, than the linear model (£225 million). But a comparison of the two charts will immediately show that the par model is considerably more stable, both within and outside estimation periods, than the linear model. In particular, the consistent negative errors shown by the Par model for 1969–71 seem to be at least partially vindicated even by the linear model when the estimation period is extended this far.

[1] This iterative procedure is a formalization of the smoothing process described in the paper. It would not stand up to statistical criticism because at (a) we are implicitly assuming multiplicative errors and at (b) additive errors. This gives more force to the example because the method patently cannot be reconciled with any stochastic assumptions and is therefore beyond the pale of conventional econometric analysis.

Chart 1. Consumers' expenditure: prediction errors using **Par model**

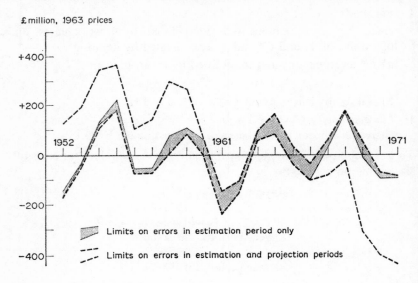

£ million, 1963 prices

Chart 2. Consumers' expenditure: prediction errors using **linear model**

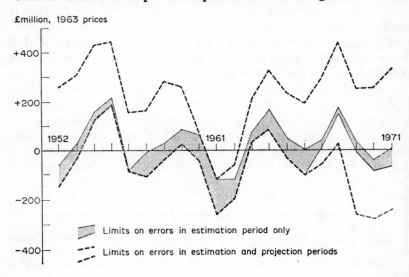

£million, 1963 prices

B. PROSPECTS FOR ECONOMIC MANAGEMENT 1972–76

by The Cambridge Economic Policy Group[1]

Section I. Par Estimates and Alternative Projections

The objectives and methodology of the present study are set out in Chapter 3A. The tables in the Appendix are the source of all the quantitative estimates given in the following sections; sources and definitions of the figures in the tables are also given in the Appendix.

Par estimates

2. The basic set of Par estimates has been constructed to abstract from short-term fluctuations in the pressure of demand and from shortfalls in the balance of payments position. The Par estimates describe the economy as it could have been in the past, or would be in the future, if demand were adjusted to maintain a steady level of unemployment (a level of $2\frac{1}{2}$ per cent has been used in this study) and if U.K. producers were always sufficiently competitive to ensure a viable balance of payments and reserve position (explicitly defined in section III).

3. Projections for the Par economy give a picture of the medium-term trends of productive potential and of claims on resources. The Par figures are not intended to represent an ideal path for the economy which economic management should aim to reach. They do provide a basic measuring rod against which a range of alternative paths for the actual evolution of the economy can be compared.

Alternative projections

4. To illustrate the implications of different strategies for managing the economy starting from its actual position in 1972, a range of alternative projections has been calculated on various assumptions about the pressure of demand and the competitiveness of the economy in international trade. Our purpose is to work out the apparent implications of different policy assumptions to see if they represent

[1] The original report was written by T. F. Cripps and C. T. Taylor. Particular responsibility for the estimates of claims on resources rests with W. A. H. Godley, T. F. Cripps and R. J. Tarling. C. T. Taylor was responsible for the analysis of non-trade items in the balance of payments. G. E. J. Llewellyn, K. J. Coutts, B. C. Moore, M. H. Pesaran and J. Rhodes all contributed to the research for this study. The report was completed early in January 1973.

feasible courses of action. If some of them lead to absurd results one must infer either that the policies in question would rapidly break down, or that the analysis is defective.

Main characteristics of the par economy, 1972–76
5. Despite the continued rise in numbers of students and pupils staying on at school, especially in 1973–74 as a result of the higher school-leaving age, the labour force potentially available for employment is expected to be at least as large in 1976 as in 1972. The average rate of productivity growth has remained at about 3 per cent per year or a little more over the last seven years and may be expected to continue at much the same rate. The Par rate of growth of G.D.P., at which the level of unemployment would remain steady, would therefore be just over 3 per cent per year. This is of course rather faster than the average rate of growth actually achieved since 1966.
6. Imports would grow at about 8 per cent per year in volume terms if the pressure of demand is held steady. To secure a reasonable balance of payments the volume of exports would have to grow slightly faster. The growth of exports required for a Par performance has accelerated steadily during the past few years because of the increasing importance and fast growth of imports of manufactures.
7. Private investment, under Par conditions, would continue to grow at nearly 6 per cent per year; and public expenditure on goods and services is projected to rise by an average of 3 per cent per year. The resources available in the Par economy would allow for private consumption to grow at an average of about 3 per cent per year, or slightly faster than it has actually grown since 1960.

The implications of growth at 5 per cent per year from 1972
8. The first set of alternative projections starts from the Government's stated objective of a 5 per cent rate of growth over the next two years which is here taken to mean that G.D.P. should expand at an annual rate of 5 per cent for two years starting from the actual position in the second half of 1972.
9. Reflation on this scale would reduce unemployment to about 400,000 by 1974 and raise the number of people at work to over 25 million. If the rate of growth of demand levelled off in 1975 to the Par growth rate of just over 3 per cent so that the level of unemployment was held steady, the average growth of G.D.P. from 1972 to 1976 would still be about 4½ per cent per year.
10. There are three important questions about such a strategy of fast

expansion. Could producers expand output at such a rapid rate? Could a tolerable balance of payments position be maintained? Could the Government secure a sufficient growth of domestic demand by its fiscal and expenditure policies?

11. There is of course no real evidence in the U.K.'s recent past about the ability of producers to achieve such a rapid expansion of output. The largest year-on-year increase in output recorded since 1950 was 5·6 per cent in 1963–64. In most other European countries faster growth rates have been achieved habitually. There is no good reason to suppose that U.K. producers could not meet such a rapid expansion of demand—although a certain degree of caution is reasonable.

12. The rapid growth assumption is bound to put considerable strain on the balance of payments. We find the underlying trends to be so unfavourable that even after allowing for a rather successful policy on prices and incomes the prospects would still be for a deficit on goods and services of some £2,100 million at 1963 values. This would imply a deficit on the current balance of payments (at current prices) of some £3,000 million in 1976. This extremely pessimistic conclusion is further discussed in section IV.

13. The balance-of-payments implications of a strategy of fast expansion are sufficiently serious to rule it out as a viable policy, unless some very powerful measures to improve the balance of trade could be put into effect.

Alternative exchange rate policies

14. There are quite important objections to any very large further depreciation of sterling. Internally, devaluation would push up import prices and make continued restraint over prices and incomes much more difficult. Further devaluation of sterling might also be resisted abroad by the other major trading countries. But since the exchange rate is conventionally regarded as the most appropriate instrument for correcting prolonged payments deficits, we have estimated the effects of a number of alternative exchange rate assumptions.

15. The rate of just under $2·35 was only reached in the last quarter of 1972. We have estimated the effects of continued depreciation of the exchange rate by 5 per cent per year relative to a weighted average of other currencies. The policy of continued depreciation does not bring about any very large improvements within the next four years because of the time lags in the response of exports. In 1976 there is a net gain of about £450 million at 1963 values or some £700 million at current prices.

16. Estimates have also been made for immediate devaluations of 15 per cent, 25 per cent and 30 per cent respectively, at the beginning of 1973. These all show much larger improvements by 1976 than a policy of gradual depreciation.

17. It must be emphasized that estimates based on these alternative exchange rate assumptions, particularly the large devaluations, completely ignore any implications for inflation and incomes policy. It is assumed throughout that domestic costs in sterling terms are held steady relative to those of our competitors measured in terms of their own currencies. From this point of view the estimates of the effects of large-scale devaluation are quite unrealistic.

Slower growth

18. The obstacles to a sustained fast growth rate are sufficiently serious to make it worth investigating an alternative projection with a lower rate. We assume a check to the growth of demand starting in 1973, so that G.D.P. grows at an annual rate of only 2 per cent from the first half of 1973. The spurt of growth already under way in 1972 and the beginning of 1973 is sufficient to reduce unemployment to about 600,000 during 1973; but by 1976 the level of unemployment would be back up to the 1972 peak and would exceed 1,000,000 by the end of that year.

19. If the exchange rate were pegged at \$2·35 there would still be a current payments deficit of about £1,800 million by 1976. This could apparently be eliminated by a devaluation of some 20 per cent in 1973.

20. The combination of slow growth with a substantial devaluation would not really provide an acceptable strategy. Unemployment would be rising from 1974 onwards and private consumption could only be allowed to grow by an average of under 2 per cent per year.

The need for new instruments of economic management

21. The various alternative projections discussed above define quite well the main options attainable using the conventional instruments of demand management and balance of payments adjustment. None of the alternatives has acceptable implications for unemployment, inflation and the growth of real incomes while achieving a tolerable balance of payments position.

22. If conventional instruments of management cannot yield acceptable results, the question of less conventional remedies must be explored. In section VI we discuss briefly the main requirements of any new instruments of control over the balance of payments.

Section II. G.D.P., Employment and Unemployment

1. The large increase in unemployment from 270,000 in 1966 to 870,000 in 1972 reflected reductions in employment both in manufacturing and in service industries. The decline in employment was larger, in relation to output, than in earlier recessions.

2. In 1972 the decline in employment was halted and probably reversed while unemployment began to fall quite steadily in the second half of the year. From the data available so far it appears that employment in the private sector outside manufacturing started to increase quite rapidly after constant decline since 1966; it also appears that there has been a substantial increase in the number of females seeking and finding employment.

Par output and productivity

3. The method used to estimate Par levels of G.D.P. and productivity is the same as that described in the earlier study, except that the parameters of the adjustment process have had to be changed in order to make sense of the recent movement of unemployment. We now assume much shorter lags in the adjustment of employment and unemployment to fluctuations in output; and the adjustment is supposed to have become steadily more elastic between 1960 and 1972.

4. Once the assumption is made that employment has been adjusted more rapidly and completely to fluctuations in demand, the recent movements of output, employment and unemployment fall into a consistent pattern. Appendix Table 1 shows that Par G.D.P. has grown at about 3·2 per cent per year throughout the period 1960–72. During the early 1960s the 'bulge' in the labour force contributed 0·4 per cent per year and Par productivity was rising by 2·8 per cent per year. As the bulge came to an end productivity growth increased to about 3·3 per cent per year, 1965–69. Since then productivity growth seems to have fallen off slightly to about 3 per cent per year.

5. For the next four years, 1973–76, we assume continued Par productivity growth at 3 per cent per year.

6. From 1972 at least up until 1980 the labour force will tend to increase for demographic reasons. A second bulge in the younger age groups is on the way as a result of the rising fertility rates in the 1950s and early 60s; the decline in fertility in the second half of the 1960s has also meant that a rising proportion of married women is coming into the labour force. The demographic bulge will easily offset the effects

of the raising of the school leaving age; by 1976 the labour force is expected to be 1 per cent larger than in 1972.

Alternative G.D.P. projections, 1972–76

7.   Under the assumption of a fast expansion of demand discussed in section I there is bound to be a rapid fall in unemployment as G.D.P. grows at 5 per cent per year for the next two years. By the beginning of 1974 unemployment should be down to 450,000—still a rather higher level than in the previous booms of 1960–62 and 1964–66.

8.   Under the alternative slow growth assumption the expansion of demand is held down to 2 per cent per year from 1973 onwards. But there is bound to be a considerable reduction in unemployment next year compared with 1972 even if substantial deflationary measures are introduced during the year. On the slow growth projection unemployment would fall to a trough of about 600,000 at the beginning of 1974 and then start to rise very rapidly, reaching 1,000,000 by the end of 1976.

Table II-1. G.D.P. and unemployment

Year	Actual G.D.P. (*compromise estimate*)	Par[1] G.D.P.	Unemployment	
			Actual first quarter-level	Mid-year adjusted for lags in the response to output (thousands)[2]
	£ million, 1963 prices			
1961	25614	24501	291	330
1965	29256 (3·4)	27912 (3·3)	303	285
1969	32055 (2·3)	31725 (3·3)		
1972	33962 (2·0)	34741 (3·1)	870	812
Fast growth assumption				
1976	40597 (4·8)	39543 (3·3)	415	403
Slow growth assumption				
1976	37926 (2·7)	39543 (3·3)	844	966

Figures in brackets are average annual growth rates.

[1] The level of G.D.P. consistent with steady 2½ per cent unemployment.

[2] Levels of unemployment resulting from past actual or projected future levels of G.D.P.

Section III. The Balance of Payments

The object of this section is to suggest a target for the balance of trade (in goods and services) in the light of expected movements in the non-trade items of the balance of payments. The non-trade flows are treated as being determined largely, although not wholly, independently of the pressure of demand in the domestic economy. Consequently the problem of managing the balance of payments is seen as essentially one of adjusting the balance of trade to meet the (given) surplus or deficit on other items, taking one year with another.

2. The procedure will be to start by briefly reviewing the actual history of the balance of payments since 1960, showing the extent of the (cumulative) deterioration in the U.K.'s external liquidity position by 1972. A 'model' balance of payments for the Par economy is then constructed for the entire period 1960–76. This is a necessary step in arriving at a target for the balance of trade (both for the past and the future) on the assumption that external payments are in approximate balance during the period. Finally some suggestions are made for a feasible trade target for 1972–76 which recognize that the economy has so far fallen short of its Par trade target, and is expected to fall even further behind by 1976.

Table III-1. U.K. Balance of Payments and Effect on Liquidity, 1960–72
(Annual averages; £ million at current prices)

	1960–63	1964–67	1968–72	1960–72
Current balance	0	−166	387	98
(of which, net I.P.D. and transfers)	262	201	239	234
Balance of long-term capital	−45	−160	14	−58
Trade credit (net)	−43[1]	−120	−128	−134
'Basic balance'	−88	−446	183	−94
I.M.F. drawing[2] rights, etc.	5	131	41	58
Net liquidity effect[3]	−83	−315	224	−36

[1] Partly estimated.

[2] Allocations of I.M.F. drawing rights, special and ordinary (net of gold contributions to I.M.F.), E.E.A. profits/losses, and revaluations affecting the reserves and short-term assets and liabilities (so far as these are identified in the official Balance of Payments Accounts: see *U.K. Balance of Payments 1972*, Table 41, and earlier editions).

[3] A negative sign here indicates a deterioration in the balance of reserves and net short-term liabilities.

The actual balance of payments since 1960

3. The principal features of the balance of payments since 1960 are summarized in Table III-I and shown in more detail in Appendix Table 4.

4. It can be seen that the balance of long-term capital averaged a deficit of some £60 million between 1960 and 1972, the net outflow showing large variations and being relatively heavy in the period preceding devaluation. By contrast, net earnings on overseas investments *minus* (net) transfers was a large and relatively steady positive item.

5. Particular mention should be made of the behaviour of net trade credit (import credit received from 'unrelated' firms, *minus* export credit granted), which has become a very large negative item in recent years.

6. Table III-1 shows that there was an average net worsening of the U.K.'s liquidity position of the order of £36 million per year between end-1959 and end-1972, or an accumulated deterioration of about £470 million. This deterioration would have been much larger had it not been for allocations of ordinary and special I.M.F. drawing rights totalling nearly £1,000 million during this period.

The Par economy's balance of payments

7. Before judging what a tolerable trade target might be in practice for the next few years, a notional balance of payments is constructed for the Par economy for the entire period 1960–76. Annual details of the main series at '1963 import values' can be found in Appendix Table 5.

8. Throughout this study, expenditures on resources are expressed at 1963 prices. In the case of balance of payments items there is often no meaningful constant price basis of measurement because many of the flows concerned are purely financial. It has proved convenient to use the import price deflator to measure all balance of payments items in terms of real import purchasing power.[1] In the tables the deflated series are defined as being measured 'at 1963 import values'.

9. Separate deflated series were produced for each of the main non-trade components published in the Balance of Payments Accounts, and these series were smoothed to estimate their trend or average

---

[1] The price deflator for imports of goods and services (1963 = 100) is put at about 140 for 1972. Projected values for this deflator vary with different assumptions about devaluation, but it is useful to bear in mind a rough scaling factor of 150 as applying on average to 1973–76.

movement. Net figures for the smoothed and deflated series are given in Appendix Table 5. These series provide the principal basis for projections to 1976; but various modifications to the trends have been introduced where information on likely new developments could be obtained.

(a) Long-term Capital

10. Perhaps the most important result of this exercise is the heavy deficit projected for the balance of long-term capital for 1973–76. It is estimated that this will average some £250 million at 1963 import values which is an unprecedented net outflow and a considerable change from the late 1960s, when the deficit was relatively modest. The movement is attributable mainly to the reduction expected in the inflow of 'oil and miscellaneous' investment, a sharp increase in the net outflow of official long-term capital due partly to the commencement of capital subscriptions to the European Investment Bank and the European Coal and Steel Community, as well as to increases in loans under the aid programme and subscriptions to the International Development Association,[1] and to an increase in outward portfolio investment not covered by overseas borrowing.

(b) Net Property Income

11. The projection of interest, profits and dividends in the context of the Par economy is complicated by the problem that, if the economy were meeting its Par targets, the net amount of short-term debt on which interest is payable would be smaller than that which has actually been incurred during the period, and net earnings on overseas investments correspondingly higher. This problem was tackled by projecting the main components of earnings on the basis of trends in their volumes since 1958, and then making an adjustment to the net figure (rising steadily to about £70 million in 1976) to allow for the lower amount of short-term external debt incurred by the Par economy. The net outcome for individual years can be seen in Appendix Table 5.

(c) Transfers

12. Government transfers (including the contribution to the E.E.C.) are projected on the basis of figures in the latest Public Expenditure White Paper.

(d) Trade Credit

13. Trade credit is another item which cannot be treated independently of the rest of the economy, since its behaviour is closely related to

[1] See White Paper *Public Expenditure to 1976–77* Cmnd. 5178, H.M.S.O., 1972.

export and import volumes, credit availability and, not least, the rate
of inflation. Accordingly, as with I.P.D. payments, alternative projections of this item were made, one relating to the Par economy and others
to conditional forecasts of 'actual' movements in exports, imports and
prices.

The Par Trade Target

14.   These estimates for non-trade items can now be brought together
and their implications for the Par economy's target balance of trade
examined. The main results are summarized in Table III-2, derived
from annual figures in Appendix Table 5.

Table III-2. The Par Trade Target
(Annual averages: £ million at 1963 import values)

	Net Property Income and Transfers	Contri- bution to E.E.C.	Balance of Long- term	Trade Credit (net)	Total of non-trade items	I.M.F. Drawing Rights, etc.	Par Trade Target
1960–63	205	—	117	−24	64	4	−75
1964–67	176	—	−100	−79	−3	124	−75
1968–72	198	—	−36	−155	7	30	50
1973–76	239	−84	−253	−236	−334	—	325
1960–76	204	−20	−121	−125	−62	39	55

15.   The main features that emerge here are firstly that the combined
non-trade items, adjusted so as to be comparable with the rest of the
Par economy, are in deficit by some £60 million per year on average
during the period as a whole. These items were in surplus in the early
years, then moved into near-balance until about 1971, and slide
progressively into very heavy deficit after that.

16.   Secondly, it can be seen that the principal factors responsible for
the deterioration projected for 1973–76, are, above all, the deficit on
long-term capital and the continuing rise in net trade credit. The
contribution to the E.E.C. budget is also a material factor. These
items in combination heavily offset the projected increase in net
property income (minus the net outflow of transfers).

17.   The selection of a liquidity target for the Par economy is a matter
for policy decision in the same sense as selection of a target for
unemployment. However, for purposes of illustration, we think it

appropriate to consider the behaviour of the Par economy on the assumption that it aims to improve its liquidity position (i.e., the balance of official reserves, including S.D.R.s and unused I.M.F. lines of credit, net of short-term liabilities in both official and un-official hands) by roughly the size of additional 'paper' and 'credit' reserves received from the I.M.F. during the period, net of revaluations affecting the reserves and liabilities, etc. This requires that the Par economy's 'basic balance' on current and long-term capital account (including trade credit) should be about zero taking the period as a whole (whether measured in current prices or at 1963 import values).

18.   Substantial allocations of credit and paper reserves were received between 1964 and 1972, but we have included nothing for this item after 1972. Some further allocations of Special Drawing Rights are probably to be expected before 1976, although for several reasons they are not likely to be as large as those received in the last few years. In view of all the uncertainties involved, it seems best not to include a favourable figure for 'drawing rights etc.' after 1972.

19.   If the Par economy is to meet the liquidity target outlined above, it must clearly be prepared to move from a moderate trading deficit in the early 1960s to very large surpluses after 1972. One of many possible courses for the balance of trade is summarized in the right-hand column of the table.

An Actual Trade Target for 1973–76

20.   The selection of an appropriate trade target for the next few years is complicated by problems which are too important to ignore. The first is that the economy in 1972 is quite far from the Par liquidity target discussed above and the second is that, as will be explained in the next section, a large deficit is projected for the balance of trade. Even if measures are applied to correct this deficit, it seems inevitable that the actual balance of payments will fall further, and more seriously, behind the Par target set for it.

21.   In the circumstances, a fairly ambitious policy would be to aim to balance the basic balance of payments over the next few years (i.e., the current account and long-term capital account, including trade credit), so avoiding further deterioration of the liquidity position, as we have defined it.

22.   It must be recognized however that unless the trade projections described in the next section are entirely wrong, it will be difficult to prevent the basic balance of payments from moving heavily into deficit in 1973 and remaining in deficit right through to 1976. It is therefore

necessary to consider how much scope there will be for financing deficits from the official reserves or with the aid of official borrowing in order to see how far the balance of payments targets could be relaxed.

23. In moving from the Par to the actual world, certain adjustments are required to the projections of non-trade flows discussed earlier. Firstly, net I.P.D. earnings received by the actual economy will be lower than those for the Par economy because the actual economy accumulates a progressively larger burden of external short-term debt.

24. Secondly, alternative projections are needed for trade credit which allow for differences in projected levels of exports and imports and movements in their prices. On the basis of the fast growth projection of the economy (see section I para. 8, *et seq.*) and assuming that the deficit on the balance of trade is held to quite moderate levels through a combination of devaluation in 1973 and other measures (for precise figures, see section VI), the deficit on trade credit would rise very sharply to well over £325 million (at 1963 import values) in 1973, reflecting the effect of devaluation in that year on import and export prices, and then fall back to about £175 million by 1976. (The average for 1971–76 would be slightly lower than for the Par economy.) Alternatively, on the basis of a slow growth of G.D.P. (see section I, para. 18), and assuming the same devaluation, net trade credit will be running slightly lower at about £165 million (at 1963 values) by 1976.

25. Further attention will be paid to the temporary relief that could be obtained from emergency policies in section VI, but it should be mentioned here that, if restrictions on long-term capital outflows are tightened, rather than relaxed as the U.K. enters the E.E.C., it might be possible to cut the projected deficit on long-term capital account by perhaps £100 million per annum (at 1963 import prices) for a number of years, without suffering much immediate reduction in earnings on overseas investments on this account.

26. The preceding considerations can be summed up as follows. The avoidance of further deterioration in the U.K.'s liquidity position would, if restrictions on capital outflows are relaxed after entry into the E.E.C., imply a trade target for 1973–76 very similar to that projected earlier for the Par economy; the main difference would be that annual I.P.D. payments would be perhaps £30 million higher, thereby making the required balance of trade about £350 million per year on average. In view of the heavy trade deficits anticipated for the next few years, this figure is of little more than academic interest.

27. The most that can be hoped for from the balance of trade is probably that it can be confined to a quite moderate deficit (in the orders of magnitude shown in Table VI-1). Table III-3 shows the implications of this outcome on the assumption that about £100 million per annum can be saved on the long-term capital account.

Table III-3. Target Balance of Payments, 1973–76
(Annual averages; £ million at 1963 import values)

Trade Balance	−300
Net property income and transfers (including contribution to E.E.C.)	90
Balance of long-term capital	−150
Net trade credit	−230
Net liquidity effect	−590

28. It can be seen that the balance of reserves and short-term debt would deteriorate on this reckoning by about £600 million per annum on average. The deterioration would be heavy at first (reflecting the timing of the trade deficits shown in Table VI-1) but would reduce to an annual rate of roughly £400 million by 1976.

29. It would be difficult to justify the adoption of a larger deficit than this for the trade target. It is hardly likely in the circumstances that much relief will be forthcoming in terms of an inflow of short-term funds, except perhaps to finance part of the projected extension in export credit. On the contrary, the emergence of large trade deficits in 1973, unless accompanied by well-timed measures to rectify the imbalance and by steps to secure emergency credits from overseas monetary institutions, is likely to provoke an outflow of funds which would add greatly to the financing problem indicated in the table. At least, the trade target can be regarded as no more than an interim one, viable only on the promise of a rapid improvement in the trade balance after 1976.

Section IV. The Balance of Trade

Between 1971 and 1972 the balance of payments deteriorated very suddenly. The 'basic balance' moved from a surplus of £1,100 million to a deficit of £400 million and the current account from a surplus of £1,000 million to a position of bare balance. The previous section has shown that a substantial surplus on trade in goods and services would be required over the next four years in order to fully protect the U.K.'s reserve position.

2. The first task is to assess the trends underlying the fluctuating balance of trade over the past twelve years. Estimates of the 'trend' trading position have been constructed, correcting the actual performance for all the short-term or fluctuating influences which it has been possible to identify. These 'trend' estimates are extrapolated into the future to provide a basis for estimating the effects of a range of alternative assumptions about actual movements of the exchange rate and G.D.P. up to 1976.

3. The purpose of the trend estimates is simply to enable us to see the longer-term underlying movement of exports, imports and the terms of trade more clearly. A second and different task is to reconstruct and project the pattern of trade in the Par economy where definite target surpluses on goods and services (specified in the previous chapter) must be achieved. The Par estimates set a standard against which the actual past or projected future trade performances can be measured, in terms both of the level of relative costs and of the real resources devoted to the balance of trade. Par estimates are calculated by estimating the level of relative costs which would be necessary, from year to year, to make the U.K. sufficiently competitive to achieve the target trade surpluses.

The trend level of imports, disaggregated by major categories

4. The growth of imports of goods and services (at 1963 prices) has shown a persistent acceleration over the past twelve years, and this acceleration is all the more marked when a rough allowance is made for the effects of variations in the pressure of demand in the U.K.

5. We have disaggregated imports into five major categories in order to obtain a clearer picture of the reasons for the acceleration in the growth of total imports.

(a) The volume of food, drink and tobacco imports has remained rather steady, insensitive to cyclical fluctuations in G.D.P., and showing almost no trend increase. The projections to 1976 assume a small decrease due to higher food production in the U.K. under the stimulus of the Common Agricultural Policy.

(b) Imports of fuels (mainly petroleum) have grown quite rapidly. After allowing for deviations of G.D.P. from Par we find a rather steady growth of about 10 per cent per year in fuel imports throughout the period 1960–72. We allow for a reduction of £300 million at 1963 prices in annual oil imports by 1976 as a result of growth of production from the North Sea oil and gas fields and a halt to the long-standing decline in output of coal. On this basis trend fuel imports will only rise by 5 per cent per year from 1972 to 1976.

(c) Imports of industrial materials (basic materials and semi-manufactures) must be adjusted for several factors. The level of these imports relative to G.D.P. depends on stockbuilding and on the volume of exports which have a much higher import component than most domestic expenditure. After allowing for these factors imports of industrial materials show a fairly steady 'trend' growth at about 6 per cent per year. This category of imports has grown faster than G.D.P. partly because it includes a large proportion of semi-manufactures which have displaced U.K. products in the home market.

6. In the first half of 1972 imports of industrial materials were surprisingly high, given the low level of industrial output and the decumulation of stocks. In projecting the future trend we have supposed that the rate of growth will not be faster than in earlier years.

(d) Imports of finished manufactures are adjusted for deviations of G.D.P. from Par with a marginal import coefficient of 10 per cent. Trend imports of finished manufactures have grown by 16 per cent per year throughout the period 1960–72 and now account for about one quarter of total imports. We assume that this trend growth rate of 16 per cent per year will continue up to 1976.

7. The rate of growth of imports of manufactures must depend to some extent on the competitive strength of U.K. producers. But it seems impossible to estimate the magnitude of any such effect, at least at the level of disaggregation used here. The devaluation of 1967 did not have any measurable effect in slowing down the growth of manufactured imports, presumably because of the presence of influences working in the other direction. Having failed to detect any significant relationship in past data (estimates of the response to a reduction in relative costs show the wrong sign), we have not made any allowance for the effect in the future.

(e) The remaining category of imports comprises services. After adjustment for deviations of G.D.P. from Par with a marginal import coefficient of 5 per cent we find a trend growth rate of 4 per cent per year.

The trend growth of total imports

8. Having adjusted the five categories of imports for various non-trend factors and then projected the trend level of each category to

1976 we obtain an accelerating trend level of total imports which grows at 4·2 per cent per year 1961–65, 5·4 per cent 1965–69, 8·6 per cent 1969–72, and is expected to grow at 7·1 per cent per year 1972–76.

9. The fast trend growth of imports poses serious problems for the U.K. because the trend growth of exports has been little more than 5 per cent per year. Rapid growth of imports of manufactures has been a general phenomenon in all the major industrial countries during the last decade. By 1970 the penetration of imports of manufactures from the other major industrial countries was still not particularly marked in the U.K. as compared with the other countries.

10. Given the uniformity of this phenomenon and the commitment to further mutual tariff reductions as the U.K. and other E.F.T.A. members join the E.E.C. it seems almost certain that imports of manufactures into the U.K. will continue to grow very rapidly over the next few years unless some effective measures are put into effect to prevent this happening.

The trend level of exports

11. The two variable factors for which exports are adjusted are cyclical fluctuations in world trade and variations in costs of production in the U.K. relative to competing industrial exporters.

(a) World trade (as measured by the total volume of industrial exports from major industrial countries) has grown on average at 9 per cent per year with rather pronounced cyclical fluctuations about the trend. The elasticity of U.K. exports with respect to world trade is estimated to be 0·5.

(b) It is very difficult to construct an adequate measure of industrial costs on an internationally comparable basis. We have therefore used G.D.P. deflators as a provisional indicator. Deflators for the U.K.'s major competitors are weighted for exchange rates changes so that relative costs are measured in a common unit of account. On this basis the U.K.'s relative costs of production remained rather steady from 1960–67, fell suddenly by almost the full amount of devaluation in 1968, started to rise quite fast in 1970–71, but were held steady by the depreciation of sterling in 1972. In 1972 relative costs, measured in this way, were still 10 per cent lower than in 1967 and the incomes freeze and $2·35 exchange rate promise a still lower level of relative costs in 1973.

12. The main evidence on the response of exports to changes in relative costs is of course the experience of the years before and after the devaluation in November 1967. Using this particular measure of

relative costs we find the following pattern of elasticities to be reasonably satisfactory:

current year 't'	0·25
year '$t-1$'	0·24
year '$t-2$'	0·14
year '$t-3$'	0·09
etc.	
long-run elasticity	0·85

13.   The trend growth of exports has been 5 per cent per year, with the U.K.'s relative costs falling by 1½ per cent per year and world trade expanding at 9 per cent per year. Under the same trend conditions we would expect exports to grow at the same rate in the future—some 2 per cent per year slower than trend imports.

The trend terms of trade

14.   To complete the analysis of the trend movement of the balance of trade in goods and services, the terms of trade (the ratio of the export to the import price deflator) must also be adjusted for various identified sources of disturbance—principally price variations due to fluctuations in the volume of world trade, the effects of devaluation, and exogenous disturbances to import prices.

15.   There is a quite perceptible correlation of U.K. import prices with fluctuations in world trade because commodity prices tend to rise and fall with world demand; using the volume of trade in manufactures as an indicator, the import price deflator is estimated to follow fluctuations in world demand with an elasticity of 0·36.

16.   Changes in relative costs are assumed to have only a very small effect on the terms of trade (an elasticity of 0·1) except when relative costs change because of differential rates of inflation (rather than exchange rate movements). There appears to be a larger but temporary effect on the terms of trade (an elasticity of 0·5) because of delays in the adjustment of import prices to domestic inflation.

17.   The terms of trade are adjusted to an estimated trend value by correcting for deviations of world trade, exchange rates and relative costs from their respective trends under the assumptions outlined above. We have also removed any residual unexplained fluctuation in the import price deflator.

The trend balance of trade

18.   The adjustments to imports, exports and the terms of trade described above provide estimates of what the balance of trade in

goods and services might have been if G.D.P. and stockbuilding were at their Par levels and if the volume of world trade, the exchange rate and relative costs all followed logarithmic trends fitted to their actual movement in 1960–72.

19.   Appendix Table 7 shows the full set of trend estimates. Between 1960 and 1971 the outcome is a small surplus on trade in goods and services which fluctuates a little from year to year because the adjustments made to actual figures have still not explained all the short-term movements of the component series. The estimates for 1972 show a sudden sharp deterioration of the trend position; the deficit is then projected to widen quite rapidly in 1973–76.

The Par balance of trade

20.   There is no reason why the trend balance of trade, as estimated here, should provide satisfactory surpluses or deficits on goods and services from the point of view of management of the balance of payments as a whole and the liquidity position. Indeed the trend balance on goods and services is projected to move into large deficits which are quite unacceptable from this point of view.

21.   Par estimates are constructed to show the underlying movement of relative costs which would be necessary to secure an acceptable balance of trade and the net resource costs (i.e., the excess of real exports over imports) associated with such a pattern of trade. For most of the 1960s it was quite reasonable to show a small deficit on goods and services. But since then, and particularly during the next few years, it will be necessary to show a surplus (rising to £400 million at 1963 values in 1976) to offset unfavourable movements in other balance of payments items and to pay for U.K. contributions to the E.E.C. budget.

22.   In the Par economy the growth of imports would gradually have accelerated from 4 per cent per year to 8 per cent per year over the period 1960–72 for the reasons discussed above.

23.   Up to 1966 actual relative costs were sufficiently competitive to achieve reasonable trade balances at the Par pressure of demand (corresponding to 2½ per cent unemployment). From then on unit costs needed to fall steadily, overtaking the fall in actual costs (which occurred suddenly as a result of the 1967 devaluation) in 1971.

24.   The estimates in Appendix Table 8 show Par relative costs already 10 per cent below actual costs in 1972, and needing to fall by about 7 per cent per year up to 1976. This rapid fall in Par unit costs is necessary to achieve a sustained growth in export volumes of some 9 per

cent per year which will secure the target trade surpluses despite a small deterioration of the terms of trade.

25. The resource costs of achieving the Par trade targets are not large because the required adjustments to the terms of trade are small. The increase in net resources required for the balance of trade from 1972 to 1976 is £600 million. Of this the higher target trade surplus itself accounts for £250 million; the remainder is needed to offset the 2·2 per cent deterioration in the terms of trade caused by the continued need to push down relative costs.

Alternative projections, 1972–76

26. For estimates of the implications of alternative growth rates of G.D.P. and different exchange rate policies starting from the actual position in 1972 we assume that world trade will recover from its present recession and will have risen 3 per cent above the 1960–72 trend in 1976. We also assume throughout that U.K. costs in own currency terms will rise no faster than those of principal competitors. In recent years inflation in the U.K. has usually exceeded that in other countries; the assumption implicit in our projections would therefore represent quite a favourable outcome of the freeze and later phases of prices and incomes policy.

27. We have constructed several projections of the balance of trade, embodying the fast and slow growth projections of G.D.P. and various alternative assumptions about the exchange rate.

28. Under the 'fixed rate' assumption sterling is pegged from the beginning of 1973 and the rate is only adjusted thereafter to compensate for any changes in parities of major competitors. Table IV-1 shows that

Table IV-1. Projections of relative costs
(Index: 1963 actual = 100)

| | | | | *1973 devaluation by* | | | |
Year	Trend value	Fixed rate	Continued Depreciation	15%	25%	30%	Par value
1972	86·2	89·0	89·0	89·0	89·0	89·0	71·6
1973	84·8	84·4	84·4	71·9	64·7	57·5	66·6
1974	83·5	84·4	80·4	71·9	64·7	57·5	62·2
1975	82·1	84·4	76·6	71·9	64·7	57·5	58·5
1976	80·8	84·4	72·9	71·9	64·7	57·5	55·4

Alternative exchange rate assumptions

this assumption implies a 5 per cent year-on-year fall in relative costs in 1973 because sterling depreciated rather late in 1972. Relative costs would then remain fixed up to 1976 because of the assumption that U.K. inflation is contained to the same rate as in other countries.

29.   Under the 'continued depreciation' assumption relative costs are pushed down by about 5 per cent each year through gradual depreciation of the exchange rate. By contrast, the first of the 'devaluation' assumptions achieves almost the same total reduction in relative costs by an immediate adjustment of 15 per cent at the beginning of 1973. Calculations have been made for two larger immediate devaluations of 25 per cent and 30 per cent respectively. The latter leaves relative costs at very nearly the estimated Par level for 1976.

30.   Table IV-2 summarizes the implications of these various assumptions. More detailed results are given in Appendix Tables 9 and 10.

Table IV-2. Projections of the balance of trade on goods and services in 1976

Assumption	Exports (£ million 1963 prices)	Imports (£ million 1963 prices)	Terms of trade (1953=100)	Balance of trade (£ million, 1963 import values)
A. *Fast G.D.P. growth*				
1. Fixed rate	11147 (5·1)	13298 (8·5)	100·1	−2144
2. Continued depreciation	11921 (6·9)	13452 (8·8)	98.6	−1698
3. Devaluation of 15% in 1973	12520 (8·2)	13572 (9·1)	98·5	−1245
4. Devaluation of 25% in 1973	13508 (10·3)	13770 (9·5)	97·4	−609
5. Devaluation of 30% in 1973	14705 (12·7)	14009 (9·9)	96·3	149
B. *Slow G.D.P. growth*				
1. Fixed rate	11147 (5·1)	12500 (6·8)	100·1	−1346
2. Continued depreciation	11921 (6·9)	12655 (7·2)	98·6	−901
3. Devaluation of 15% in 1973	12520 (8·2)	12775 (7·4)	98·5	−447
4. Devaluation of 25% in 1973	13508 (10·3)	12972 (7·8)	97·4	188
5. Devaluation of 30% in 1973	14705 (12·7)	13212 (8·3)	96·3	947

Figures in brackets are average growth rates 1972–76, per cent per year

Given the fixed exchange rate, exports would still grow slightly faster than trend from 1973 onwards because of the assumed recovery in world trade. Continued depreciation of the exchange rate could push the growth of exports up to nearly 7 per cent per year at the cost of a small deterioration in the terms of trade. Immediate devaluation could have much more dramatic effects on the growth of exports, producing average growth rates to 1976 of 8 per cent, 10 per cent, or 13 per cent per year respectively. Fast growth of exports would be achieved at the cost not only of deterioration in the terms of trade but also of some acceleration of the growth of imports.

31.   After allowing for deterioration of the terms of trade, the only projection to show a surplus on goods and services by 1976 is the one which assumes an immediate devaluation of 30 per cent. Under the alternative assumption of very slow growth of G.D.P. (and hence rising unemployment) the projected growth of imports is reduced by about $1\frac{1}{2}$ per cent per year; but even then large deficits on goods and services are still expected in 1976 unless an immediate devaluation of 15 per cent is assumed.

32.   It has already been emphasized in section I that the estimates of the effects of devaluation are particularly hypothetical, and it was also made clear there that the projections assuming fast growth of G.D.P. are implausible because the Government could not maintain a policy of fast growth of demand if the balance on goods and services continued to deteriorate very rapidly.

More favourable estimates for the balance of trade

33.   These estimates do of course depend entirely on some assumptions, particularly about the persistence of past trends, which cannot be made with real confidence. The following paragraphs indicate the quantitative significance of some of the more vulnerable assumptions.

34.   The response of exports to changes in relative costs is particularly uncertain because past evidence is limited. The projected trend of exports is especially critical. It might easily be 1 per cent per year more favourable than our estimate, in which case the balance on goods and services would be improved by about £400 million (in 1963 values) in 1976.

35.   It seems rather unlikely that the trend growth of imports will be much lower than we have projected. The quantitative significance of any prospective reduction in costs is the less for imports than for exports because manufactures comprise a smaller part of the total.

36.   The terms of trade in 1976 might quite easily turn out 2 per cent

more favourable than our estimates, bringing an improvement of about £250 million (in 1963 values) to the balance on goods and services. 37. Considering the uncertainty over exports and the terms of trade, it is quite likely that under any given conditions the out-turn on the balance on goods and services in 1976 could be £600–£700 million more favourable than the estimates given here. It is also quite likely that the out-turn could be that much worse. But the trends are so unfavourable that even if the figures for the balance of trade in table IV-2 were written up by £700 million (at 1963 values) the deficits would still be unacceptably large except under those projections which assume immediate further devaluation of the exchange rate.

Section V. Public Expenditure, Investment and Private Consumption

This section estimates how available resources might be divided up between the public and private sectors, and between consumption and investment, given the level of G.D.P. and the net resources devoted to the balance of trade. After reviewing the claims of the public sector and of private investment it will be possible to see how much is left over for private consumption, and to examine the implications for the growth of personal incomes.

Public expenditure
2. It is well known that it can be rather misleading to measure the share of resources appropriated by public expenditure at constant 1963 prices. In current price terms the share taken by the public sector tends to grow more rapidly because a substantial proportion of public expenditure is incurred for services such as administration, health, education and defence in which little or no productivity growth is imputed. The 'relative price effect'—i.e. the extra growth of the public sector's share of resources when measured at current prices—is normally of the order of about 1 per cent per year for all public expenditure on goods and services; the effect is attributable to current rather than investment expenditures.
3. Estimates published in the White Paper (Cmnd. 5178) imply that when measured at 1963 prices public expenditure on goods and services will grow between 1972 and 1976 at almost the same rate as Par G.D.P. There will be rather faster growth of current expenditure and slower growth of investment than in the past.
4. Table V-1 shows past and projected ratios of public expenditure to G.D.P., both at constant 1963 prices and in current price terms. The

latter figures for 1976 are based on estimates of the relative price effect in the White Paper.

5. The share of resources absorbed by the public sector (measured at current prices) increased significantly between 1961 and 1965 and again between 1965 and 1969. The reason for the small size of the increase in the ratio of public expenditure to G.D.P. since 1969 is that the relative

Table V-1. Public expenditure on goods and services
(£ million 1963 market prices)

Year	Current expenditure	Investment in dwellings	Other fixed investment	Total public expenditure on goods and services	Total as % of G.D.P. at factor cost	
					At 1963 prices	At current prices
1961	4933	315	1644	6892	26·9	26·4
1965	5396	526	2061	7983	27·3	28·2
	(2·3)	(13·7)	(5·8)	(3·7)		
1969	5806	686	2297	8789	27·4	30·3
	(1·8)	(6·9)	(2·7)	(2·4)		
1972	6249	546	2598	9393	27·7	30·8
	(2·5)	(−7·3)	(4·2)	(2·2)		
Fast growth assumption						
1976	7000	537	3020	10557	26·0	30·1
	(2·9)	(−0·4)	(3·8)	(3·0)		
Slow growth assumption						
1976	7000	537	3020	10557	27·8	32·2
	(2·9)	(−0·4)	(3·8)	(3·0)		

Figures in brackets are average growth rates, % per year

price effect has been very much smaller than usual; and this can only have happened because the pay of public sector employees has risen unusually slowly relative to other incomes. If the pay of public employees were to catch up again in relative terms, the current-price ratio of public expenditure to G.D.P. in 1976 could be nearly 1 per cent higher than the figures projected in the table.

Private investment
6. The level of private housebuilding in 1972 has been about 20 per cent higher than in the previous year, while other private fixed investment has risen by only 4 per cent above the very depressed 1971 level and is still lower than in 1970. Using the same methods as in the earlier

paper to adjust private investment for variations in the pressure of demand, the underlying Par growth rate since the middle 1960s is estimated to have been just under 6 per cent per year.

7. In the past, booms in private housebuilding such as those in 1964 and 1968 have been followed by downturns of some severity, but the level of private housebuilding is unlikely to decline now because of the strong incentives to the private sector provided by government housing policy. Given the low levels of public sector housebuilding forecast in Cmnd. 5178, total investment in housing in 1976 is expected to be no higher than the previous peak in 1968, even under the assumption of fast growth of G.D.P.

Table V-2. Private investment and stockbuilding
(£ million, 1963 prices)

Year	Fixed investment	Stockbuilding	Total investment	Total as % of G.D.P. at factor cost
1961	2956	352	3308	12·9
1965	3449	436	3885	13·3
	(3·9)		(4·1)	
1969	3923	441	4364	13·6
	(3·3)		(2·9)	
1972	4232	100	4332	12·8
	(2·6)		(−0·2)	
Fast growth assumption				
1976	5638	493	6131	15·1
	(7·4)		(9·1)	
Slow growth assumption				
1976	5141	187	5328	14·0
	(5·0)		(5·3)	

Figures in brackets are average growth rates, % per year.

8. Other private fixed investment will grow more rapidly, recovering from very depressed levels in 1971 and 1972. An increase of 7 per cent is expected next year and a further increase of about 12 per cent in 1974. Under the slow growth assumption little further increase is expected, but under the stimulus of fast growth in demand private fixed investment is expected to continue to grow at 6 per cent per year up to 1976.

9. The recovery in demand in 1972 and 1973 will probably lead to substantial stockbuilding in 1973. Published estimates show very large reductions in stocks in the first three quarters of 1972. But recent

research[1] suggests that the official estimates of the stock appreciation component of the increase in value of stocks have been too high in recent years, and consequently that stockbuilding has been underestimated. Revised estimates (see Appendix Table II) imply a rather stable ratio of end-year stocks to G.D.P. over the whole period 1960–72 and stocks do not appear to be very far below their normal levels relative to output even at the end of 1972.

10. Total private investment, including stockbuilding, absorbed a very low share of output in 1972. Even under the slow growth assumption the ratio of private investment to G.D.P. is expected to rise sharply from under 13 per cent in 1972 to nearly 15 per cent in 1974; with fast growth in demand the ratio would rise to about 15½ per cent in 1974.

Private Consumption

11. To calculate Par levels of private consumption and the future growth of consumption consistent with different assumptions about the growth of G.D.P. and about the balance of trade, consumption must be treated as the residual component of demand. It is implicitly assumed that consumption is stimulated or restrained by fiscal or monetary action so as to achieve the given overall growth of demand for G.D.P.

12. Under Par conditions the rate of growth of private consumption must normally be slightly less than the rate of growth of G.D.P. because of the tendency for investment to take a rising share of the available resources and because of the increased target surpluses on goods and services needed to maintain a reasonable balance of payments position. Over the past twelve years private consumption has actually grown at an average rate of 3 per cent per year; the growth rate was much lower than this when the balance of payments position improved, during 1967–71, and rather faster in years such as 1972 when the balance of payments position was allowed to deteriorate.

13. Table V-3 gives summary projections for private consumption in 1972–76 under various different conditions; a full set of estimates will be found in Appendix Tables 11–14.

14. For the period up to 1976, the fast G.D.P. growth assumption will naturally permit quite rapid growth of private consumption. But only if the balance of payments could be allowed to go into massive deficit (as under (b) and (c) in Table V-3) could consumption grow as fast as output. If a reasonable balance of payments position is to be achieved

---

[1] A project at the Department of Applied Economics sponsored by the Department of Trade and Industry has been investigating the measurement of stock appreciation by companies.

(as for example under (a) in the Table), the average growth of consumption will have to be restrained to about 3 per cent per year, considerably less than the assumed $4\frac{1}{2}$ per cent per year growth of G.D.P., in order

Table V-3. Resources available for private consumption
(Expenditures at factor cost: £ million, 1963 prices)

Year	G.D.P.[1]	Public expenditure	Private[2] investment	Balance[3] of trade	Private consumption
Actual					
1961	25609	6639	3149	−286	16107
1965	29118	7683	3700	−402	18138
					(3·0)
1969	31939	8408	4153	18	19359
					(1·6)
1972	33726	9037	4105	−710	21294
					(3·2)
Par					
1972	34741	9037	4652	−48	21100
Fast growth assumption					
1976	40465	10157	5828		
(a) devaluation of 15% in 1973				306	24174
					(3·2)
(b) continued depreciation at 5% per year to 1976				−1847	26328
					(5·4)
(c) fixed exchange rate, 1973–76				−2446	26926
					(6·0)
Slow growth assumption					
1976	37802	10157	5052		
(a) devaluation of 15% in 1973				178	22416
					(1·3)
(b) continued depreciation at 5% per year to 1976				−1050	23644
					(2·7)
(c) fixed exchange rate, 1973–76				−1648	24242
					(3·3)

Figures in brackets are average growth rates, % per year.
[1] Expenditure estimate of G.D.P. at factor cost.
[2] Including stockbuilding.
[3] Exports less imports of goods and services, at factor cost.

to leave adequate resources for private investment, stockbuilding and net exports.

15.   Under the slow growth assumption, Table V-3 shows a very low average growth rate of consumption (1·3 per cent per year under (a)

in the Table) unless the balance of payments could be allowed to run into huge deficit.

16. The main squeeze on private consumption comes in 1973–74. Whether under the fast or slow growth assumptions, there would be large increases in investment and stockbuilding in these two years as compared with 1972. Public expenditure is also forecast to rise particularly fast. If progress is to be made towards putting the balance of payments to rights, there will have to be a virtual standstill in private consumption for at least the next year because it is already over 3 per cent higher than the average level in 1972.

17. Once the disposition of resources has been put into a more sustainable pattern, with larger provision for investment and net exports, private consumption could of course be allowed to start to grow once more at almost the same rate as G.D.P.

Consumption and fiscal policy

18. The real income of the personal sector varies in relation to G.D.P. not only because of taxation and transfers from the public authorities but also on account of changes in the ratio of import prices to domestic prices and because of variations in the share of income accruing to companies as undistributed profits. To see how the growth of personal income and hence consumption may have to be stimulated or restrained relative to G.D.P. we have made estimates of the likely effect of some of these influences on personal consumption.

19. The Par estimates for 1973–76 show an increasingly deflationary terms of trade effect because of the need for continued reductions in relative costs to maintain the external position. The projections suggest that very slight fiscal stimulus might be needed after 1973 to keep demand growing at the Par rate.

20. The Par figures show the implications of assuming that the economy follows a path of steady growth and balance of payments equilibrium. Alternative projections starting from the actual position in 1972 (see Appendix Table 15) have quite different implications for the consumption gap and fiscal policy, depending on what is assumed to happen to the balance of payments. Without large devaluation continued fiscal stimulus is required to sustain the growth of demand in the face of rapidly widening deficits on trade in goods and services. If very large devaluations are assumed, the growth of consumption must be restrained in order to leave room for fast growth of exports within the assumed overall totals for G.D.P.; most of the necessary deflation of domestic demand is projected to come from the terms of trade effect.

Section VI. Alternative Policies

1. The calculations described in the previous sections imply that the Government's objective of a fast expansion of G.D.P. at 5 per cent per year up to the end of 1974 would reduce unemployment to about 400,000; there is no reason to suppose that this would indicate an excessively high pressure of demand in the economy. Expansion could then continue up to 1976 at the Par rate of 3½ per cent per year without further reducing unemployment.

2. If the end-1972 exchange rate were maintained and prices and incomes policies were quite successful in restraining U.K. inflation (see section IV for the detailed assumptions), the projections show that fast expansion of G.D.P. would lead to a large deficit on trade in goods and services in 1973 widening to over £2,000 million (at 1963 import values) in 1976. Projections of property income, transfers and capital movements (section III) imply that the U.K.'s external liquidity position could only be fully protected by surpluses on trade in goods and services, rising to about £400 million (at 1963 import values) in 1976. The minimum target which could be accepted for that year would be a deficit on goods and services of not more than £100 million. The analysis therefore indicates that a strategy of fast expansion without new measures to protect the balance of payments would be impossible to carry through.

3. Further depreciation of the exchange rate would cause inflationary pressure because of the rise in prices of food and other imports and would jeopardize the success of prices and incomes policy. Even if the inflationary consequences of devaluation could be avoided, the alternative projections under various assumptions about the exchange rate imply that an immediate devaluation of nearly 30 per cent would be needed to achieve the minimum balance of payments target under the strategy of fast expansion of G.D.P. But in fact such a large devaluation would certainly be followed by domestic inflation and must be considered unacceptable.

4. Projections assuming a strategy of severe deflation, restraining the growth of G.D.P. to less than the Par rate (so that unemployment started rising again) still show large and increasing deficits on trade in goods and services for 1973–76 unless an immediate devaluation of nearly 20 per cent is assumed. These projections also imply that if the growth of G.D.P. were to be reduced to 2 per cent per year after a large devaluation, the growth of personal incomes and consumption would have to be restrained to an intolerably low rate (averaging 0·9 per year between 1972 and 1974).

5. None of the various strategies for the management of demand and the balance of payments examined in these projections provide acceptable results over the next four years. There are many less conventional measures which could in principle be applied to help to avoid a balance of payments crisis without sacrificing the objectives of low unemployment and a reduced rate of inflation of costs and prices. We shall not attempt to assess the merits of particular measures here. The remainder of this section will outline the requirements for a viable strategy of economic management and hence suggest the kinds of effects which any new set of policies should be designed to achieve.

The availability of resources

6. Our starting point is the assumption that fast growth of G.D.P. is necessary, both in order to reduce unemployment to a more acceptable level and in order to provide sufficient resources to leave something over for growth of private consumption after other claims on resources have been met.

7. The target growth of G.D.P. is taken to be that projected under the fast growth assumption of the previous chapters, and it is assumed that public sector expenditure, private investment and stockbuilding will be allowed to grow at the rates estimated in section V. The remaining resources then have to be allocated between the foreign balance and private consumption.

The balance of trade

8. It was indicated in section III that there is some scope for interim relaxation of the long-term target for the balance of trade in goods and services. There are first of all two items in the estimated capital flows which can be adjusted to some extent. If strict controls on outward direct investment are maintained (and the relaxation of controls on outflows to the E.E.C., beginning in 1974, is postponed) the projected net outflow of long-term capital might plausibly be reduced by some £150 million (at current prices) in 1976. One might also allow for the fact that a considerable portion of the extension of trade credit is normally financed through foreign borrowing by the banks. Since this borrowing is short-term it was not included in the credit items influencing the liquidity position. But provided there is some confidence in the long-term viability of the management of the balance of payments it may be acceptable to allow another £150 million per year for this borrowing.

9. Finally it must be recognized that the U.K. can draw on a consider-

able fund of credit from central banks and international institutions for a number of years provided there is a convincing plan to restore the balance of payments position. We assumed in section III that quite large deterioration of the liquidity position is possible over the next few years providing that a trend towards recovery is established and the net reserve effect is reduced below £500 million per year by 1976.

10.   Putting these items together, the 1976 target for the balance on goods and services can perhaps be relaxed by some £800 million at current values or £500 million at 1963 import values. The minimum target for goods and services is therefore a deficit of £100 million (at 1963 import values) rather than a surplus of £400 million.

Table VI-1. Projected balance on goods and services, 1972–76

year	Exports	Imports	Terms of trade	Balance of trade (£ million, 1963 values)
	(£ million, 1963 prices)		(1963 = 100)	
1972	9127	9595	102·3	−260
1973	9916	10457	100·0	−543
1974	11092	11288	98·3	−388
1975	11856	11863	98·4	−200
1976	12520	12427	98·5	−100

See text for assumptions underlying these projections

11.   The next step is to make an assumption about the maximum effective stimulus to exports which could reasonably be given in the present circumstances. Here we adopt the export growth estimated to result from a devaluation by 15 per cent at the beginning of 1973; the stimulus could of course in fact be given at least in part by other measures. The implied growth rate is over 8 per cent per year, almost the same as that achieved after the 1967 devaluation. The terms of trade are assumed to deteriorate slightly because of the measures taken to stimulate exports.

12.   Under the above assumptions the volume of imports of goods and services could be allowed to rise to £12,400 million at 1963 prices in 1976, a level 30 per cent higher than in 1972. After providing for imports of food, fuels, industrial materials and services, this leaves nearly £2,900 million (at 1963 prices) for imports of finished manufactures compared with £2,000 million actual imports in 1972.

13.   These figures imply that the average rate of growth of imports of finished manufactures must be restricted to just over 9 per cent per

year in volume terms, whereas in the absence of any special measures they could have been expected to grow at nearly 18 per cent per year, given the fast growth of G.D.P. The implied import saving is nearly £1,000 million (at 1963 prices) in 1976.

14. Table VI-1 gives the year by year movement of the balance of trade expected if exports are stimulated as indicated above and imports of finished manufactures are constrained to rise by just over 9 per cent in volume each year.

The prospects for private consumption

15. The resources available for private consumption can now as usual be found as the residual element of expenditure on G.D.P. The average growth rate is about 4·3 per cent per year, considerably faster than has been achieved in any previous four-year period.

16. As was indicated in section V, the impact of the 1972 budget has already raised consumption by the end of 1972 at least 3 per cent above its average for the year. This means that, compared with the present position, there would have to be a virtual freeze on consumption for the next twelve months, despite the fast growth of output and employment. Bearing in mind the need to insulate the domestic economy from any sharp increases in the prices of food, fuel and basic materials it would clearly be desirable to force up the prices of other imports very sharply, both in order to constrain the growth of import volume and to provide a deflationary effect on domestic demand.

17. More room for expansion of consumption could have been provided if the public sector were not committed and already engaged in an unusually rapid increase in expenditure on goods and services. It seems that as in previous reflations the increase in public expenditure has come at the worst possible moment.

Statistical Appendix

Expenditure, output, employment and balance of payments estimates for 1960-76

Contents:

Tables:

SOURCES AND DEFINITIONS

Table 1. G.D.P., employment and unemployment

Year	Y	U	U'	E	E'	Y*	P*	E*
1960	24957	363	318	24122	24366	23716	0·995	23835
1961	25614	291	330	24512	24561	24501	1·023	23950
1962	25909	353	474	24591	24487	25313	1·051	24080
1963	26913	546	446	24424	24643	26151	1·081	24200
1964	28433	386	334	24774	24957	27017	1·111	24322
1965	29256	303	285	25067	25166	27912	1·142	24443
1966	29780	274	403	25225	24966	28820	1·180	24434
1967	30305	480	517	24810	24709	29758	1·218	24424
1968	31447	539	530	24649	24635	30725	1·258	24414
1969	32055	525	544	24627	24575	31725	1·300	24404
1970	32725	556	605	24543	24256	32700	1·340	24403
1971	33056	634	782	24083	24070	33705	1·381	24403
1972	33962	870	812	24062	24004	34741	1·424	24402
Growth rates								
1961–65	*3·4*	—	—	*0·6*	*0·6*	*3·3*	*2·8*	*0·5*
1965–69	*2·3*	—	—	*−0·4*	*−0·6*	*3·3*	*3·3*	*0·0*
1969–72	*1·9*	—	—	*−0·8*	*−0·8*	*3·1*	*3·1*	*0·0*
Fast growth								
1973	36001	777	564	23970	24491	35739	1·467	24362
1974	37801	436	403	24804	24828	36820	1·512	24357
1975	39146	383	403	24842	24952	38130	1·558	24477
1976	40597	415	403	25018	25114	39543	1·605	24634
Growth rate								
1972–76	*4·6*	—	—	*1·0*	*1·1*	*3·3*	*3·0*	*0·2*
Slow growth								
1973	35738	777	625	23970	24361	35739	1·467	24362
1974	36453	534	708	24595	24180	36820	1·512	24357
1975	37182	812	832	23931	24035	38130	1·558	24477
1976	37926	844	966	24097	23899	39543	1·605	24634
Growth rate								
1972–76	*2·8*	—	—	*0·0*	*−0·1*	*3·3*	*3·0*	*0·2*

Table 2. Public expenditure

Year	CG	IDG	IKG	IG	G
1960	4760	301	1505	1806	6566
1961	4933	315	1644	1959	6892
1962	5089	357	1672	2029	7118
1963	5170	380	1754	2134	7304
1964	5249	499	1980	2479	7728
1965	5396	526	2061	2587	7983
1966	5551	594	2197	2791	8342
1967	5860	665	2496	3161	9021
1968	5882	707	2489	3196	9078
1969	5806	636	2297	2933	8739
1970	5878	597	2374	2971	8849
1971	6082	540	2517	3057	9139
1972	6249	546	2598	3144	9393
Growth rates					
1961–65	*2·3*	*13·7*	*5·8*	*7·2*	*3·7*
1965–69	*1·8*	*4·9*	*2·7*	*3·2*	*2·3*
1969–72	*2·5*	*−5·0*	*4·2*	*2·3*	*2·4*
1973	6515	561	2792	3353	9868
1974	6653	551	2927	3477	10130
1975	6829	540	2971	3511	10340
1976	7000	537	3020	3557	10557
Growth rate					
1972–76	*2·9*	*−0·4*	*3·8*	*3·1*	*3·0*

Table 3. Gross fixed capital formation

Year	IG	IDP	IKP	II	Y	IDP*	IKP*	I*	Y*
1960	1806	533	2079	4418	24957	484	1950	4239	23716
1961	1959	541	2415	4915	25614	521	2055	4535	24501
1962	2029	531	2332	4892	25909	523	2166	4718	25313
1963	2134	533	2327	4994	26913	485	2283	4902	26151
1964	2479	636	2699	5814	28433	547	2560	5586	27017
1965	2587	636	2813	6036	29256	574	2520	5681	27912
1966	2791	585	2810	6186	29780	546	2601	5938	28820
1967	3161	610	2838	6609	30350	578	2722	6460	29758
1968	3196	637	3112	6945	31447	609	3065	6870	30725
1969	2933	552	3371	6856	32055	571	3237	6742	31725
1970	2971	520	3589	7080	32725	542	3575	7088	32700
1971	3057	594	3387	7038	33056	635	3413	7105	33705
1972	3144	710	3522	7376	33962	770	3694	7607	34741

Growth rates

1961–65	7·2	4·1	3·9	5·3	3·4	2·5	5·2	5·8	3·3
1965–69	3·2	−3·5	4·6	3·2	2·3	−0·1	6·5	4·4	3·3
1969–72	2·3	8·8	1·5	2·5	1·9	10·5	4·5	4·1	3·1

Fast Growth

1973	3353	690	3773	7816	36001	679	3912	7943	35739
1974	3477	744	4279	8501	37801	700	4133	8311	36820
1975	3511	767	4610	8889	39146	722	4381	8614	38130
1976	3557	791	4847	9194	40597	744	4679	8980	39543

Growth rate

1972–76	3·1	2·7	8·3	5·7	4·6	−0·9	6·1	4·2	3·3

Slow Growth

1973	3353	679	3773	7804	35738	679	3912	7943	35739
1974	3477	684	4211	8372	36453	700	4133	8311	36820
1975	3511	680	4285	8476	37182	722	4381	8614	38130
1976	3557	672	4469	8698	37926	744	4679	8980	36543

Growth rate

1972–76	3·1	−1·4	6·1	4·2	2·8	−0·9	6·1	4·2	3·3

Table 4. Actual balance of payments
(£ million at current prices)

Year	BT	PIA	GT	PT	B	Long-term investment overseas (net)	Trade credit (net)	BB	D	Net liquidity effect	Ditto cumulative
1960	-407	233	-94	13	-255	-197	-20	-472	—	-472	-472
1961	-147	254	-118	17	6	62	-42	26	—	26	-446
1962	-101	334	-121	10	122	106	-22	206	—	206	-240
1963	-137	398	-132	-5	124	-150	-89	-115	20	-95	-335
1964	-602	393	-163	-10	-382	-342	-46	-770	—	-770	-1105
1965	-300	435	-177	-7	-49	-182	-46	-277	—	-277	-1382
1966	-101	387	-180	-22	84	-70	-204	-190	356	166	-1216
1967	-462	379	-188	-44	-315	-46	-185	-546	169	-377	-1593
1968	-372	335	-179	-55	-271	27	-253	-497	-196	-693	-2286
1969	173	497	-177	-49	444	-33	-161	250	85	335	-1951
1970	393	494	-172	-34	681	-39	-204	438	488	926	-1025
1971	784	470	-200	-14	1042	359	-261	1140	-293	847	-178
1972	-238	515	-212	-25	40	-245	-210	-415	125	-290	-468

Table 5. Par balance of payments
(£ million at 1963 import prices)

Year	BT	PIA+GT+PT	EEC	B	Long-term investment overseas (net)	Trade credit (net)	BB	D	Net liquidity effect	Ditto cumulative
1960	−75	210	—	135	−118	−6	11	4	15	15
1961	−75	208	—	133	−126	−12	−5	4	−1	14
1962	−75	203	—	128	−118	−51	−41	4	−37	−23
1963	−75	198	—	123	−105	−26	−12	4	−8	−31
1964	−75	188	—	113	−116	−84	−87	124	37	6
1965	−75	173	—	98	−120	−46	−68	124	56	62
1966	−75	170	—	95	−104	−100	−109	124	15	77
1967	−75	172	—	97	−58	−86	−47	124	77	154
1968	−50	175	—	125	−58	−145	−78	30	−48	106
1969	0	185	—	185	−3	−75	107	30	137	243
1970	50	202	—	252	−5	−164	88	30	118	361
1971	100	211	—	311	−24	−170	117	30	147	508
1972	150	215	—	365	−91	−221	53	30	83	591
1973	250	218	−45	423	−171	−209	43	—	43	634
1974	300	230	−65	465	−246	−231	−12	—	−12	622
1975	350	245	−95	500	−280	−249	−29	—	−29	593
1976	400	263	−130	533	−314	−255	−36	—	−36	557

Table 6. Balance of trade, actual 1960–72

Year	X	M	TT	BT	WX	UC
1960	5327	5669	0·986	−415	0·850	1·018
1961	5487	5628	0·998	−150	0·870	1·011
1962	5578	5736	1·010	−103	0·943	1·017
1963	5809	5946	1·000	−137	1·013	1·000
1964	6044	6520	0·982	−584	1·138	0·993
1965	6343	6577	0·992	−288	1·243	1·002
1966	6631	6753	1·004	−96	1·350	1·002
1967	6655	7182	1·014	−431	1·433	0·987
1968	7469	7706	0·990	−313	1·655	0·860
1969	8170	7935	0·989	142	1·868	0·854
1970	8621	8358	1·005	303	2·028	0·851
1971	9046	8744	1·031	581	2·173	0·891
1972	9127	9595	1·023	−260	2·282	0·890
Growth rates						
1961–65	*3·7*	*4·0*	*−0·2*	—	*9·3*	*−0·2*
1965–69	*6·5*	*4·8*	*−0·1*	—	*10·7*	*−3·9*
1969–72	*3·8*	*6·5*	*1·1*	—	*6·9*	*1·4*

Table 7. Balance of trade, trend 1960–76

Year	$\widehat{X}$	$\widehat{M}$	$\widehat{TT}$	$\widehat{BT}$	$\widehat{WX}$	$\widehat{UC}$
1960	5053	5195	1·004	−123	0·801	1·046
1961	5393	5299	1·003	110	0·876	1·029
1962	5550	5631	0·999	−86	0·958	1·012
1963	5870	5780	1·003	108	1·048	0·996
1964	6062	6069	0·993	−47	1·146	0·980
1965	6434	6252	0·989	110	1·253	0·965
1966	6836	6617	0·994	175	1·370	0·949
1967	7029	7001	0·986	−74	1·499	0·934
1968	7488	7446	1·014	145	1·639	0·919
1969	7877	7725	1·001	159	1·792	0·905
1970	8258	8263	1·020	163	1·960	0·890
1971	8847	8941	1·020	88	2·144	0·876
1972	9253	9906	1·011	−549	2·345	0·862
1973	9644	10536	1·010	−794	2·564	0·848
1974	10137	11318	1·010	−1083	2·804	0·835
1975	10656	12158	1·009	−1406	3·067	0·821
1976	11202	13033	1·008	−1738	3·354	0·808
Growth rates						
1961–65	*4·5*	*4·2*	*−0·4*	—	*9·4*	*−1·6*
1965–69	*5·2*	*5·4*	*0·3*	—	*9·4*	*−1·6*
1969–72	*5·5*	*8·6*	*0·3*	—	*9·4*	*−1·6*
1972–76	*4·9*	*7·1*	*−0·1*	—	*9·4*	*−1·6*

Table 8. Balance of trade, Par 1960–76

Year	X*	M*	TT*	BT*	WX*	UC*
1960	5094	5191	1·004	−75	0·801	1·050
1961	5150	5277	1·010	−75	0·876	1·104
1962	5521	5604	1·002	−75	0·958	1·037
1963	5611	5741	1·010	−75	1·048	1·064
1964	5981	6032	0·996	−75	1·146	1·006
1965	6195	6225	0·993	−75	1·253	1·002
1966	6558	6614	0·997	−75	1·370	0·984
1967	7111	7069	0·984	−75	1·499	0·915
1968	7351	7518	1·016	−50	1·639	0·939
1969	7742	7756	1·002	0	1·792	0·912
1970	8169	8267	1·018	50	1·960	0·871
1971	8947	8973	1·014	100	2·144	0·823
1972	10254	10030	0·993	150	2·345	0·716
1973	11126	10721	0·986	250	2·564	0·666
1974	12142	11603	0·980	300	2·804	0·622
1975	13281	12604	0·975	350	3·067	0·585
1976	14487	13664	0·971	400	3·354	0·554
Growth rates						
1961–65	*4·7*	*4·2*	*−0·4*	—	*9·4*	*−2·4*
1965–69	*5·7*	*5·7*	*0·2*	—	*9·4*	*−2·3*
1969–72	*9·8*	*8·9*	*−0·3*	—	*9·4*	*−7·7*
1972–76	*9·0*	*8·0*	*−0·6*	—	*9·4*	*−6·2*

Table 9. Balance of trade: Projections 1972–76—Fast growth assumption

	Year	X	M	TT	BT	WX	UC
Fixed rate	1972	9127	9595	1·023	−260	2·282	0·890
	1973	9524	10585	1·016	−908	2·510	0·844
	1974	10250	11616	0·999	−1379	2·887	0·844
	1975	10704	12419	1·000	−1718	3·157	0·844
	1976	11147	13298	1·001	−2144	3·453	0·844
Growth rate	*1972–76*	*5·1*	*8·5*	*−0·5*	—	*10·9*	*−1·3*
Continued	1972	9127	9595	1·023	−260	2·282	0·890
Depreciation	1973	9524	10585	1·016	−908	2·510	0·844
	1974	10375	11641	0·994	−1329	2·887	0·804
	1975	11097	12497	0·990	−1511	3·157	0·766
	1976	11921	13452	0·986	−1698	3·453	0·729
Growth rate	*1972–76*	*6·9*	*8·8*	*−0·9*	—	*10·9*	*−4·9*
1973 devaluation by 15%	1976	12520	13572	0·985	−1245	3·453	0·719
Growth rate	*72–76*	*8·2*	*9·1*	*−0·9*	—	*10·9*	*−5·2*
1973 devaluation by 25%	1976	13508	13770	0·974	−609	3·453	0·647
Growth rate	*1972–76*	*10·3*	*9·5*	*−1·2*	—	*10·9*	*−7·7*
1973	1972	9127	9595	1·023	−260	2·282	0·890
devaluation	1973	10485	10777	0·978	−526	2·510	0·575
by 30%	1974	12374	12041	0·961	−148	2·887	0·575
	1975	13658	13010	0·962	130	3·157	0·575
	1976	14705	14009	0·963	149	3·453	0·575
Growth rate	*1972–76*	*12·7*	*9·9*	*−1·5*	—	*10·9*	*−10·3*

Table 10. Balance of trade: Projections 1972–76—Slow growth assumption

	Year	X	M	TT	BT	WX	UC
Fixed rate	1972	9127	9595	1·023	−260	2·282	0·890
	1973	9524	10495	1·016	−818	2·510	0·844
	1974	10250	11165	0·999	−928	2·887	0·844
	1975	10704	11796	1·000	−1096	3·157	0·844
	1976	11147	12500	1·001	−1346	3·453	0·844
Growth rate	*1972–76*	*5·1*	*6·8*	*−0·5*	—	*10·9*	*−1·3*
Continued	1972	9127	9595	1·023	−260	2·282	0·890
Depreciation	1973	9524	10495	1·016	−818	2·510	0·844
	1974	10375	11190	0·994	−878	2·887	0·804
	1975	11097	11875	0·990	−889	3·157	0·766
	1976	11921	12655	0·986	−901	3·453	0·729
Growth rate	*1972–76*	*6·9*	*7·2*	*−0·9*	—	*10·9*	*−4·9*
1973 devaluation by 15%	1976	12520	12775	0·985	−447	3·453	0·719
Growth rate	*1972–76*	*8·2*	*7·4*	*−0·9*	—	*10·9*	*−5·2*
1973 devaluation by 25%	1972	9127	9595	1·023	−260	2·282	0·890
	1973	10181	10627	0·989	−555	2·510	0·647
	1974	11680	11451	0·972	−93	2·887	0·647
	1975	12675	12190	0·973	148	3·157	0·647
	1976	13508	12972	0·974	188	3·453	0·647
Growth rate	*1972–76*	*10·3*	*7·8*	*−1·2*	—	*10·9*	*−7·7*
1973 devaluation by 30%	1976	14705	13212	0·963	947	3·453	0·575
Growth rate	*1972–76*	*12·7*	*8·3*	*−1·5*	—	*10·9*	*−10·3*

Table 11. Expenditure on G.D.P., actual 1960–72

Year	C	CG	I	S	X	M	A	R	Y
1960	18445	4760	4418	641	5327	5669	3272	307	24957
1961	18876	4933	4915	352	5487	5628	3326	5	25614
1962	19280	5089	4892	75	5578	5736	3329	60	25909
1963	20130	5170	4994	223	5809	5946	3467	0	26913
1964	20830	5249	5814	677	6044	6520	3712	51	28433
1965	21197	5396	6036	436	6343	6577	3713	138	29256
1966	21628	5551	6186	301	6631	6753	3817	53	29780
1967	22118	5860	6609	228	6655	7182	3956	−27	30305
1968	22687	5882	6945	289	7469	7706	4155	36	31447
1969	22800	5806	6856	441	8170	7935	4199	116	32055
1970	23413	5878	7080	433	8621	8358	4406	64	32725
1971	24032	6082	7038	155	9046	9744	4582	29	33056
1972	25500	6249	7376	100	9127	9595	5031	236	33962
Growth rates									
1961–65	*2·9*	*2·3*	*5·3*	—	*3·7*	*4·0*	*2·8*	—	*3·4*
1965–69	*2·9*	*1·8*	*3·2*	—	*6·5*	*4·8*	*3·1*	—	*2·3*
1969–72	*3·8*	*2·5*	*2·5*	—	*3·8*	*6·5*	*6·2*	—	*1·9*

Table 12. Expenditure on G.D.P., Par 1960–76

Year	C*	CG	I*	S*	S*	M*	A*	Y*
1960	17544	4760	4239	305	5094	5191	3036	23716
1961	17971	4933	4535	314	5150	5277	3124	24501
1962	18495	5089	4718	323	5521	5604	3229	25313
1963	19233	5170	4902	332	5611	5741	3355	26151
1964	19318	5249	5586	342	5981	6032	3426	27017
1965	20075	5396	5681	351	6195	6225	3562	27912
1966	20732	5551	5938	361	6558	6614	3706	28820
1967	20820	5860	6460	372	7111	7069	3797	29758
1968	21756	5882	6870	382	7351	7518	3998	30725
1969	23040	5806	6742	393	7742	7756	4243	31725
1970	23900	5878	7088	404	8169	8267	4471	32700
1971	24871	6082	7105	416	8947	8973	4743	33705
1972	25202	6249	7607	428	10254	10030	4969	34741
1973	25618	6515	7943	440	11126	10721	5182	35739
1974	26326	6653	8311	452	13142	11603	5462	36820
1975	27356	6829	8614	465	13281	12604	5811	38130
1976	28495	7000	8980	478	14487	13664	6233	39543
Growth rates								
1961–65	*2·8*	*2·3*	*5·8*	—	*4·7*	*4·2*	*3·3*	*3·3*
1965–69	*3·5*	*1·8*	*4·4*	—	*5·7*	*5·7*	*4·5*	*3·3*
1969–72	*3·0*	*2·5*	*4·1*	—	*9·8*	*8·9*	*5·4*	*3·1*
1972–76	*3·1*	*2·9*	*4·2*	—	*9·0*	*8·0*	*5·8*	*3·3*

Table 13. Expenditure on G.D.P.: Projections 1972–76—Fast growth assumption

	Year	C	CG	I	S	X	M	A	R	Y
Fixed rate	1972	25500	6249	7376	100	9127	9595	5031	236	33962
	1973	27325	6515	7816	705	9524	10585	5417	117	36001
	1974	28909	6653	8501	844	10250	11616	5863	123	37801
	1975	30763	6829	8889	607	10704	12419	6355	128	39146
	1976	32876	7000	9194	493	11147	13298	6949	132	40597
Growth rates	*1972–76*	*6·6*	*2·9*	*5·7*	*—*	*5·1*	*8·5*	*8·4*	*—*	*4·6*
Continued Depreciation	1972	25500	6249	7376	100	9127	9595	5031	236	33962
	1973	27325	6515	7816	705	9524	10585	5417	117	36001
	1974	28792	6653	8501	844	10375	11641	5847	123	37801
	1975	30394	6829	8889	607	11097	12497	6301	128	39146
	1976	32146	7000	9194	493	11921	13452	6837	132	40597
Growth rates	*1972–76*	*6·0*	*2·9*	*5·7*	*—*	*6·9*	*8·8*	*8·0*	*—*	*4·6*
1973 devaluation by 30%	1972	25500	6249	7376	100	9127	9595	5031	236	33962
	1973	26433	6515	7816	705	10485	10777	5294	117	36001
	1974	26927	6653	8501	844	12374	12041	5581	123	37801
	1975	27993	6829	8889	607	13658	13010	5948	128	39146
	1976	29516	7000	9194	493	14705	14009	6435	132	40597
Growth rates	*1972–76*	*3·7*	*2·9*	*5·7*	*—*	*12·7*	*9·9*	*6·3*	*—*	*4·6*

Table 14. Expenditure on G.D.P.: Projections 1972–76—Slow growth assumption

	Year	C	CG	I	S	X	M	A	R	Y
Fixed rate $2·35	1972	25500	6249	7376	100	9127	9595	5031	236	33962
	1973	27004	6515	7804	632	9524	10495	5362	117	35738
	1974	27312	6653	8372	496	10250	11165	5584	119	36453
	1975	28556	6829	8476	237	10704	11796	5946	121	37182
	1976	29599	7000	8698	187	11147	12500	6329	124	37926
Growth rates	*1972–76*	*3·8*	*2·9*	*4·2*	*—*	*5·1*	*6·8*	*5·9*	*—*	*2·8*
Continued Depreciation	1972	25500	6249	7376	100	9127	9595	5031	236	33962
	1973	27004	6515	7804	632	9524	10495	5362	117	35738
	1974	27194	6653	8372	496	10375	11190	5567	119	36453
	1975	28187	6829	8476	237	11097	11875	5892	121	37182
	1976	28869	7000	8698	187	11921	12655	6218	124	37926
Growth rates	*1972–76*	*3·2*	*2·9*	*4·2*	*—*	*6·9*	*7·2*	*5·4*	*—*	*2·8*
1973 devaluation by 25%	1972	25500	6249	7376	100	9127	9595	5031	236	33962
	1973	26395	6515	7804	632	10181	10627	5278	117	35738
	1974	25977	6653	8372	496	11680	11451	5394	119	36453
	1975	26708	6829	8476	237	12675	12190	5674	121	37182
	1976	27370	7000	8698	187	13508	12972	5988	124	37926
Growth rates	*1972–76*	*1·8*	*2·9*	*4·2*	*—*	*10·3*	*7·8*	*4·4*	*—*	*2·8*

Table 15. The consumption gap, 1972–76

	Year	Required consumption	Generated consumption	Initial gap	Terms of trade	Rent and food	Final gap
Par	1972	25202	25942	−740	−576	—	−164
	1973	25618	26687	−1069	−748	−138	−183
	1974	26326	27494	−1168	−915	−300	47
	1975	27356	28472	−1116	−1072	−337	293
	1976	28495	29528	−1033	−1230	−375	572
Fast growth							
Fixed rate	1972	25500	25500	—	—	—	—
	1973	27325	26834	491	−115	−138	744
	1974	28909	28042	867	−207	−300	1374
	1975	30763	29040	1723	−173	−337	2233
	1976	32876	30116	2760	−136	−375	3271
Continued depreciation	1972	25500	25500	—	—	—	—
	1973	27325	26834	491	−115	−138	744
	1974	28792	28042	750	−343	−300	1393
	1975	30394	29040	1354	−453	−337	2144
	1976	32146	30116	2030	−572	−375	2977
1973 devaluation by 30%	1972	25500	25500	—	—	—	—
	1973	26433	26834	−401	−1124	−138	861
	1974	26927	28042	−1115	−1257	−300	442
	1975	27993	29040	−1047	−1261	−337	551
	1976	29516	30116	−600	−1267	−375	1042
Slow growth							
Fixed rate	1972	25500	25500	—	—	—	—
	1973	27004	26687	317	−115	−138	570
	1974	27312	27287	25	−202	−300	527
	1975	28556	27934	622	−166	−337	1125
	1976	29599	28605	994	−129	−375	1498
Continued depreciation	1972	25500	25500	—	—	—	—
	1973	27004	26687	317	−115	−138	570
	1974	27194	27287	−93	−333	−300	540
	1975	28187	27934	253	−436	−337	1026
	1976	28869	28605	264	−544	−375	1183
1973 devaluation by 25%	1972	25500	25500	—	—	—	—
	1973	26395	26687	−292	−814	−138	660
	1974	25977	27287	−1310	−914	−300	−96
	1975	26708	27934	−1226	−897	−337	8
	1976	27370	38605	−1235	−878	−375	18

Sources and definitions

All series in £ million, 1963 prices unless otherwise indicated

Table 1   G.D.P., employment and unemployment

Y Gross domestic product at factor cost.
Average of expenditure, income and output indices linked to expenditure estimate for 1963; expenditure estimates incorporate revised stockbuilding series (see section V).

U Wholly unemployed, Great Britain, excluding school leavers, seasonally adjusted average for first quarter (thousands).

U' Unemployment adjusted for lagged response to output
$$U'_t = 0 \cdot 625 U_{t+1} + 0 \cdot 375 U_t$$

E Employees in employment, plus self-employed and armed forces, Great Britain, March figure (thousands).

E' Employment adjusted for lagged response to output
$$E'_t = 0 \cdot 625 E_{t+1} + 0 \cdot 375 E_t$$

Y^* Par G.D.P. at factor cost.
Estimated for 1961, 1965, 1969 and 1971 by the formula
$$Y^* = Y/[1 + \beta_y (0 \cdot 025 - U'/25000)]$$

Values are interpolated for intermediate years and extrapolated for 1960 and 1972.

β_y Elasticity of output with respect to adjusted unemployment, declining from 4 in 1960 to 3 for 1972–76.

P^* Par output per head (£ thousand, 1963 prices).
Estimated for 1961, 1965, 1969 and 1971 by the formula
$$P^* = Y/[E' + \beta_p (625 - U')]$$

Values are interpolated or extrapolated for other years.

β_p Elasticity of productivity with respect to adjusted unemployment, declining from 1·8 in 1960 to 0·8 for 1972–76.

E^* Par employment (thousands) $E^* = Y^*/P^*$.

Projections for 1973–76

E^* is extrapolated by allowing for demographic changes, trends in participation rates and the effects of higher educational enrolment and P^* is projected to grow at 3 per cent per year. Given assumed values for Y, levels of U' and E' (and hence also U and E) are solved from the formulae given above.

Table 2   Public expenditure

CG Public authorities' current expenditure on goods and services.

IDG Public authorities' fixed capital formation in dwellings.

IKG Other fixed capital formation by public authorities (excluding steel industry).

IG Total public authorities' fixed capital formation
$$IG = IDG + IKG.$$

G Total public sector expenditure on goods and services
$$G = CG + IG.$$

Projections for 1973–76

Estimates in the White Paper on Public Expenditure are adjusted to calendar years and to a 1963 prices basis.

Table 3 Gross fixed capital formation

IDP Private gross fixed capital formation in dwellings.
IKP Other private gross fixed capital formation (including public sector steel industry).
I Total gross fixed capital formation
$$I = IDP + IKP + IG$$
IDP^* Par private gross fixed capital formation in dwellings
$IDP^* = IDP + 0 \cdot 0446(Y^* - Y)$ + adjustment for variations in mortgage interest rate
IKP^* Par other private gross fixed capital formation
$$IKP^* = IKP + 0 \cdot 2607(Y^* - Y)_{-1} - 0 \cdot 0997(Y^* - Y)_{-2}$$
I^* Par total gross fixed capital formation
$$I^* = IG + IDP^* + IKP^*.$$

Projections for 1973–76

IDP^* is extrapolated assuming very small trend growth after 1972. IKP^* is calculated by the formula
$$IKP^* = -2210 + 0 \cdot 2607 Y^*_1 - 0 \cdot 0997 Y^*_2 + 15\,(t - 1948)$$
+ adjustment for extra steel and oil investment

Values for IDP and IKP are solved from the formulae given above.

Table 4 Actual balance of payments

BT Balance of trade on goods and services.
PIA Property income from abroad, net.
Interest, profits and dividends earned overseas, net of overseas tax, minus payments overseas, net of U.K. tax.
GT Government transfers abroad, net.
Excludes payments to E.E.C.
PT Private transfers abroad, net.
B Current balance of payments

Long-term investment overseas, net

Inflows of direct, portfolio, 'oil and miscellaneous', and official long-term investment from overseas, minus outflows. Foreign currency borrowing by U.K. banks to finance investment overseas is counted as long-term inward investment.

Trade, credit, net

> Import credit received from unrelated firms, minus export credit granted. Values for 1960-62 are estimated on the basis of changes in imports and exports, assuming constant credit/trade ratios.

BB Basic balance of payments

> B + long-term investment overseas, net + trade credit, net

D Allocations of I.M.F. drawing rights, special and ordinary (net of gold contributions to the I.M.F.), E.E.A. profits/losses and revaluations affecting the reserves and short-term assets and liabilities, so far as these are identified in the official Balance of Payments accounts. (See *U.K. Balance of Payments, 1972*, Table 41, and earlier editions.)

Net liquidity effect

> Changes in the balance of official reserves (including special I.M.F. drawing rights and unused lines of credit at the I.M.F.) minus net short-term external liabilities in official and private hands. Identically equal to $BB + D$. A minus sign indicates a deterioration in the balance.

All values are at current prices.

Table 5 Par balance of payments

BT The Par economy's required balance of trade on goods and services. In principle, the target is set so as to make Par *BB* zero, given other balance of payments flows. The smoothed target shown here broadly meets this condition for 1960-76 as a whole, while confining the required annual improvement in trade to well within £100 million in most years. The target is no more than a broad order of magnitude, and its precise annual values are not important.

EEC The U.K.'s net contribution on current account to the E.E.C. budget. Estimates in the White Paper on Public Expenditure were expressed at 1963 import prices (see below).

Other headings correspond to those in Table 4. However, all past flows have here been smoothed to estimate their trend or average movements and are expressed at *1963 import values*. The latter are defined as current values deflated by the price deflator for U.K. imports of goods and services, 1963 = 100.

Projections for 1973-76

PIA Values of the principal components of interest, profits and dividends were projected separately on the basis of logarithmic trends in their real values. Adjustments were made for additional interest and profits payable on inward investment in North Sea oil and gas, and for lower growth of interest payments on short-term debt accumulated by the Par economy. It was assumed that the Par economy would have some £1,500 mn of net short-term liabilities (at 1963 values) less than the actual economy by 1976, and that interest would be saved in that year equivalent to about 5 per cent of this amount. A low rate of interest was selected because it was assumed that some of the projected difference in the liquidity position would reflect higher reserves or official short-term lending at low rates of interest by the Par economy.

GT Projected on the basis of estimates in the latest Public Expenditure White Paper.

Long-term investment overseas

Direct investment was projected on the basis of logarithmic trends in real flows. Separate projections were made for investment in E.E.C. and non-E.E.C. areas and adjustments were made to reflect relaxation of restrictions to the E.E.C. after 1974.

Outward oil and miscellaneous investment was projected on the basis of the trend in accumulated net assets for this item. (The down trend in annual investment in oil etc. since the early 1960s is not expected to continue.)

Inward oil and miscellaneous investment was made to fall from a trend level of £240 million in 1972 to some £190 million in 1976, reflecting a fall-off in investment in the North Sea by foreign companies.

Official long-term investment was projected mainly on the basis of estimates in the Public Expenditure White Paper, converted to 1963 import values. This item includes U.K. capital subscriptions to the European Investment Bank and the E.C.S.C.

Trade Credit

Movements in Par import and export credit (ΔT_M and ΔT_x) were projected as follows:

$$\Delta TM = \cdot 08(\Delta M)$$
$$\Delta TX = \cdot 25(\Delta X)$$

where M and X are Par imports and exports respectively, adjusted to current values. (Par imports and exports at 1963 prices are given in Table 8.) Net trade credit is then $\Delta T_M - \Delta T_x$, expressed at 1963 import prices.

Tables 6–10   Balance of trade

Actual Series:

X Exports of goods and services.

M Imports of goods and services.

TT Terms of trade (index, 1963 = 100).
     Ratio of price deflator for exports of goods and services to price deflator for imports of goods and services.

BT Balance of trade on goods and services at 1963 import values

$$BT = X.TT - M$$

WX Volume of world trade.
     Summary index of manufactured exports for 11 industrial countries, average of quarterly values; source: linked series from U.N. Monthly Bulletin.

UC   Relative costs.
       Index of U.K. G.D.P. deflator relative to a weighted average of the
       G.D.P. deflators of 6 other major countries with geometric weights
       equal to 1963 shares of trade in manufactures, corrected for exchange
       rate changes (multiplied by RX).
RX   Relative exchange rate.
       Index of U.K. dollar exchange rate relative to a weighted average
       of the dollar exchange rates of 6 other major countries with geometric
       weights equal to 1963 shares of trade in manufactures.

Trend series (see section IV):

$$\left.\begin{array}{l}\widehat{WX}\\ \widehat{UC}\\ \widehat{RX}\end{array}\right\}\text{log trend values fitted to actual data, 1960--72}$$

$$\hat{X}=X\left(\frac{\widehat{WX}}{WX}\right)^{0\cdot5}\left(\frac{\widehat{UC}}{UC}\right)^{-0\cdot25}\prod_{j=-1}^{\infty}\left(\frac{\widehat{UC_{-j}}}{UC_{-j}}\right)^{-0\cdot4\,(0\cdot6)^{j}}$$

$$\hat{M}=M+0\cdot27(Y^{*}-Y)+0\cdot25(S^{*}-S)+0\cdot20(\hat{X}-X)$$

       – adjustments for effects of import surcharge 1964–67 and imports
       of U.S. aircraft.

$$\widehat{TT}=TT\left(\frac{\widehat{UC}}{UC}\right)^{0\cdot5}\left(\frac{\widehat{UC_{-1}}}{UC_{-1}}\right)^{-0\cdot4}\left(\frac{\widehat{RX}}{RX}\right)^{0\cdot4}\left(\frac{\widehat{RX_{-1}}}{RX_{-1}}\right)^{-0\cdot4}\left(\frac{\widehat{WX}}{WX}\right)^{-0\cdot36}$$

       × adjustment for unexplained variation in import price deflator.

$$\widehat{BT}=X.\widehat{TT}-M$$

Par series (see section IV):

*WX** trend value $(=\widehat{WX})$.
*UC** values are estimated to yield approximately the target balance of
       trade, *BT**, after taking account of the effects on exports and the
       terms of trade assuming the same elasticities as for *X*.

*RX** $RX.\dfrac{\widehat{UC}}{UC^{*}}$

*M** $\hat{M}+0\cdot20\,(X^{*}-\hat{X})+$ imports of U.S. aircraft.

*X** $(BT^{*}+M^{*})/TT^{*}$

*TT** $\widehat{TT}\left(\dfrac{UC}{\widehat{UC}}\right)^{0\cdot5}\left(\dfrac{UC^{*}}{\widehat{UC}}\right)^{-0\cdot4}\left(\dfrac{RX^{*}}{\widehat{RX}}\right)^{0\cdot4}\left(\dfrac{RX^{*}_{-1}}{\widehat{RX}_{-1}}\right)^{-0\cdot4}$

*BT** target balance of trade (see section III).

Projections for 1973–76

       Values of $\hat{X}$ and $\widehat{TT}$ are extrapolated from the trend 1960–72. $\hat{M}$
       is projected on the basis of a disaggregated study of the trend growth

of imports and incorporated an allowance for savings due to North Sea oil and gas, and higher domestic output of coal and food. All other items are solved using the formulae given above to adjust the trend projections.

Tables 11–14   Expenditure on G.D.P.

C   Consumers' expenditure.
S   Physical increase in stocks and work-in-progress, revised (see section V).
A   Adjustment to factor cost.
R   Residual error (compromise less expenditure estimate).
C* Par consumers' expenditure, obtained as a residual.
S* Par physical increase in stocks and work-in-progress

$$S^* = S + 0.276(Y^* - Y) - 0.092(Y^* - Y)_{-1} - 0.186(Y^* - Y)_{-2}$$

A* Par adjustment to factor cost.
Adjustment to factor cost is decomposed into net indirect taxes falling on private consumers' expenditure, public current expenditure, gross fixed capital formation and exports. The Par adjustments for all but private consumers' expenditure are obtained by applying the ratio of the factor cost adjustment at 1963 rates to expenditure at 1963 prices to the Par series. The ratio used for Par private consumers' expenditure is obtained by fitting a curve to estimates of past ratios derived as residuals.

Projections 1973–76

Consumers' expenditure is estimated as a residual, given projections of other categories of expenditure and extrapolating the Par estimate of its net indirect tax content. In the case of alternative projections starting from the actual position in 1972 a small residual error has been retained to improve comparability of past and future figures.

Table 15   The Consumption gap

Required consumption	Consumers' expenditure as a residual in the expenditure accounts (defined as C).
Generated consumption	Private consumption generated by the flow of incomes, assuming the current real burden of taxation and the terms of trade expected for 1972.
Initial gap	Difference between required and generated consumption.
Terms of trade effect	The effects on consumption of changes in import prices relative to home costs.
Rent and food	Effects of higher food prices due to movement to the Common Agricultural Policy and of higher rents to be changed for local authority housing.
Final gap	Initial gap less terms of trade effect and rent and food.

4: A Tabular Comparison of the Three Models

P. Mottershead

This chapter presents a tabular comparison of the three models, and appends to it some of the more technical points raised in the discussions. The information about the models which can be displayed in this way is, of course, limited; it is not possible to show, for example, how 'Par' figures are calculated from actual figures—a central feature of the 'Par' model. The table, therefore, should be treated as a summary of certain differences between the models—but not as a comprehensive account of all differences.

There follows a record of that part of the discussion which concerned the treatment of some of the important variables.

Observations

Contingency Reserve and Shortfall
All three models naturally use the Public Expenditure White Paper, and there was some discussion of the treatment of particular items, notably the contingency reserve and the shortfall. One participant suggested that neither item could be considered meaningful in the forecasting sense and consequently both should be omitted from calculations, using the total of the programmes as the best estimate of probable future expenditure.

The Par Group suggested that as the contingency reserve had in previous years been largely hypothecated to the real uprating of National Insurance, and in the current White Paper it had been substantially hypothecated to the control of Nationalized Industry prices in relation to their wages and other costs, it really belonged to the transfer category of public expenditure. This meant that it was in fact ignored in the Par model, because the model has no tax loop and consequently transfers are not brought into the system. The shortfalls belong to the category of public expenditure on goods and services and are deducted from the public expenditure projections in each year.

Wealth Term and Non-durable Consumption

One participant queried the use of a wealth term in the determination of consumption of non-durables in the growth project model. The author replied that consumption of non-durables was at first taken to be a function of permanent and transitory income and permanent and transitory wealth. Transitory wealth was later removed as statistics were poor and it did not perform well, but the permanent wealth term, comprising mainly accumulated savings, was retained as it did stand up well to *ex post* verification.

Export Elasticities

It was noted by one participant that the export unit value indices which are used in the calculation of export elasticities are far from comparable between different countries. Although one could assume that the quality of the various indices remained constant relative to each other, it would be better to have some idea of what relative prices really were. There were some international investigations of the comparability of indices and these should be used.

Shifting exchange rates had provided more data for the study of elasticities, but they have also raised the problem of the correct numeraire for measuring changes in the sterling exchange rate. The simple dollar equivalent was surely no longer sufficient and the use of a weighted exchange rate was advocated.

Export Prices

There was considerable discussion about the different treatment of exports and export prices, particularly in relation to a devaluation. The Treasury model used a projection of world G.D.P. prices with an implicit trend for world export prices to arrive at U.K. export prices. The Par model did not have export prices as such but operated in terms of costs, because the Par group thought that the concept of a price elasticity for exports did not comprehend the whole mechanism of balance of trade adjustment. In the case of a devaluation, for example, the shift to profit might be as important as a change in price in stimulating an increase in exports. It was basically a matter of convenience that the whole of the adjustment from a devaluation was put on the export side and the Par modellers stressed that this should not be taken to mean that they believed that a substantial devaluation would have no effect on import volumes.

The Stone model had a two-stage approach to the export forecast.

COMPARISON OF THE MODELS

Aspect	Model I Treasury	Model II Stone	Model III Par
Level of Aggregation	Aggregate model	Disaggregated by 35 industries	Aggregate Model
DEMAND SIDE Private consumption	Normally determined as a residual after investment, balance of payments and public sectors satisfied. Desired consumption is a function of real disposable income and past consumption. Real disposable income is derived from total personal income by deducting direct taxes.	Divided into 41 categories of consumers' expenditure. These categorized into durable/non-durable. *Non-durable* a function of lagged consumption and real disposable income with wealth term included. *Durable* expenditure estimated by stock adjustment model and divided into three: (a) Motor vehicles; (b) Furniture and floor coverings; (c) Electrical and radio goods.	Consumers' expenditure calculated as a residual after other categories determined. 'Generated' consumption determined by output, pressure of demand and terms of trade.
Public consumption	Determined from the Public Expenditure White Paper projections with allowance for imputed rent.	Determined from the Public Expenditure White Paper projections. Divided into: (a) Defence; (b) N.H.S.; (c) Education, and (d) Other.	Determined from the Public Expenditure White Paper projections.
Private investment (fixed)	Private dwellings and land transfer costs exogenously determined. Apart from this five divisions are made: (a) Manufacturing: plant and machinery; (b) Manufacturing: vehicles; (c) Manufacturing: other new building; (d) Distribution investment; and (e) Other non-manufacturing investment. (a) (b) and (c) determined from manufacturing output, (d) and (e)	Divided into expenditure on each of nine asset types. Replacement investment is a function of capital life. Extensions investment is a function of the change in investing industry output, except in declining industries.	Divided into two sections: (a) Dwellings (b) Other Determined from output and interest rates.

Stockbuilding	Determined from output using a simple stock adjustment model.		Determined from output.
Public fixed investment	Determined from the Public Expenditure White Paper plans.		Determined from the Public Expenditure White Paper plans.
Exports	Divided into three: (a) Goods; (b) Private services; and (c) Government services. (a) and (b) determined from world trade and relative prices. (c) exogenously determined.	Forecasts of exports for given levels of world trade and prices are provided by the National Ports Council. The effects of departures from the given price levels are calculated from estimates of price elasticities for exports.	Determined from world trade and relative costs.
Imports	Divided into three: (a) Goods; (b) Private services; and (c) Government services. (a) determined from total final expenditure and relative prices; (b) determined from G.D.P.; (c) exogenously determined.	The general form for each import is a function of total demand for the importable and its relative price. Agricultural imports are dependent on government policy.	Determined from output, stocks and exports. Projected from disaggregated study of the trend growth of imports.
Adjustment to factor cost	The current price factor cost adjustment is forecast by projecting each tax/subsidy separately and allocating the yield of each between the components of demand by fixed proportions. The constant price factor cost adjustment is assumed to be the same proportion of each expenditure category as in the price base year.	Derived as the difference between G.D.P. estimate at factor cost (the sum of industrial net outputs plus ownership of dwellings, government and personal sector wage bill) and G.D.P. estimates at market prices.	Decomposed into: (a) Private consumers' expenditure; (b) Public current expenditure; (c) Gross fixed capital formation; (d) Exports. Adjustments to (b) (c) and (d) use 1963 ratio. Adjustments to (a) use a more complex form by fitting a curve to estimates of past ratios.

Aspect	Model I Treasury	Model II Stone	Model III Par
BALANCE OF PAYMENTS External capital flows	Determined exogenously.	Determined exogenously.	Projected from trends. Government flows from the Public Expenditure White Paper.
Interest, profits and dividends (I.P.D.)	Net I.P.D. credits are a function of current price world trade, with a proportion deducted for tax. The 3 components of net I.P.D. debits are calculated separately as a per cent of the national total, tax is then deducted.	Interest payments exogenously determined. Profits and dividends paid abroad and received from abroad related to stock of investment and profits.	Projected separately from trends.
SUPPLY SIDE Employment	Function of output, lagged employment, normal hours and productivity. (Since this paper was presented this sector has been modified to distinguish between government employment and output and that of the rest of the economy).	Growth of employment in each industry depends on the industry's investment and its growth in output. Government employment is exogenous. Total employment is limited by the estimated working population.	Function of output and productivity. Future working population related to demographic changes, trend participation rates and higher educational enrolment.
Productivity	Represented by the inclusion of two time trends, starting in 1958 and 1963 respectively.	Calculated for each industry by dividing output by employment. *Not* projected on trend.	3 trends to represent past productivity. Par output per head projected to grow at 3 per cent per annum.
PRICES Home Prices	Consumption, investment and stockbuilding prices determined as a function of domestic wage costs and import costs. Government prices from a weighted average of consumer prices and average earn-	Industrial prices are calculated on a full-cost basis for each industry. Profits are taken as a fixed share of value added.	

	The separate determination of current and constant price G.D.P. effectively determines the overall level of prices. A profit share can be imposed in the estimation of current price G.D.P.		
Export prices	Derived from G.D.P. prices and competitors' export prices.	Price indices are calculated by solving functions for the demand and supply of exports. They are closely related to world prices for some commodities.	
Import prices	Assumed to grow at same rate as competitors' export prices.	Determined exogenously for 86 import groups.	
Terms of trade			Determined by exchange rate and relative costs. [G.D.P. at U.K. factor cost relative to weighted average of G.D.P. deflator of 6 other major countries.]
TAXES	Projected in one of two ways: (a) by assuming ratio of taxes to income is constant; (b) by applying present taxes at announced rates to the projections of income.	Direct personal tax revenues are calculated by applying tax rates to single and married persons, each classified by 25 income groups and types of income. Corporate tax revenues are calculated from estimates of taxable income including industrial profits. Indirect tax revenues calculated by applying rates to individual categories of consumers' expenditure or other expenditure where appropriate.	No tax loop in Par model, but tax implications derived from the difference between desired and generated consumption.

The first was a projection at given exchange rates and given price relationships. The exchange rates and the price relationships can then be altered and, through imposed elasticities, the effects of this can be examined. These elasticities are in respect of world prices and also in respect of the price of goods going to the home market. This could take account of the shift to profit after a devaluation which could be an important motive in stimulating an increase in exports.

Capital Stock Valuations

In the discussion about investment forecasting, there was considerable interest in the problems of measuring capital. This arises in all three models, but in particular the Stone model uses vintage production functions with productivity consequently dependent upon investment in new machinery.

Suggestions for improving investment equations included the use of international comparisons. Complaints were also made of the unreliability of existing capital stock figures and suggestions were made that more information could be gathered by the Census of Production. Existing capital stock valuations were started in this country when Barna in the 1950s took a sample of fire insurance valuations. The C.S.O. also started a perpetual inventory method but there was a considerable gap between the two. The perpetual inventory method came in for some criticism, and some participants expressed strong doubts about the validity of any valuations of the capital stock. Price indices for capital goods which were a prerequisite for valuations could not take adequate account of quality changes. In particular the perpetual inventory method was unsound in that it was based on arbitrary valuations made of capital installed during the war, and there was no way in which it could be known how much of this capital was in fact obsolete after the war.

Some people thought that it was necessary to have some idea of the value of capital in order to decide on a correct weighting procedure for capital of different vintages. Those who were against this thought that more information simply on the age of capital assets, perhaps in the form of a census of machinery, would be desirable.

Part II
Discussion of the Macro-Models

This part includes two discussion papers on the macro-models which were presented to the Conference; one by Mr. Budd of the Treasury on whether or not there is such a thing as medium-term policy, and one by Mr. Woodward of the Department of Applied Economics on disaggregation. We have also included here a paper prepared by the National Economic Development Office on the industrial assessment which they were then making, and on the use which they made both of macro-economic models and of industrial models in the preparation of this assessment.

At the end of this section there is a report on the discussion of the macro-economic models and of the N.E.D.O. assessment. The discussion of the industrial models is reported separately (page 226); and some of the more technical points made in the discussion have been attached as notes to the comparative table (page 124.) The various arguments are not attributed—though obviously when one or other model was defended against some criticism, it was usually defended by one of the people working on that model. Some of the discussion is reported in direct speech for stylistic variety, since long sections of indirect speech are rather wearisome to read.

The basic papers were circulated some time before the Conference; and various members of the National Institute prepared a set of discussion papers on them. Most of these papers are not reprinted here; the various points made have been incorporated into the discussion. However, one paper by Mr. Worswick, on productivity in the Par economy, together with a reply from Mr. T. F. Cripps, is included as an Appendix (page 231).

5: Economic Policy and the Medium Term[1]

A. P. Budd

I. The Medium Term in General

My first point is that there is no such thing as medium-term economic policy.

The difficulty of defining medium term policy is in itself illuminating. Formally we can think of economic policy as the choice of values of policy variables through time in order to achieve desired values of target variables through time. (As a matter of detail, actions are not necessarily simultaneous with decisions. Decisions will frequently determine values of policy variables in advance.) The overall objective of economic policy (readily stated in theory but impossible to define in practice) is to maximize the value of a utility function of outcomes through time.

Given the formal definition, how can we identify part of economic policy as being medium term policy? We can define the short term as covering, say, the next two years and the medium term as covering all subsequent years, but we would only be able to identify a distinct medium-term policy if we could divide decisions into those that influence outcomes in the next two years but not later and those that influence outcomes beyond the next two years but not earlier. We might be able to categorize some decisions in this way, but the great bulk of decisions have both short-term and medium-term effects and it is neither practical nor useful to classify them as short or medium term.

The only sense in which it is useful to talk of 'medium-term economic policy' is as a shorthand for those aspects of current economic policy in which medium-term outcomes are taken into account. It cannot be emphasized too strongly that medium-term policy is not about decisions taken in the medium term; the medium term, like tomorrow, never comes. The point is that there is only one economic policy; we can ask how much it does or should take account of the medium term but we cannot extract part of it and examine it as medium-term policy.

[1] I am grateful to several members of H.M. Treasury and particularly to Sir Bryan Hopkin and Mr. Andrew Britton for helpful comments on earlier drafts. However the views expressed in this paper should be regarded as my personal ones.

133

Although I believe that it is misleading to imagine that there is a separate branch of economic policy which can be called medium-term policy, there is still the important question of what part consideration of the medium term should play in current economic policy. One way of establishing the need to consider medium-term outcomes is by describing a world in which they were ignored. In such a situation economic decisions would be taken as if the world were coming to an end after two years. (If it were generally believed that the world would end after two years, individuals too would behave rather differently, but that need not concern us.) Presumably the main objective of economic policy in such cases would be to ensure that precisely no resources were left after two years while trying to avoid their exhaustion before the two years were up. The effects of such a policy (assuming of course that the world did not end after two years) would represent an extreme form of what is described as 'sacrificing medium-term goals to short-term ends'. In the extreme case there would be disastrous loss of potential output in year three as a result of depletion of capital and natural resources during years one and two.

I have introduced the expression 'sacrificing medium-term goals to short-term ends' and it seems worthwhile considering in some detail what it means, since it is presumably an important justification for medium-term models that they help to prevent it happening. In our formal definition of economic policy we can distinguish between the objective function and the technical constraints subject to which it is maximized. (Here again there are difficulties in practice. The technical constraints include the policy instruments and their effects, but the distinction between targets and instruments is often blurred. Tax rates, for example, are frequently treated as targets rather than instruments.) 'Neglect of the medium term' could either refer to the choice of the objective function or it could refer to errors caused by neglecting the interdependence of objectives through time.

When 'neglect of the medium term' refers to the choice of the objective function, the critic is in effect saying that the policy-makers have the wrong objective function. They are too myopic, or have too high a discount rate, or pay too much attention to winning the next election, or whatever. While such criticisms may be perfectly valid it is not clear that the development of medium-term economic models will improve matters. Indeed an extreme definition of the boundaries of economics would imply that economists, as such, have no particular contribution to make on the subject.

It is extremely difficult to judge whether apparent neglect of the medium term is the result of policy-makers' objectives rather than a failure to understand the technical constraints of the economy. For example few would deny that the attempt to maintain the exchange rate of the pound up to 1967 was costly in terms of output foregone but we do not know to what extent policy-makers took these costs into account. There is the further complication of unavoidable uncertainty about the future, so that a reasonable decision *ex ante* may turn out to have been an error *ex post*.

It is in the area of improving our knowledge of interdependence through time that we must hope for the greatest benefits from medium-term models. We require knowledge of the medium-term implications of current actions or (which is the same thing) of the required policies to achieve medium-term objectives. This amounts to the platitude that we need to know the structure of the economy. In what particular ways do we want medium-term models to help us? The conventional medium-term objectives are those in which, for technical or political reasons, only very small changes can be achieved in the short run. The medium-term objective par excellence is the rate of growth of productive potential. In the short run it is taken as datum, in the long run it may be possible to influence its value. This is a case in which we are woefully ignorant about the relationship between current actions and medium-term outcomes. Is it better to have a sustained rapid growth of demand (to provide a buoyant atmosphere for investment) or a prolonged deflation (to encourage the abandonment of inefficient business practices)? Is it better to have a high share of wages (to encourage labour-saving investment) or a high share of profits (to encourage business confidence)? How much do we gain from more universities? How much do we lose by not having co-ordinated investment plans? The list of questions could be extended. Probably one could only hope to agree on the near truism that more investment *of the right kind* would be a good thing.

While the need for answers to such questions is well recognized, there is another possible use for medium term models which receives less attention. We normally think of the stabilization of the levels of unemployment, of the balance of payments and of the value of the domestic currency as short-term objectives. But how do we choose the target values of these economic variables, and how rapidly do we try to stabilize them? It seems that the basis of the choice must lie in understanding the medium-term behaviour of the economy. This does not mean that we need to forecast the conjuncture of the economy in five years' time (we would have very little success if we tried). The period over which we attempt to control the economy will depend on the short-term dynamic behaviour of the economy, our ability to forecast exogenous variables and the properties of the instruments at our disposal. An understanding of the medium-term behaviour of the economy should help to tell us what the values of the target variables should be in the short term. In practice stabilization policy could be operated over a period of two years or less without implying that unemployment and the balance of payments, for example, should be brought to their medium-term target values within two years. A successful medium-term model should provide the framework within which short-term economic policy is conducted. (I leave open the question of whether the medium-term model should be separate from the short-term model.)

The conclusions I draw from this general section are as follows. It is misleading to think of a separate branch of economic policy called medium-term policy since its most important property is that it is part of current decisions. At best 'medium-term policy' can be used as a shorthand to describe medium-term aspects of current decisions. It is tempting to divide the objectives of economic policy into those which can be ignored in the short term and those which can be ignored in the medium term. The growth of productive potential might be placed in the first category; the level of unemployment in the second. This kind of division can be harmful because the medium-term objectives may be neglected in the heat of the moment and we may forget that the short-term objectives should be determined within the framework of a medium-term policy.

We talk rather glibly of the sacrifice of the medium term to the short term without being very precise about what it means. We could perhaps suggest that the first task for medium term models is to demonstrate that *for a given objective function* better outcomes can be achieved by applying the acquired knowledge of the longer-term behaviour of the economy.

II. The Medium Term in U.K. Economic Policy

The kind of economic policy I shall be discussing is the central task of macro-economic co-ordination and control, in other words the kind of actions and decisions normally associated with the Treasury's role in economic management. In this part I discuss the part played by medium-term considerations in economic policy in the U.K.

In the first part of the paper I described an extreme version of neglect of the medium term. It cannot be suggested that the U.K. economy is run as if the world were going to end after two (or even five) years. Some recent economic decisions have been justified largely by reference to their long-term implications. Entry to E.E.C. is the classic example, but it is also true of the reform of the tax system. Measures to provide incentives or encourage investment are taken at least as much for their medium- and long-term effects as for their effect in the short term.

At the moment, the area in which the medium term is most fully taken into account is in the planning of public expenditure. This also happens to be the area in which the Treasury's medium-term model is most directly involved. Most of the remainder of this paper is concerned with the medium-term planning of public expenditure but I also consider how the scope of medium-term policy (in the sense defined in Part I) could be extended.

One would certainly expect public expenditure to form a major part of medium-term economic policy. It uses, directly and indirectly, almost one half of total domestic resources. Much of its content is concerned with the long-term development of the economy. I should emphasize that I am not concerned here with the planning of individual public expenditure projects; from the overall economic policy point of view we are concerned with the economic effects of the aggregate level of public expenditure.

The question, what should the aggregate level of public expenditure be, falls rather uneasily between the fields of economics and politics. We have found, for example, that the academic experts in public finance admit that it is an interesting and important problem but do not believe that their techniques are relevant to its solution. They are interested in the choice between projects rather than in their total value. But even if we admit that the decision about the level of public expenditure is ultimately a political one, there is still the extremely important task of presenting the economic background for the decision in an effective way.

It is easiest to start with a brief description of the administrative process under which public expenditure decisions are considered. The Public Expenditure Survey system produces estimates of public expenditure *on the basis of existing policies*. The exact definition of existing policies is a matter for discussion, and sometimes for dispute, between the Treasury and the spending departments. While the Survey discussions are in progress, the expenditure programmes are fed as exogenous variables into the medium-term model. There is a joint presentation to

Ministers of the estimates of public expenditure and of medium-term economic assessments which take them into account.

We can assume that the correct decisions have been taken about the allocation of total public expenditure into different programmes; our object is to provide a basis for a decision about its overall level. (It is, of course, for Ministers to decide the allocation of a total among programmes, and to choose—where the situation imposes such choice— between the disadvantages of not fulfilling their policy aims in the spending programmes and the risks of allowing the total to rise above the overall level derived from the wider economic projections.) I am also assuming that the planning of public expenditure is at least *intended* to involve medium-term commitments (though this need not mean that its exact value is determined five years in advance).

The outstanding feature of public expenditure is that it represents a major claim on total resources. The first question is how this claim can be presented and judged against other claims. One way of demonstrating the problem would be by attempting to provide a forecast of the economy as we think it will develop over the next five years, on the assumption that there will be no further policy changes (an extension of the kind of short-term forecast we produce). There are two objections to doing this. The first is that there would be little point in judging the aggregate level of public expenditure against a state of the economy that would not be allowed to occur. Policy changes will be made over the next five years and it would be wholly artificial to assume unchanged policy. The second objection is that it would be extremely difficult to predict the conjuncture of the economy over a period as long as five years given the existence of random shocks and the difficulty of forecasting exogenous variables.

For these reasons, we examine the impact of public expenditure in the medium term on an economy in which medium-term objectives are assumed to be achieved. (I discuss below whether we can usefully determine what policy changes will be necessary to achieve this objective.) It is obviously no simple matter to define this ideal state of the economy even if, in the first place, we are only trying to determine its level of output. To illustrate the difficulties, total output is determined by the target level of unemployment; we need to decide what the target level of unemployment is and what level of output is associated with it. Let us make the heroic assumption that we know what the target level of unemployment should be so that we can concentrate on the technical problem of determining the level of output. First of all there is a conceptual problem. The relationship between unemployment and output is a dynamic one with long lags. Do we take this into account in determining output and unemployment or do we treat 1978, say, as a fictional year in which adjustments are complete (or asymptotically so)? I think the question is very difficult, but let us assume we have solved it. The determination of output for a given level of unemployment depends on some knowledge of the dynamic system, and on a particular knowledge of the growth of productive potential. We are very conscious that this is an area in which we would like to improve our understanding of the medium-term behaviour of the economy. We are trying to take into account the different rates of growth of productivity between sectors (particularly between the public and other sectors), but we have not yet been able to incorporate investment successfully into our determination of productive potential.

In assessing the economic impact of public expenditure programmes for the medium term we expect usually to pay most attention to the final year of the survey, five years ahead (the impact of the programmes in the conjunctural situation of the short term is a different subject). For given targets for unemployment and the balance of payments, the model can determine the level of output and the required allocation of resources to the balance of trade. Given the uncertainties about productive potential and world trade, for example, we produce several 'variant' cases. (The problem of whether the final year of the assessment period is an actual or an 'imaginary' year tends to be even more acute in the case of the balance of trade.) We thus have total output and the claims on resources by public expenditure and the balance of trade. In the case of private investment, the relevant concept is the required level of private investment to sustain the target level of growth of output. In principle output should be a function of investment as well as vice-versa (this is also true, of course, of public investment) but meanwhile we try to produce an investment forecast which can reasonably be interpreted as an investment requirement.

By subtraction the resources available for consumption are determined as a residual. The result is the kind of 'Resources Table' presented in the 1972 Public Expenditure White Paper [Cmnd. 5178]. The relevant way of summing the demands of public expenditure is a matter of political preference. The definition used in the White Paper includes the indirect demands from current grants to persons (pensions, unemployment benefits, etc.) with the result that the residual for 'consumption' is smaller than the Blue Book figure for consumers' expenditure. The Resources Table presents the medium-term implications of public expenditure plans in terms of claims on available resources; it emphasizes the choice between public expenditure and private consumption. We can leave aside the difficult problem of how the choice is made; as economists we can consider our task completed when we have presented the options in a coherent way.

The Resources Table is a rather crude—if robust—way of considering the medium-term implications for resource allocation of public expenditure plans. Among the other implications we might be expected to consider are the effects on taxation, the effects on the rate of inflation and the effects on the balance of payments. To take taxation first, an initial point to make is that the Resources Table in itself cannot provide even a rough and ready guide to what changes (if any) in taxation would be necessary in order to keep demand in balance with the projected supply of resources; it shows only the quantity of resources available for privately-financed expenditure and not what demand for such resources emanating from consumers may turn out to be.

There are two major difficulties in considering tax implications of public expenditure plans. The first is that the taxation requirement in the medium term, for a given level of public expenditure, will depend on the conjunctural situation at that time; we do not expect to be able to forecast the conjuncture several years ahead. We might be able to get round this difficulty by limiting our ambitions to forecasting the underlying required tax position, that is by assuming not only that medium-term objectives are achieved but also that endogenous demands, such as consumption, reflect their long-run behaviour. But even this simplification would not allow us to estimate required tax *rates*. To do this we need to overcome the second major difficulty, which is that forecasts of tax revenues are very sensitive to assumptions about the rate of inflation. There is no simple solution to the problem of forecasting tax revenues on the basis of fixed tax rates. As an analytical device we can consider taxes in a broader sense, for example as a proportion of total personal income; but given the difficulty of forecasting inflation, we cannot forecast the tax take resulting from a given tax rate structure, nor can we translate from an estimate of the tax requirement to an estimate of tax rates.

The range of uncertainty is so wide that the operational value of any medium-term tax projections must be in doubt even if we try to simplify the problems in the ways described above. At the moment there is a great deal of work to be done in developing the techniques and in deciding how the results can usefully be presented to the policy-makers.

Judging the medium-term effects of public expenditure on the rate of inflation and on the balance of payments presents even greater problems. Theoretically we can distinguish several reasons why the level of public expenditure might affect prices. The first is that if the growth of productivity in the public sector is lower than that in the rest of the economy, the G.D.P. deflator will be larger, *for a given level of money wages*, the larger the share of public expenditure in G.D.P. It is difficult to see that this presents a problem in its own right. If there is a differential growth of productivity between the public sector and other sectors, we need to take it into account, but changes in the G.D.P. deflator caused simply by switches between public and private expenditure must be less important, from the policy point of view, than changes in individual price indices.

A second possible link between public expenditure and prices is the effect on prices of the aggregate level of demand. Normally we would not regard this as a medium-term problem since we assume that we shall take the correct steps to remove excess demand. However there are those who argue that, beyond a certain point, attempts to increase the share of public expenditure in G.D.P. are bound to be inflationary (because the increased taxes will always be passed on in the form of higher prices and wages) and that it should be possible to predict when that point will be reached. This is certainly the type of issue that a medium-term model should attempt to explore though we are not at present able to do so.

A third possible link is between the public sector borrowing requirement and the rate of inflation. Apart from the extreme difficulty of forecasting the public sector borrowing requirement five years in advance, we do not at present have any relationships in the model between monetary variables and either real variables or price changes. It is very difficult to say where one might put this in the list of priorities for future development of the model.

The present Treasury medium-term model does not project imports in sufficient detail to estimate the impact of public expenditure on the balance of payments or on the required balance of trade. It is, of course, a matter of debate whether the import content of public expenditure is of interest *per se* or whether we merely want to improve the forecast of total imports. In either case, this is possibly an area in which progress could be made.

I have said that we assume that medium-term objectives are achieved. By this I mainly mean that we assume that stabilization policy will be successful. There remains the question of whether we derive useful results from determining the required changes in policy instruments.

We cannot hope to forecast the conjunctural position five years ahead and it is not obvious that it would be helpful even if we could.

As I said in Part I of this paper it may well be optimal to conduct stabilization policy over a two-year horizon. If this is true, there is no purpose in trying to estimate the required changes in stabilization instruments four or five years ahead. This means that we are not trying to determine a medium-term demand management policy, for example, in the sense in which we have a short-term demand management policy. What we can try to do is to investigate the underlying tendency towards excess demand or excess supply (using a highly artificial definition of 'unchanged taxes') for a given public expenditure programme. At the moment any such attempts must be subject to enormous margins of error and we cannot claim that we can do it successfully.

Are we right to limit the use of a medium-term model to examining the implications of public expenditure? The answer must depend very much on what we are technically capable of doing. I pointed out that the examination of public expenditure is the main area in which the Treasury's medium-term model is used. This implies that where other medium-term implications are considered in current policy, they are considered without using the medium-term model. They are either derived from the short-term model or they are derived from quite separate sources. I believe that this represents a reasonable assessment of the limitations of the present model and it also indicates where we might hope to make further developments. An important area is in the selection of targets for short-term stabilization policy. We do not really know enough about the technical constraints which determine the feasible medium-term objectives of unemployment, inflation and the balance of payments (one area that I have not discussed at all is the possibility of measures to reduce the sustainable level of unemployment). Nor, as I have said, do we know enough about the required instrument changes to raise the rate of growth of productive potential.

Finally, it can be said that the use of what is really an extended version of a short term Keynesian macro-economic model is bound to limit our ability to provide useful guidance on the medium-term implications of current decisions. We are very much limited to the discussion of problems on the demand side and can only talk in very general terms about supply conditions. It may be that the greatest potential gains to economic management for the medium term lie in the investigation of supply conditions, though it must also be admitted that the gains are extremely uncertain.

6: The Role of Disaggregation [1]

V. H. Woodward

I. Summary

The paper is in three main sections. Section II considers factors which give rise to the need for disaggregation. These are divided between disaggregation needed to calculate the effects of different policy instruments and disaggregation needed to study different policy goals. The main policy goals are growth and the distribution of income. A model capable of answering most questions relevant to medium-term policy requires disaggregation of incomes, expenditures and outputs. Section III considers the practical application of medium-term models and factors influencing their level of aggregation. Two separate applications are identified, assessments of future public expenditure and assessments of growth prospects. A weakness of the former type of assessment, as practised so far, has been the failure to take into account the distributional effects of changes in expenditure and the way in which it is financed. Assessments of growth prospects have so far been of limited value, partly because of technical deficiencies. Both types of assessment have, in addition, suffered from political sensitivity to revealing official plans.

Section IV discusses the future of medium-term assessments. The advantages of one centralized model sufficiently disaggregated to help formulate virtually all medium-term policies are discussed. An important part of its operation would be the willingness of the government to reveal, in broad terms, its taxation policy in the medium term and to commit itself to pursuing other policies required to achieve medium-term objectives. The major obstacle seen to the technical development of medium-term assessments is the absence of the necessary data. An essential requirement for the future development of medium-term assessments is a disaggregated set of national accounts.

[1] This paper arises out of research carried out jointly with members of the Project, which is under the general direction of Professor Richard Stone. The author, however, is solely responsible for the views put forward.

143

II. Disaggregation and Medium-Term Assessments

The role of disaggregation depends basically on the objectives of medium-term assessments. The government accepts the responsibility of trying to achieve certain goals through its policies. At the risk of oversimplification, most government policies can ultimately be said to be concerned with the maximization of the rate of growth consistent with a politically acceptable distribution of income. Policy goals as conventionally understood often include price stability, control of inflation, a satisfactory balance of payments position, etc. But all these

Table 1. Public Sector Expenditure and Financing
(Per cent of G.N.P. at current factor cost)

	1950	1960	1970
Expenditure			
Current expenditure on goods and services	21.6	18·6	20·9
Capital formation	5·1	7·1	9·5
Capital transfers	0·9	0·4	1·7
Grants and subsidies	13·1	9·4	12·4
Interest and dividends	5·3	5·2	4·9
Total expenditure	46·0	40·7	49·4
Financing			
Direct taxation	19·4	15·9	23·4
Indirect taxation	17·7	14·8	19·5
Gross trading income	2·9	3·1	3·5
Rent, interest and dividends	2·1	2·6	3·5
Capital taxes and transfers	2·4	1·1	1·6
Net borrowing	1·6	3·1	−2·0

Source: National Income and Expenditure

factors are of concern essentially because of their effects on the growth or distribution of income. The growth of income is defined in this paper, for convenience, as the growth of G.D.P. although it is recognized that this yardstick has its limitations. Similarly, the distribution of G.D.P has limitations as a measure of the welfare of particular income groups. Study of the distribution of income discussed in this paper is not necessarily concerned with the re-distribution of income from rich to poor; the main concern is with the distribution of income among households with different characteristics.

Government tax and expenditure policies exert a powerful influence on both the growth and distribution of income. Table 1 shows public expenditure as a per cent of G.N.P. in 1950, 1960 and 1970.

Expenditure was exceptionally high in 1950 because of defence spending; in 1960 it amounted to over 40 per cent of G.N.P., rising to nearly 50 per cent in 1970. Taking a narrower definition, expenditure on goods and services was over 25 per cent of G.N.P. in 1960, rising to over 30 per cent in 1970. The main sources of finance for this expenditure were, of course, direct and indirect taxation.

The evolution of expenditures over time and the way in which they are financed are bound to have a big impact both on the growth and distribution of original income generated by the private sector, even if tax and expenditure policies remain unchanged. The income tax system has this effect first because there are different rates of tax for different slices of income and secondly because allowances are fixed in nominal terms so that both real growth in the economy and inflation result in a higher incidence of income tax. This is compensated to the extent that indirect taxes are specific and so the tax yield, which is related to the physical quantity consumed, declines in relation to other taxes. The net effect on revenue thus depends on the ratio of direct and indirect taxes to income, the ratio of *ad valorem* to specific indirect taxes, changes in the pattern of consumer spending and the rate of inflation and real growth.

In planning its future expenditure policies the government has a clear interest in ensuring that policy changes explicitly aimed at influencing the distribution of income are not counteracted by effects of inflation and real growth in the economy. Changes in the distribution of income resulting from a proposed policy change may themselves have an influence on the growth rate, by, for example, reducing incentives or they may, by generating wage claims, alter the rate of inflation. Apart from these distributional effects, government expenditure may have a direct bearing on the growth of original income generated by the private sector because its level itself leads to inflation or because of its demands on certain resources, e.g. skilled manpower. In addition, many measures are designed, by varying the composition of expenditure or incidence of taxation, to influence the growth of the economy. On the expenditure side examples are investment grants or allowances, employment premiums, etc; on the taxation side selective employment tax, protective duties, etc.

Both the scale and complexity of public expenditure and revenues suggest that some disaggregation is needed in medium-term assessments if the effects of government policies on the economy are to be calculated accurately. We would expect the importance of disaggregation to be greater than for short-term forecasts because over a five-year period alternative assumptions have a larger cumulative effect and because structural change will be more important. Thus, alternative assumptions about the rate of inflation will have a large effect on tax yield and a distinction between *ad valorem* and specific taxes is essential. Over this period of time there can be substantial shifts in the composition of expenditure according to movements in relative prices or the rate of growth of real incomes; some disaggregation of expenditure is therefore necessary to capture the effects of the changing incidence of indirect taxation. Some disaggregation of personal income may also be necessary because of the complexity of the income tax system.

So far we have been considering the extent of disaggregation needed to calculate the impact of different policy instruments. The policy goals themselves may suggest that disaggregation is needed in other areas. For example, it is necessary to distinguish the nationalized industries so that their investment programmes can be separately considered, and to examine separately the scale of subsidies required for agriculture. In these instances disaggregation of output projections is needed. But unless the demands on these industries and the level of imports are to be determined in relation to the growth of total G.D.P. it is necessary to disaggregate expenditure into categories which are matched on the output side. Apart from industries where government involvement is obvious there are other instances where disaggregated output projections may be required. A distinction between manufacturing and services, for example, suggests itself because of the emphasis given to policies in recent years aimed at influencing the deployment of labour between these two sectors.

Disaggregation of incomes is necessary if policies which influence the distribution of income are to be pursued in a systematic manner. Disaggregation of incomes by institutional sector is generally adopted in medium-term models, allowing a division of income, for example, between the personal and corporate sectors. Of most importance to the study of income distribution, however, is the subdivision of personal sector income by household type and income group. It is desirable for example, to distinguish between pensioner households and households with different numbers of dependents. Disaggregation of incomes in this way, however, only allows partial examination of income distribution questions. It is necessary to calculate the expenditure of different households so that the effect of changes in commodity prices and indirect taxation on their real income can be examined. The study of income distribution policies, therefore, can only be carried out properly in conjunction with a model which disaggregates expenditure as well as income.

To what extent should a single model of the economy be constructed which is capable of providing a basis for most medium-term policies? Few would disagree that the disaggregation of output and expenditure should be the ideal. The main reasons for not constructing models generally disaggregated in this way are (1) the assessment is concerned with a particular question and it is a waste of resources to disaggregate further than strictly necessary; (2) the available data does not allow disaggregation of output and expenditure projections. In the past, computation problems would have prevented the construction of models disaggregated on a large scale; this is not the case today. For official assessments there would appear to be substantial advantages to be gained from developing a central disaggregated model which could provide the means for coordinating public and private sector plans. This is discussed in section IV.

The development of disaggregated medium-term assessments is influenced by political sensitivity to the revelation of the detailed effects of government policies since the time span of a medium-term assessment covers the life of a government. A secondary factor is the uncertainty attached to any projection, particularly because many factors are beyond government control. Another point is that it is politically difficult to introduce a new type of assessment. But the possibility that political sensitivity may hinder the development of assessments which could prove to be of considerable practical value should not be overemphasized. It should always be possible to find some form of presentation that is politically acceptable.

III. Medium-Term Assessments in Practice

Medium-term assessments are relatively recent in origin, dating from the early 1960s. Two distinct types of assessment can be identified. One is to examine the time path of the economy to see whether its development in response to short-term policies meets medium-term objectives, particularly in the light of planned public expenditures. These assessments tend to be highly aggregated. The other main use of medium-term assessments is to examine the prospects for increasing the rate of growth, either by considering the effect of varying exogenous assumptions such as the growth of world trade or by changes in government policies or the behaviour of the private sector. The emphasis of such assessments is naturally on the response of supplies to changes in demand, so a key feature of them has been the disaggregation of industrial output.

Although in principle both types of assessment distinguished above rely on a projection of trends in the economy based on policies required to achieve the same basic objectives, they have in practice been carried out separately. There are two reasons for this. First, in constructing a model primarily concerned with the growth of public expenditure it is natural that no reason should be seen for the disaggregation of expenditure further than the major components shown in the national accounts except in so far as the level of aggregation is known to bias the results. Moreover, decisions about the phasing of expenditure need to be based on an annual model, whereas assessments concerned with stimulating the rate of growth have been based on target year models because of the limitations of disaggregated data. Second, and more fundamental, is that the two types of assessment have been made with a view to influencing the actions of different decision-takers. The Treasury assessments made to help plan public expenditure have been for the government's benefit and little information is published about them. On the other hand, official assessments which examine growth prospects have been made primarily to influence behaviour by the private sector.

Growth prospects
The motive for the introduction of medium-term assessments of growth prospects was dissatisfaction with Britain's slow growth rate relative to other industrialized countries. The Department of Economic Affairs was set up in 1964 to take over responsibility for economic growth. The National Plan [1] was published only a year later. Although earlier exercises had been carried out by the National Economic Development Office (N.E.D.O.[2]), both the political commitment and resources devoted to the Plan were much greater. The level of G.D.P. was to be increased by 25 per cent over the period 1964–70. The advantage of setting a target rate of growth was that it removed uncertainty. The absence of such a target, it can be argued, leads to different assumptions being made by entrepreneurs, with the possibility that bottlenecks or excess capacity result if firms proved to be optimistic or pessimistic in the light of events. Moreover, if the target rate of growth was set higher than had been achieved in the past, *but was feasible*, it was hoped that the act of planning future investment, together with emphasis on attaining a target, would act as incentives to improve efficiency and so raise the overall growth rate.

The Plan described itself as 'a commitment to action by the Government'. As an expression of the government's intention to achieve the target, planned public sector expenditures were adjusted upwards to levels consistent with faster growth. Government policies in other areas, however, were not adjusted. If the government had really been committed to achieving the target, incentives for private sector investment might have been made available on much more favourable terms. The main area where no commitment was made, however, was direct tax rates. This reflects the official view that a distinction can be made between taxation policy which is used to adjust the level of demand in the short term and public expenditure policy which is used to influence the longer-term development of the economy. In the area of tax rates the government did not give the Plan its full backing and, faced with the choice of devaluation or deflation less than a year after its publication, chose to sacrifice growth for a fixed exchange rate. The policy of maintaining a fixed exchange rate may have led to greater fluctuations in domestic demand than would otherwise have been the case. These fluctuations undoubtedly had an adverse effect on the stable growth of private sector investment. A question which is raised, therefore, is whether indicative planning exercises can hope to be successful without some commitment by the government about the effects of all government policies, including direct tax rates, on the future growth in demand. This is discussed further in the next section. Apart from this reason for its failure, the National Plan had several technical drawbacks. Further discussion of the Plan is restricted to these; its many other aspects have been discussed extensively elsewhere [13]. It is important to separate its technical deficiencies from the political reasons for its failure. If it can be shown that its technical limitations can be reduced the way may be open for the introduction of some form of indicative planning involving disaggregation in the future, though not necessarily along the same lines as the National Plan. While disaggregated assessments have been carried out since the National Plan [3], they have been framed in such a way as to commit neither the government nor the private sector to any form of action. While this is primarily for political reasons the technical deficiencies of the Plan are partly responsible. The main purpose of carrying out an economic assessment, however, is to provide the basis for a course of action and so disaggregated assessments made since the National Plan must be regarded as of limited value. The reason for continuing assessments in this form seems to be that the government saw the value of maintaining the tripartite system of consultation which was built up and culminated in the publication of the National Plan. The N.E.D.O. industry committees enabled a wide variety of micro-economic problems to be discussed.

The framework of the Plan was based on the projection of an input-output table for 1960 (itself an updated version of the only published official table for 1954) to the base date of the plan, 1964. Given the growth and composition of demands to 1970, industry outputs and investment levels could be calculated. An essential part of such an exercise, even if the data are up to date, is to check the feasibility of the output projections because the figures which emerge for individual industries are often crucially dependent on the projection of the input-output coefficient matrix which reflects changes in technology. In addition, to ascertain the growth of capacity needed to meet planned outputs, the size of existing capacity and its utilization had to be ascertained. Published official statistics are wholly inadequate in this respect. Consultation with industry was therefore an essential part of the preparation of the National Plan both to determine changes in input-output coefficients and the growth of investment needed to meet planned outputs. In practice the consultation procedure was used to determine output levels as well. One reason was because of the inadequacy of the data on which the projections were based. Not only was it highly suspect because it was out of date but also the disaggregation was not fine enough for the figures emerging for individual industries to mean anything to most representatives of industry. The result was that when consultation got under way the initial output projections were revised substantially. As all this was carried out in less than a year there was no time to use the consultation procedure to revise the output projections of one industry so that they were compatible with the views of another. Instead, the central team had to make arbitrary adjustments to ensure overall consistency. The result was a set of projections in which it is unlikely that either the central team or industry placed much confidence.

The further development of the model of the economy on which the National Plan was based was described by B. C. Brown [4] in 1968. It was now entirely computerized but still remained the simplest kind of input-output model. The model was given assumptions about the growth of total G.D.P. by main category of expenditure, total imports and the level of total employment. These were presumably derived from the aggregated model which traced out the time path to the target year, mentioned in connection with public expenditure assessments in the next section. Also given was the input-output coefficient matrix, industry productivity levels and the commodity composition of demand. The model yielded projections of industry output and employment for thirty industrial sectors. Some of the projections were constrained to independent estimates made by other Departments, notably those for agriculture and energy industries. The projections of output and employment then had to be scaled to agree with the aggregated model. The model worked everything out at constant prices only. With the abolition of D.E.A. in 1968 the staff were divided between the Treasury which took over the annual medium-term model and the newly created Ministry of Technology, which took over the input-output model. The decision to separate official medium-term work in this way was understandable. One of the major criticisms of the National Plan was that it was too aggregated. The input-output table for 1963 had at last become available, distinguishing 70 sectors, and it was decided to base future work on this. By moving the input-output model to the Ministry of Technology advantage could be taken of contacts with industry and statisticians dealing with industrial statistics. On the other hand, the opportunity of developing the conceptual framework of the disaggregated model was lost. This would have allowed it to incorporate more complex relationships so it could be more than a mere adjunct to an aggregated annual medium-term model, which gives rise to the serious problem of reconciling inconsistencies. Information about the official input-output model was next given by A. A. McLean [5] in 1971 when the model had moved to the Treasury. Most of the time since its progress was previously reported appears to have been spent on developing the data needed to operate the same basic model at the 70 sector level. The only conceptual advance the model had made was to free the constraint on the growth of total imports, although it was not mentioned whether the resulting estimate of the aggregate level of imports was used to revise the initial projection of imports, emanating from the annual aggregated model, and so influence all the projections made by the latter. The estimate of imports in the input-output model relied on the projection of import proportions. It was hoped that these would be replaced by import functions, explaining imports at a disaggregated level by demand and relative prices, but this would not be possible until a price circuit was introduced into the model. The present official input-output model does not display very substantial conceptual advance over that used to prepare the National Plan. The main emphasis has been on further disaggregation of the same basic model.

A much more ambitious approach to disaggregated medium-term projections is embodied in the Cambridge Growth Project (Stone) model of the economy. This is the only other model in Britain which is disaggregated and which is concerned with growth prospects for the whole economy. The official input-output model was originally based on one of the first versions of the Stone model. But the development of the respective models diverged before the time of the National Plan. This was because instead of developing an annual aggregated model to trace out the time path and using input-output techniques to disaggregate the target year projections, Stone resources were devoted to introducing more complex relationships into the disaggregated model. In the absence of a disaggregated set of national accounts this involved a willingness to develop disaggregated data, which occupied a considerable amount of the Project's time. The main results of this separate development are (1) the Stone model does not raise problems of reconciling aggregated and disaggregated projections and (2) the Stone model allows interaction between demands and supplies to influence projections for individual industries to a much greater extent than is the case with the official model. The stages in the development of the Stone model were as follows. The first major development beyond methods used to construct the National Plan was the introduction of a price circuit which allowed imports and exports to vary with the level of demand and relative prices. This model was used to explore the effects of devaluation in a projection of the economy to 1972 [6]. One of the major limitations of the model at this stage was that it could only be used to examine the effects of a selected growth rate on the structure of the economy on the assumption that productivity trends at a disaggregated level continued in the future as they had done in the past. Recent developments have removed these limitations. The model now links estimates of output and expenditure with the generation and distribution of income. The main effect of this is to make consumers' expenditure endogenous. The growth rate is conditional on government policies and other variables taken as exogenous such as part of investment, the rate of inflation and the growth of world trade. Productivity growth is estimated by using past relationships between the rate of growth of output, investment and labour demand at an industry level. This model can be used to examine a wide variety of problems of interest in the medium-term, e.g. the effects of changes in specific government tax or expenditure policies on the growth rate. As it is completely computerized, simulation of the effects of alternative policies or values for exogenous variables is relatively easy. The model can be used to carry out disaggregated projections of the economy on a specific set of assumptions about future values for exogenous variables but with government policies unchanged. The extent to which objectives are met in the future, e.g. for employment or the balance of payments, dictates the need for policy changes, the size and nature of which have to be made explicit. The effects of the policy changes on the levels of output and employment of individual industries can be examined. This model was used to carry out a medium-term assessment after the 1972 Budget [7].

If some form of indicative planning exercise were based on a model of the economy constructed along the lines of the Stone model, the nature of this new exercise would necessarily be very different from the National Plan. The emphasis of the National Plan was on action by the private sector to achieve the targets. In the new exercise it would be necessary to spell out the precise assumptions made about all government policies because the projections for individual industries would be conditional upon them. Emphasis would be on the use of government policies to stimulate the growth rate. The effects of short-term demand management policies on medium-term growth prospects could be traced through to the implications for output and employment at an industry level. Explicit assumptions would be made about size and effects of price changes throughout the economy, the determination of future productivity growth, import demand propensities, the future pattern of consumer spending and savings behaviour of the personal and business sectors. All these assumptions would be based on econometric analysis of past data.

The basic objective of an exercise of this kind would not be primarily to set a target rate of growth. A target necessarily implies something which has not been achieved in the past with the consequent danger of setting sights too high and undermining confidence in the assessment. It also leads to political difficulties if not achieved. The implementation of an exercise of this kind, however, would in its initial stages lead to political difficulties because of the new approach towards revealing government policies over a longer period of time than practised at present, particularly on the taxation side. If established as annual exercises however, these difficulties would diminish. The main objective of such an assessment would be to provide one framework through which both public and private sector plans could be reviewed. This is discussed further in section IV.

Public Expenditure
Since Plowden [8], official medium-term assessments of all public expenditure in relation to resources have been made but information was only published about them in 1963 [9] and 1966 [10] until the annual

Public Expenditure White Papers appeared from 1969 [11]. The first expenditure White Paper, published in 1963, indicated both the criteria the government believed appropriate in determining the *total* level of public expenditure and the information it was prepared to reveal about its medium-term assessment. The growth of public expenditure should be related to the growth of the economy as a whole. Attention focuses on the ratio of public expenditure to G.N.P. If, in a forward assessment of the economy, this ratio is expected to rise the share of resources available to the private sector has to fall. This will generally imply that an increase in taxation is needed. The White Paper presented estimates of public expenditure in total and by programme for two years 1963/4 and 1967/8 but the only information given about the growth of resources was that 'the Government are aiming at a rate of growth of G.N.P., at constant prices, of 4 per cent a year'. As expenditure was planned to grow by 4·1 per cent a year the White Paper concluded 'it is unlikely that a development of public expenditure on the scale implied will leave much scope for a reduction in the burden of taxation'. The information presented in this White Paper did not allow rational discussion of the growth of expenditure in relation to resources. This was partly because expenditure was not divided between economic categories so the different economic impact of transfers, for example, could not be separated from expenditure on goods and services. As figures for only the current year and terminal year were presented it was not possible to consider the effect of varying the time path of expenditure.

These criticisms were largely overcome by a Green Paper *Public Expenditure—A new presentation* [12] which presaged publication of expenditure figures in more detail. This pointed out that after the Plowden Report extensive development of public expenditure statistics had been undertaken and, because confidence could now be placed in the system of forward planning, publication of more detailed figures was now possible. Expenditure plans were to be published for the next five years and revised and rolled forward one year in successive White Papers. Projections of all receipts were to be shown. The reason given for this, however, was only to allow the reader to adopt whatever definition of expenditure he preferred. Major presentational improvements were to be made. Expenditure was to be shown by economic category and a new concept 'the relative price effect' was to be introduced in order to allow for different price movements of goods and services purchased by the public sector relative to those purchased by the private sector, without revealing the government's assumptions about future price changes. The first of these annual White Papers appeared in 1969. This did not reveal details of the assessment on which the planned expenditures were based. It contained projections of receipts for only two years ahead, based on constant tax rates. Even this limited information on receipts was not present in the 1970 White Paper.

Since 1970 the content of the White Papers has been substantially the same but in 1972, in response to pressure from the Select Committee on Expenditure, a limited amount of information about the medium-term assessment on which the plans were based was published. The approach used was to postulate a growth of Gross Domestic Product and to deduct the claims of private investment needed to achieve the growth rate and the claims made by the balance of trade and public expenditure. The residual equals the resources available for 'privately financed consumption'. The conclusion was that under two alternative assumptions about the growth rate the growth of privately financed consumption 'should be acceptable by past standards'. This information is so limited that it only represents an advance over past information published, giving the ratio of public expenditure to G.N.P. in that, now some details about the official medium-term assessment have appeared, it is likely that more will be revealed in the future. What is required is an assessment of the future growth of the economy, based on existing policies, and policy changes needed to meet desired objectives. In such an assessment public expenditure appears as a demand on resources and so directly influences the growth rate, and its ratio to G.D.P. is one of the desired objectives.

The technical basis of these assessments is of interest because the policy goal, the ratio of public expenditure to G.D.P., suggests the model of the economy on which they are founded can be relatively simple. Table 2 shows some of the main characteristics of three medium-term models that could be used to assess future public expenditure, with particular emphasis on the level of aggregation. Details of the Treasury model refer to the one described elsewhere in this volume. A comprehensive comparison of the structure of these three models is beyond the scope of this paper. A main point of difference between them, however, is their level of aggregation. Comment will be restricted to this topic although they certainly differ in many other respects. The Par model is the least disaggregated, prices and incomes not being introduced explicitly. The level of aggregation in the Treasury model mainly differs from this in that it does incorporate prices and incomes. The Stone model is radically different from both of these because output, expenditure and incomes are disaggregated to a much greater extent

Table 2. Medium-term models compared[1]

	Model		
	Par[2]	Treasury[3]	Stone[4]
Main characteristics			
Annual or target			
Treatment of	Annual	Annual	Target
productivity	Exogenous	Exogenous	Endogenous
Treatment of prices	Not introduced explicitly	Factor cost prices calculated for final demand categories —import prices and proportions and domestic average earnings taken as exogenous	Commodity prices determined by share of imports and cost composition of domestic commodity output-import prices and domestic average earnings taken as exogenous.
Monetary sector	None	None	None
Level of aggregation			
Industrial output	1	1	35 industries × 45 commodities
Expenditure:—			
Consumers	1 (residual)	1	Durable and non-durable expenditure separate 42 categories × 45 commodities
Government	1	2	4 categories × 45 commodities
Investment[5]	1	11	35 industries × 8 assets × 45 commodities
Exports	1	2	45 commodities
Imports	5	2	86 commodities
Incomes	Not introduced explicitly	Six institutional sectors	Eight institutional sectors. Household income disaggregated into 8 types of income and 25 income groups

[1] In each case details are given for the latest reported version.
[2] *Prospects for Economic Management 1972–76.* Mimeographed. Department of Applied Economics, Cambridge, January 1973.
[3] A. A. McLean, 'Medium Term Projections in the Treasury,' pp. 9 *et seq.* above.
[4] T. S. Barker, 'An Input-Output Model of the British Economy, pp. 25 *et seq.* above.
[5] Excluding stockbuilding.

and also because it is solved only for a target year. All of the models can be used to do a projection of trends in the economy on the basis of an existing set of policies and changes in policies needed to meet objectives for the balance of payments and employment. The question is how does the level of aggregation influence the results? It would clearly be difficult, if not impossible, to produce an empirical answer to this question based on a comparison of results because of differences between the three models in their conceptual framework and data base. But something can be learned by considering how the level of aggregation in the different models may affect estimates of the growth of G.D.P. and its main components. This does not lead to the presumption that estimates from any of the three models are better than one another. The purpose is to indicate areas where further research is needed.

The main difference between the Par model and the Treasury model, in respect of the level of aggregation, arises because the former has no explicit assumptions about prices and incomes. To the extent that relative price changes are judged to be important, adjustments are, of course, made to the composition of expenditure in the former model. For example, the effect on real consumption of changes in import prices relative to home unit costs is allowed for. Adjustments are made to allow for certain changes in the distribution of income, e.g. for the effect of *real* fiscal drag and for changes in the share of retentions by companies. The absence of an explicit price circuit and estimation of incomes does raise the possibility of error by omission. For example, the Par model appears to make no allowance for the effects of fiscal drag due to inflation alone. In simulations of the effect of wage inflation proceeding at an annual rate of 5 per cent faster than our competitors', 1972–75 (the type of simulation exercise relevant to policy) the Stone model suggested the *initial* effect of this inflation on consumers expenditure over the period due to fiscal drag would amount to about £300m. at 1963 prices. It is fair to say, however, that in the Stone model, this was swamped by the magnitude of the effects arising from a deterioration in the balance of trade. This point, however, does suggest the possibility of omitting significant relationships if prices and incomes are not treated explicitly. Moreover, the omission of incomes in the Par model limits its use to a consideration of government expenditure on goods and services, rather than all public expenditure, and prevents a consideration of the magnitude of particular tax changes needed to alter the level of consumption if the model results suggest this is necessary.

Differences between the two aggregated models in the detail of investment are not important—the extra number of categories distinguished in the Treasury model arises because of the disaggregation of public investment which is exogenous to the model. The only substantial difference is in the treatment of imports. The reason for disaggregation in the Treasury model is to distinguish between imports of goods and imports of services. Imports of goods are related to total final expenditure and a relative price term, the coefficient of which is imposed on the basis of analysis carried out with the official input-output model. The Par model disaggregates total imports into food, etc., fuels, industrial materials, manufactures and services, and projects trends in each in relation to trends in G.D.P. Unlike the official model, import volumes are assumed to be unresponsive to domestic prices relative to prices of competing imports.

The greater disaggregation in the Stone model is likely to lead to differences in results, compared with the other two models, for several reasons. The basic difference is that demands and supplies are reconciled at a disaggregated level. This enables the model to treat productivity growth as endogenous because production functions operate at an industry level. Aggregate employment resulting from Stone projections is likely to differ from the other two models. The extent of the differences should, in theory, depend on the magnitude of structural change and the difference between overall productivity growth rates. Differences in employment projections yielded by the aggregated models compared with the Stone model may be more marked because of the different treatment of productivity growth when the aim is to simulate the effects of alternative assumptions. This is because of the interaction between demands and supplies at a disaggregated level and because the level of productivity varies with the level of output in the Stone model. In the Stone model, changes in productivity at an industry level result in changes in the price of output which will lead to changes in the volume of imports and exports as both are sensitive to relative prices.

The estimation of taxes in the Treasury model and the Stone model is substantially different. In the Treasury model indirect taxes are projected in some detail but they can only be related to past trends and aggregate variables such as consumers' expenditure. In the Stone model indirect taxes are estimated separately on each commodity or category distinguished in the model and this allows the effects of indirect tax changes on prices to be followed through in detail. The personal income tax system is incorporated in much more detail in the Stone model than in the Treasury model. This may be particularly important in a comparison of the two models when simulations involving substantially different rates of inflation are carried out, because of the effects of 'fiscal drag'.

In the Stone model consumers' expenditure in aggregate is estimated separately for expenditure on durable and non-durable goods. This distinction is particularly important when simulations of the model involving substantially different growth rates are being carried out.

Expenditure on these two broad groups is further broken down, into forty-one categories in all, according to income and price elasticities measured from past data. The division of consumer demands between imports and domestic output is primarily determined by demand and price elasticities. The effect of these elasticities is a major source of difference between the Stone model and the two aggregated models.

The main issue centres around the estimation of imports because export levels are more dependent on exogenous assumptions. The Stone model is likely to lead to a different estimate of import volumes from the other two models because demand elasticities operate at a disaggregated level. Moreover in [14] evidence is given that higher average import demand elasticities result from the sum of disaggregated functions compared with an aggregated import function. There is not necessarily a difference in estimates of imports in the three models through differences in demand propensities because this depends on the specification of the function in the aggregate models and the time period over which relationships were estimated. The response of import volumes to relative prices assumed in the three models is likely to be a greater source of discrepancy. It is well known that import price elasticities estimated from aggregated import functions are small. A crucial area is the estimation of imports of manufactures. Stone estimates, based on disaggregated data for imports of manufactures up to 1966 [15] record an overall price elasticity of -1.6. The elasticity for manufactures in aggregate was -0.8. The Par model, working with more recent data for imports of manufactures in aggregate, incorporates an elasticity of zero. These differences in import price elasticities will lead to substantial differences in the response of the respective models to variations in the exchange rate. These differences in elasticities cannot be reconciled at present because of lack of disaggregated data on imports after 1966.

The preceding discussion suggests that if these three models are used to assess the ratio of planned public expenditure to G.D.P., on the basis of existing policies or changes in policies needed to meet employment and balance of trade objectives, they are likely to yield different results because of their respective levels of aggregation. A question which should be pursued, however, is whether consideration of this ratio is the appropriate criterion for determining the future level of public expenditure. In all three models the means of financing expenditure is assumed to affect personal sector behaviour only in so far as it influences aggregate consumption through the direct relationship between consumers' expenditure and disposable income. There are two reasons for introducing a different criterion for the determination of public expenditure levels.

Excluding defence and administration, one motive for carrying out public expenditure is because it is thought desirable to change the distribution of income (in its broadest sense) in the short term or longer term. State-run health and particularly education schemes are examples of longer term influences on the distribution of income. An important reason for their inception was the mal-distribution of income, which prevented equality of opportunity. It is even possible to look at the short term effect of these policies by imputing a benefit to households in different income groups according to their use of these services, and, by comparing their contribution to them through taxation, to assess the distributional effects. If the distributional effects are zero, which may be the case as incomes grow in the future, one of the main reasons for public provision of these services will cease to exist. Of course other reasons, such as avoiding duplication, will remain but against these must be set probable restriction of choice, as well as other factors. If the criterion for determining total public expenditure continues to be its ratio to G.D.P., rational consideration of the desirability of public rather than private sector provision of services cannot be made. The present criterion over-emphasizes the use of medium-term assessments for the *control* of the level of public expenditure *relative* to private and inhibits a consideration of the optimum *absolute level* of public expenditure.

Some public expenditures are made explicitly with a view to altering the distribution of income, e.g. most transfers and investment in housing. The latter account for around 17 per cent of G.N.P. at factor cost. The distribution of income is also influenced by the direct and indirect tax systems, local authority rates and policies for charging for goods and services provided both by public authorities and the nationalized industries. The rational allocation of expenditure should be based on an examination of the effects of all these policies on income distribution. Otherwise it is more difficult to formulate long-term policies to change income distribution in the way desired. A decision to increase family allowances may be nullified by the direct or indirect tax systems, changes in the method of financing nationalized industries investment, an increase in charges for school meals, changes in local authority rates, etc. It is not enough to analyse the effect of policy changes designed to influence income distribution at the point of time such changes are made. For example, if personal direct tax rates or allowances are changed in a budget, the Financial Statement contains tables showing the effect on take-home pay of the changes. With substantial changes in taxation or the exchange rate the underlying position of the economy can be transformed and perhaps only a year later the incidence of taxation is higher than it was before due to the progressive system. The impact of government policies on the distribution of income is far greater than trends in original income. The medium-term is the appropriate time horizon for considering how changes in income distribution can be brought about. Policies for improving the lot of low-paid workers, pensioners, etc. can be viewed alongside the trend in the growth of income and the overall effects of tax and expenditure policies. The need to bring income distribution questions explicitly into medium-term assessments is amply evidenced by the present crisis in industrial relations. There may be a solution in demonstrating that government policies are equitable between different income groups or social classes.

Second, if the criterion for determining the future level of public expenditure is simply its projected ratio to G.N.P., the distributional effects on the rate of growth brought about by the expenditure policies and the implicit structure of taxation may not properly be taken into account. Public expenditure plans themselves may be a prime cause of inflation. Table 1, for instance, showed that public expenditure as a share of G.N.P. rose by 10 per cent during the 1960s, from 40 per cent of G.N.P. in 1960 to 50 per cent in 1970. Some evidence for this view is given in *Do Trade Unions Cause Inflation?* [16] where the responsibility for the recent rapid inflation was attributed to the Government due to increases in the incidence of direct taxation rather than to wage bargaining by the trade unions. Further evidence for the possible importance of public expenditure plans as a crucial factor in influencing the rate of wage inflation is given by a recent O.E.C.D. study, *Expenditure Trends in O.E.C.D. Countries, 1965–80* [17]. The report notes that while private consumption has retained its share of G.N.P. at constant prices in O.E.C.D. countries since 1955, its share of G.N.P. at current prices declined in all countries. If the share of 'pure' private consumption, i.e. consumption not paid for out of transfers received from the public sector, is considered the decline was even more marked. This shift away from 'privately financed' consumers' expenditure was only made possible by a sharp increase in taxes paid by households. In the words of the report: 'Inflation . . . is also the mechanism by which efforts to alter the distribution of income or expenditure which are not accepted by those concerned are partially or fully frustrated . . . Thus if higher taxes designed to finance new or improved public programmes provoke successful claims for higher money incomes, the consequent rise in costs will tend to reduce, in real terms, the amount of new services which can be financed out of the increased public revenue.' As inflation is the single most important economic problem facing the country today this further points to the necessity for more detailed consideration of both the criteria for determining total expenditure, its incidence and the way in which it is to be financed. This problem can only be properly studied with a model which disaggregates original income by industry of origin. It may be possible to establish relationships between increases in money earnings and factors specific to individual industries, such as productivity growth or trade union bargaining power.

None of the present models used in assessments of public expenditure is capable in its present form of examining the full distributional effects of policies in the medium term. It would be necessary to allocate public expenditure and receipts to households in different income groups and with different characteristics. Such an analysis is carried out *ex post* and published annually in *Economic Trends* [18].

IV. The Future of Medium-Term Assessments

Assuming that necessary data became available, how might medium-term assessments be expected to develop?

Two perennial problems facing the economy which medium-term assessments may help to solve are the growth of private sector investment and wage inflation. A major factor influencing the growth of investment appears to be future expectations about the growth of demand. Public sector policies have a major impact not only on the future level of demand but also on its composition. Projections of the level of output and components of demand at an industry level, on assumptions about specific government policies in force, might be of considerable value for planning an orderly growth of private investment. These projections would be produced by a model of the economy based on analysis of economic relationships in the past and would be conditional on the stability of these relationships, government policies in force and assumptions about external factors, such as the growth of world trade. They would need to be revised annually because any of these conditions might be falsified by events. The projections would in no way be targets but would represent the position of the economy 3–5 years ahead, abstracting from cyclical change. Emphasis would be given to the government implementing policies to achieve the outcome, although the projections would incorporate the specialist knowledge of central economic policy makers, representatives of government departments and state and private industries. Apart from projections of output and demand such a model would be used for many other purposes, e.g. to study industry productivity levels with a view to implementing policies to encourage faster productivity growth.

The rate of wage inflation is influenced by many factors but public sector tax and expenditure policies are likely to be among the most important. Projections showing that the impact of these policies on the distribution of income was equitable might improve industrial relations. These projections could emanate from the same model used to project industry outputs and be consistent with the latter. This would facilitate study of the wider problems of income distribution and the formulation of long-term income policies.

Two questions arise about these proposed projections: their relationship to short-term forecasts and their implications for the revelation of government policies. Short-term forecasts would remain an essential part of policy making. Medium-term projections based on existing policies would provide a longer time horizon for stabilization policy. As knowledge advances it may become possible to formulate stabilization policy with a medium-term model which attempts to track the actual path of the economy, on a set of conditional assumptions. Until that time short-term and medium-term assessments will necessarily be carried out separately. The system proposed, however, places much greater emphasis on medium-term objectives in the formulation of economic policies. Information published by the government about the future growth and distribution of income is seen as an important means of attaining these objectives. Projections showing the trend growth of the economy, i.e. abstracting from cyclical change, on the basis of *existing* policies could be published. Several difficulties arise here. There is the conceptual problem of relating the actual position of the economy to the trend position on unchanged policies. A difficulty arises in defining the meaning of unchanged policies. A strict definition would assume that tax allowances and current transfers remain fixed in money terms but this would lead to absurd results because of inflation and real growth in the economy. While a limited amount of information about medium-term projections on unchanged policies (suitably defined) might be released to justify policy changes for short-term demand management, emphasis would be placed on projections under the assumption that necessary policy changes were made to meet medium-term objectives, notably full employment and an adequate balance of payments position. These projections would show industry outputs, the composition of demand and the distribution of income by sector, with the household sector being analysed by income group. It would be necessary to supplement the projections with similar information estimated for the base year on the assumption that full employment was achieved. In addition, the actual position of the economy in the base year would be shown. The greatest difficulty facing the development of such a system would be the relationship between tax policies for demand management and those dictated by the planned growth of public expenditure. Tax changes departing from the medium-term objectives could be justified on the grounds of necessity for short-term demand management policy, which may require an increase in taxation. But when the short-term position improved and a relaxation of fiscal policy became possible the pattern of taxation should logically revert to that specified for medium-term policies, if the level and composition of planned public expenditure remained unchanged. The system proposed would tend to discourage the use of short-term tax changes discriminating against particular areas of demand or supply because the longer-term effects on income distribution would be revealed. This system would involve much less emphasis being given to the budget as a means of pursuing economic and social policies. Indeed, it is doubtful whether the present system, through which decisions to change expenditures and revenues are made at separate times of the year, could be perpetuated. The system proposed might be expected to place emphasis on measures needed to stimulate the future growth rate and discussion of major social questions concerning the distribution of income. Its strength would be to provide a single framework through which virtually all economic and social policies could be analysed.

Consultation with both sides of industry would be an important part of the planning process but it would not be used to determine output and employment at an industry level. It would be confined to technical aspects of the projections and an appraisal of the results of projections at the basic level of aggregation adopted in the central model. Consultation would operate through a system of sub-models, which are both receivers and providers of information. The sub-model, given the same information as the central model, may produce different aggregate estimates of output and employment by virtue of its disaggregation. This will dictate the need to change coefficients in the central model which may well have repercussions for the original final demand estimate. Iterations between the two models continue until they provide the same aggregate results.

The level of aggregation in the central model would distinguish 30–40 industrial sectors. The optimal level of aggregation is dependent on many factors. On the demand side, the incidence of consumers' expenditure on different products may indicate that a certain level of aggregation is desirable. On the supply side, the subsidy system or import propensities may indicate that another level of aggregation is appropriate. In addition, the level of aggregation may be influenced by the extent to which the sum of disaggregated estimates yields different results, which are believed to be more reliable than an aggregate estimate. The further question of data availability arises. There is therefore no easy answer to the optimal level of aggregation. The level of disaggregation chosen will depend on the variable which is being considered. Yet a complete model has to be founded on one basic classification although sub-classifications and sub-models can be accommodated where appropriate.

A practical solution effectively determines the level of aggregation adopted in the central model. If the purpose of the model is to study the effects of government macro-economic policies on growth prospects the complexity of this is such that there is a limit to the effective functioning of a team and this will restrict the amount of disaggregation possible. The model needs to be sufficiently disaggregated to study broad structural change in the economy and yet small enough to enable half a dozen people to understand how it works thoroughly, so that changes in personnel do not disrupt the work programme. On this criterion the number of sectors distinguished should not be more than 30–40. As already suggested, many problems may demand greater disaggregation. A solution is to develop sub-models which can be constructed by teams with specialist knowledge which have a particular interest in further disaggregation.

One of the principal obstacles to the development of disaggregated medium-term assessments along these lines arises from the limitations of official data. A model which seeks to establish relationships between the supplies and demands of particular commodities requires accurate data for the past which are consistent over time. The extent of the inconsistencies in disaggregated data is discussed in [22]. It will clearly be a major task to reconcile them. Official policy appears to be to develop periodic input-output tables distinguishing between ninety sectors. The result of this may be to limit the resources available for ensuring consistency of disaggregated data over time which would be easier if a smaller number of sectors formed the basis for official input-output tables.

The development of such a system would require a good deal of further research on disaggregated model building. A precondition for this and for official use of such a system would be a rationalization of statistical information on a massive scale and a greatly increased use of computers within government. Major advances have been made in both these areas in recent years. The reorganization of public expenditure statistics has been a minor revolution [19]. Adequate computer facilities do exist [20]. But there is a need for the coordination of official statistics so they are all compatible with a common framework. They all need to be available, in the first instance, on a common basis, i.e. for a calendar year and for the United Kingdom, although departmental considerations may indicate an alternative is necessary, e.g. Ministry of Agriculture data are generally available for England and Wales on a crop-year basis. Apart from this there needs to be a common classification and the national accounts provide the logical framework. Hence, statistics of past and projected public expenditure by programme should be exactly compatible with the national accounts classification and price basis. It would be necessary to go further than this under the proposed system, and analyse past and projected public expenditure on goods and services by its industrial composition. An analysis of central government expenditure on this basis was carried out recently [21] but there is no indication it is to be done regularly. Although it was the official intention to carry out a similar analysis of local authority expenditures as far back as 1968 [4] no progress appears to have been made so far. Income distribution statistics are also deficient. Inland Revenue Surveys of Personal Income yield more or less satisfactory data for incomes in middle- and upper-income groups. Information about lower-income groups is limited. The only comprehensive source is the Family Expenditure Survey but this only covers about 7,000 households. It is also the only comprehensive source of information on expenditure by income group which is essential to any study of income distribution. A very substantial increase in the sample size of the Family Expenditure Survey would be necessary if the present system were adopted. It would be necessary to match the Inland Revenue and Family Expenditure data, which are complementary to one another.

The major development on the statistical front, however, would be to move to a disaggregated set of national accounts. This does not simply involve an input-output table which is constrained to be compatible with the present aggregated national income and expenditure statistics. It requires building up these aggregates by reconciling demands and supplies at a disaggregated level. The necessity for this approach is discussed in [22]. A precondition for a disaggregated set of national accounts is an annual Census of Production, which has in fact been carried out since 1970. The level of disaggregation would be determined

Diagram 1. Information Flow to and from a Disaggregated Model for Macro-economic Policy and Control of Expenditure

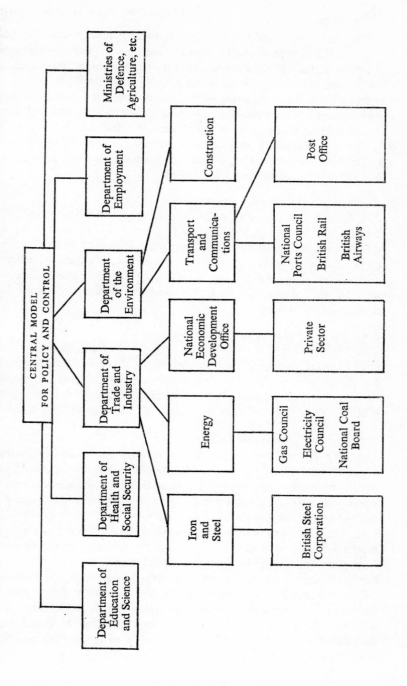

by the requirements of a central model used for macro-economic policy and control of expenditure. It was argued that 30–40 industrial sectors is appropriate. Apart from industrial disaggregation, disaggregation by sector and income group would be necessary.

In order to illustrate some of the merits of a disaggregated information system for medium-term assessments we should consider how it would operate on the basis of the existing structure of government. This is shown in diagram 1. Its purpose is to indicate areas of major interest to different government departments, rather than to give an all-embracing picture. Reading from left to right:

Department of Education and Science
A sub-model of the educational system might be constructed. Work has already been done in this area [23] but it would need to be compatible with the central model. The main purpose for dialogue with the central model, however, would be for the control of expenditure because educational decisions are likely to have relatively little influence on medium-term developments in the economy, other than imposing a demand on resources.

Department of Health and Social Security
This Department has responsibility for the implementation of many policies concerned with income distribution. It is also partly responsible for the *ex post* analysis of income distribution published annually in *Economic Trends*. It would be the logical candidate for taking responsibility for the construction of an income distribution sub-model.

Department of Trade and Industry
The Department has major responsibilities for industrial statistics which in itself would place it in a key position in a disaggregated information system for economic policy. In addition to this, it has the responsibility for regulating the state energy industries and formulating fuel policy. An official sub-model of the fuel economy already exists [24]. Its value must be severely limited by the absence of a central disaggregated model which would distinguish individual fuel and power industries. Such a model, compatible with the central model, would form the basis for planning future investment programmes. Similarly, a sub-model might be developed to assess iron and steel investment programmes. A further major responsibility of the Department is acting as a liaison with the private sector. It would be in a position to develop sub-models at an industry level in cooperation with the National Economic Development Office.

National Economic Development Office
This agency would provide the key link between the private and public sectors. Its central role would be to assess the implications of the published projections of industry output and the distribution of income with both sides of industry. In addition it would act as a forum for consultation on technical aspects related to sub-models, generating part of the interchange of information with the central model.

Department of the Environment
The Department might develop a sub-model for the formulation of transport policy based on transport demands, the industrial component of which can be estimated from disaggregated industry projections. This could be used to formulate investment plans for state-run transport industries. Sub-models might also be constructed for the Post Office and the construction industry.

Department of Employment
The Department would provide technical information to the central model concerning many aspects of employment. It has an interest in developing a sub-model to study employment projections yielded by the central model in order to see if the occupational implications are feasible. Another possible labour bottleneck is the regional distribution of employment. A disaggregated model has obvious relevance for regional policy in Britain since the problem is, to a large extent, a structural one.

Ministries of Defence, Agriculture, etc.
Several other government agencies may have an interest in constructing sub-models. For the Ministry of Defence this would be primarily for the purpose of the control of expenditure. The construction of a sub-model for agriculture, however, would be important for the operation of economic policy because of the magnitude of the subsidy system and the impact of food imports on the balance of payments. The Ministry of Agriculture should find such a sub-model invaluable for the formulation of its detailed policies. Extensive work has already been carried out on such a sub-model [25].

References

1. *The National Plan*, Cmnd. 2764, H.M.S.O., 1965.
2. *The Growth of the Economy to 1966*. National Economic Development Council. H.M.S.O., 1963.
3. *The Task Ahead—An economic assessment to 1972*. Department of Economic Affairs, H.M.S.O., 1969.

4. BROWN, B. C. 'The Use of Input-Output Methods in D.E.A.' In *Input-Output in the United Kingdom*, ed. Dr. W. F. Gossling, Cass, London, 1970.
5. McLEAN, A. A. 'Forecasting by Input-Output'. Paper prepared for the 1971 Norwich Conference on Input-Output and Throughput.
6. BARKER, T. S. and LECOMBER, J. R. C., 'Exploring 1972' No. 9 in *A Programme for Growth*. D.A.E., Cambridge, Chapman and Hall, 1970.
7. BARKER, T. S. and WOODWARD, V. H. 'Inflation, Growth and Economic Policy in the Medium Term.' *National Institute Economic Review*, No. 60, May 1972.
8. CHANCELLOR OF THE EXCHEQUER. *Control of Public Expenditure.* Cmnd. 1432. H.M.S.O., July 1961.
9. *Public Expenditure in 1963/4 and 1967/8.* Cmnd. 2235. H.M.S.O., 1963.
10. Cmnd. 2915, H.M.S.O., 1966.
11. CHANCELLOR OF THE EXCHEQUER. *Public Expenditure 1968/9–1973/4.* Cmnd. 4234. H.M.S.O., Dec. 1969.
12. CHANCELLOR OF THE EXCHEQUER. *Public Expenditure: A New Presentation.* Cmnd. 4017. H.M.S.O., April 1969.
13. *Inquest on planning in Britain.* P.E.P. No. 499, 1966. (See also P.E.P. Nos. 487 and 493.)
14. BARKER, T. S. 'Aggregation Error and Estimates of the U.K. Import Demand Function.' In *The Econometric Study of the United Kingdom*, ed. K. Hilton and D. Heathfield, London, Macmillan, 1970.
15. BARKER, T. S. 'The Determinants of Britain's Visible Imports, 1949–66.' No. 10 in *A Programme for Growth*. D.A.E., Cambridge, Chapman and Hall 1970.
16. JACKSON, D., TURNER, H. A. and WILKINSON, F. *Do Trade Unions Cause Inflation?* D.A.E. Occasional Paper No. 36, C.U.P., 1972.
17. *Expenditure Trends in O.E.C.D. Countries, 1965–80.* Paris, O.E.C.D., 1972.
18. 'The Incidence of Taxes and Social Service Benefits in 1971,' *Economic Trends*, February 1972.
19. REES, C. M. 'Public Expenditure Statistics.' *Statistical News*, February 1969.
20. KUNZLE, G. 'Treasury Computer Facilities for Economic Forecasting.' *Statistical News*, November 1970.
21. 'Commodity Analysis of Central Government Current Expenditure on Goods and Services.' *Economic Trends*, August 1971.
22. WOODWARD, V. H. 'The reliability of the U.K. National Accounts and their use in medium-term assessments of the economy.' Paper prepared for 13th General Conference of the International Association for Research in Income and Wealth, Balatonfüred, Hungary, 1973.
23. REDFERN, P. 'Input-output analysis, and its application to education and manpower planning.' C.A.S. Occasional Paper No. 5, H.M.S.O. 1967.
24. FORSTER, C. and WHITTING, T. 'An integrated mathematical model of the fuel economy' *Statistical News*, November 1968.
25. McFARQUHAR, A. M. M. and EVANS, M. C. 'Projection models for U.K. Food and Agriculture.' *Journal of Agricultural Economics*, No. 3, 1971.

7: Industrial Assessments and the use of Macro-Economic Models

J. R. S. Homan and S. Hampson

1. The National Economic Development Council has from its inception been particularly concerned with raising the rate of economic growth and with the improvement of British industrial performance. It is therefore interested in constraints on future growth and how to tackle them, and in the structural problems that may require positive actions for their solution. Such matters can only be effectively considered and dealt with over the medium term. The Council's work accordingly needs to be based on informed views on the medium-term prospects for individual industries, and for the U.K. economy as a whole.

2. In the present context we are concerned with one aspect of the Council's work—its medium-term industrial assessments. Such assessments are now being made of the prospects for twelve industries up to 1977,[1] representing one quarter of G.D.P.; they were commissioned by the Council in January 1972 and will be completed by mid-1973. As the work is still in progress, we cannot yet report on our results; this paper concentrates on our approach to the work and on the use being made of economic models.

The purpose of industrial assessments
3. All the Office's assessment work starts from the proposition that our main concern is with faster growth and improved economic performance; except over a very short period, the former cannot be sustained without the latter. This means that we need to obtain as much meaningful data as possible on the recent performance and problems of the industries under study, and then to look at the future for each industry under four main headings:

(i) the changing composition of final and intermediate demand for

[1] See Appendix A for a list of the industries covered.

industries' products, both in the U.K. and in the main export markets;

(ii) the opportunities for specialization to take advantage of changing international patterns of demand, based on a dynamic analysis of comparative advantage;

(iii) the problems of improving domestic economic performance, especially raising the productivity of labour, and improving the management of other inputs, notably capital;

(iv) supply constraints, including labour, especially skilled labour, financial resources and plant and equipment, and methods of tackling them.

4.   It will be evident from this list that structural change is a central issue, and one of our objectives is to detect through industrial consultations probable major shifts in resources at an early stage, so that the appropriate policy measures can be devised and actions taken by management, unions and Government. Insofar as this can be done, it should help to minimize the undesirable social as well as economic consequences of the under-utilization of resources.

5.   Equally, it is evident that much of our work must be qualitative. This must be so if we are to attempt to consider all the factors affecting industrial economic performance, which include such matters as attitudes towards different kinds of work, problems of industrial organization and management control, as well as the more purely economic factors. Moreover, the ground under us is shifting all the time, and our approach has therefore to be dynamic.

6.   The proposals that emerge at the end of the analysis, and which are concerned with possible ways of tackling constraints on growth and of improving economic performance, may be directed towards companies, unions, industries or the Government. Whilst the central purpose of assessment work is to lead to effective action, it serves at least two other important ends.

7.   The first of these is to provide flows of information at the micro-economic level, i.e. industries and industrial subsectors, to all those concerned with policy-planning at this level, who include, besides industrial organizations, trade unions and individual companies, Government departments concerned with industrial policy.

8.   The second is to provide information as to the possible future course of the sectors of the economy under study for those concerned with macro-economic policy, in particular the Government, the C.B.I., and the T.U.C. as members of the N.E.D.C. Something more will be

said about the difficulties of developing meaningful 'micro-macro' links later on in this paper, but the importance of this aspect of the work should be emphasized here.

The current industrial assessments

9.   The current industrial assessment work has evolved and changed considerably since its three predecessors—the early N.E.D.O. 4 per cent Growth Plan of 1962/63, the D.E.A.'s National Plan of 1964/65, and *The Task Ahead* industrial assessments of 1969/70. The current assessments do not set out to provide a comprehensive plan, being relatively modest in scope and selective in their industrial coverage.

10.   The current assessments cover only those industries thought likely to be most significantly affected by E.E.C. entry: they account for the bulk of U.K. manufacturing and agriculture. They concentrate on the major industrial problems and changes likely to arise over the next five years, especially as a result of E.E.C. entry, and also because of recent economic developments in the U.K. and internationally. They examine the implications of the changes for investment and manpower problems and policy, and seek to identify the available strategies to meet these changes if sustained higher growth is to be achieved.

11.   It is not the primary intention of the current assessments to produce forecasts. The approach is to provide an analysis at sector level of recent developments and medium-term possibilities to 1977, at two different but illustrative rates of growth of $3\frac{1}{2}$ per cent and 5 per cent per annum; one well within the country's productive potential, the other at the upper limit.

The use of models

12.   In building up a picture of industrial potential and future industrial issues from its detailed work on individual industries, the Office is making use of macro-economic models in the following ways.

13.   In the first place, all the individual industry assessments are based on the two sets of alternative illustrative projections of the trends in the main macro-economic aggregates to 1977, supplied by H.M. Treasury. Secondly, with some outside assistance, we are experimenting with the use of the Treasury's 70×70 input-output model as a complement to results obtained by industrial consultation, to provide parallel sets of estimates of future rates of growth for individual industries. We are also making use of the available work on trade flow analysis as a check on the results of industrial consultation on the prospects for trade.

14.   In addition, the Office is developing a number of sectoral models of different types for specific industries, including input-output models and models of financial flows. One of these, the textile industry input-output model, is described in a separate paper by M. J. Bramson and Caroline Miles.

Illustrative macro-economic projections
15.   Although the review is not a comprehensive exercise expected to yield a set or sets of consistent results for the whole economy, it is obviously essential that all industries taking part in it agree to common assumptions about likely future overall growth rates and their components, preferably incorporating alternative 'higher' and 'lower' case outcomes. Only if the individual industry results are built up on a common framework are the results likely to be reasonably compatible. Without this degree of compatibility it would not be possible to present a coherent picture of the total demand, trade and output of all the industries studied, their likely future aggregate demand for resources, and the consumer goods industries' demands on the intermediate and capital goods industries.

16.   The illustrative projections, together with common assumptions, were designed to give industry working parties just such a common base of expectations of macro-economic developments in the medium-term. The common assumptions are based on the continuance of present domestic and international policies and trends, except where changes are known to be going to occur.

17.   Quantitative projections for assessment industries are being generated from these common assumptions, which consist of the trend growth of G.D.P. in constant price terms, at the two illustrative rates of $3\frac{1}{2}$ per cent and 5 per cent, the growth of world trade, total investment and private and public consumption. These assumptions are almost entirely demand-oriented, and the process of industrial consultation will add indications of the supply-side reactions and implications at sector level. Basic demand aggregates affecting investment- and consumption-oriented industries are thus provided. The Public Expenditure White Paper[1] has since augmented input assumptions for investment-oriented industries. Disaggregated illustrative projections of the growth of consumers' expenditure have been provided; this work and its status is described in the section of the paper on the input-output model.

[1] *Public Expenditure to 1976–77*, Cmnd. 5178, H.M.S.O., Dec. 1972.

Quantitative sector projections and industrial consultations

18. The next step is for the Office to draw up provisional reports embodying calculations, hypotheses and qualitative analyses at industry and sector level, for discussion with review working parties. These consist of representatives of management and unions and also government officials concerned with the particular industry under review.

19. In general, the Office is assembling, from the work done by individual industry groups, sets of the possible 1977 values for a number of significant variables, based on the common illustrative projections. These variables include U.K. and export demand for the products of the industry and its subsectors, imports, exports, domestic output, manpower requirements and the level of investment needed to achieve the projected level of output.

20. Analysis by industry groups starts generally from a range of regression models of past behaviour; the complexity of these models depends on the adequacy of accessible data on the industry. These analyses are subjected to the close scrutiny and judgement of the assessment working parties, to ensure that informed industrial experience and knowledge about the likely effect of significant changes and developments in the economic and industrial environment are taken into account.

21. Where an industry is going through a period of rapid change, which may be a change in its product structure, its characteristic production functions, its organization or its environment, the past is likely to prove a more than usually unsatisfactory guide to the future. This is basically why some assessment working parties are not able to make projections on the basis of historical data. Even where reasonably clear trends can be identified, and this is not always possible, the working parties concerned do not accept that these trends are likely to continue.

22. Several examples occur in the present assessment. The environment within which the U.K. agricultural and food manufacturing industries operate is being entirely changed by the Common Agricultural Policy of the E.E.C. Another example is textiles, where the working parties concerned have come to the conclusion that the projection of historical time series data for individual sectors could be dangerously misleading, for reasons that will be spelt out in their report. They have therefore encouraged the development of a sector level input-output model which will, it is hoped, help to clarify the picture of the way the industry as a whole, and its different sectors, are likely to develop over the next five years.

The input-output model

23. Consistency between the various industry results is clearly desirable, but is difficult to achieve. A first step is to have a way of checking the compatibility and plausibility of these results, and we are seeking to make use of input-output analysis experimentally for this purpose.

24. The input-output model being used is basically that developed in the Treasury, who have made it available to the Office and have also helped with technical facilities. It is essentially an orthodox, static model; the central equation is:

$$Q=[I-A+\hat{m}]^{-1}f$$

Q = vector of total outputs
I = unit matrix
A = commodity-commodity coefficient matrix
$\hat{m}$ = diagonalized vector of import proportions
f = final demand vector, the sum of several individual vectors.

The model has been described by A. A. McLean.[1]

25. The model, with its ancillary routines, is designed to produce a vector of the total demands on the domestic output of individual industries from a set of final demand aggregates. As a first step, the final demand aggregates are translated into vectors of final demands for individual commodities. The processes used to do this vary as between different functional categories. These vectors of individual final demand are then aggregated across commodities to give the required final demand vector, f, for use in the equation given above.

26. The processes whereby the means of spreading the demand aggregates are derived are outlined below. To translate the investment final demand aggregates into investment in commodity terms, the historic commodity investment patterns are projected, with adjustments for special knowledge, and transformed into proportions of the overall totals. For stockbuilding, the weighting system which determines the proportions used in spreading the aggregates is derived from the expected relative growths in the domestic output of each commodity. For exports, the past data, in absolute terms, are projected and the future pattern of demands used as weights for spreading the export aggregates.

27. The public and private consumption vectors were produced at N.E.D.O. rather than generated within the model: the former because

---

[1] 'Forecasting by Input-Output.' Paper delivered to Norwich Conference on Input-Output and Throughput, September 1971 (publication forthcoming).

it was not otherwise available to us, and the latter because it was felt that the usual techniques were not adequate when relative prices might be expected to change quite markedly as a result of the imposition of V.A.T. and the E.E.C. Common Agricultural Policy.

28. The public consumption vector was generated in two stages. The first stage was to divide the illustrative projection of public consumption between the four main headings; defence, local authority expenditure, health, and other. A view was taken on the relative magnitude of these items by reference to the Public Expenditure White Paper. The four sub-aggregates were then divided amongst commodities in much the same proportions as in 1968, although some of the proportions, notably in the food categories, were adjusted in the light of industrial comment.

29. Considerably more work has been done on private consumption, which is much the largest component of final demand and where, in consequence, potentially greater benefits can be derived from improvements. The Linear Expenditure System (L.E.S.) has been used for the non-durable items, and individual stock adjustment equations for the durable items. The coefficients of the L.E.S., and a preliminary set of relative prices, were made available to us by the Department of Applied Economics at Cambridge. These were discussed within the Office and at some assessment working parties, following which some fairly substantial changes were made, especially in the food categories.

30. The Office is also consulting consumer-oriented industries not covered by the assessments on the private consumption vector. This should help to avoid the danger that relative prices of assessment industries will be revised upwards at the expense of other industries.

31. The first of the provisional results of the individual industries' work are now available for comparison with the input-output results. In general, the discrepancies are larger than might have been hoped for, but there does not seem to be any systematic bias. However, only as more results become available will a clearer picture emerge.

Future developments

32. The current assessments will shortly be completed, and one of our tasks will be to examine the effectiveness of the methods we have used and to seek to improve them. So far as the quantitative techniques are concerned there are likely to be a number of uses which we shall hope to develop in the future. Before outlining them, it is worth reiterating that by its nature much of the Office's work has to be qualitative. The principal object of the quantitative techniques is to

contribute to the development of informed judgments of industries' medium-term prospects through industrial consultation.

33. One major area in which we hope to do further work is in the development of methods to check the compatibility and plausibility— and ultimately the consistency—of industrial results and to relate these results to the macro-economic inputs. The input-output model we are using has certain shortcomings, but this does not mean that the approach is wrong or that the model is not susceptible of improvement. In particular, we are planning further quantitative input-output model work, especially on the investment side, as it seems clear that this is an area in which current models are particularly weak. At the same time we believe that industrial consultation may help to improve the structure of such models.

34. We also hope to continue to work on our existing sectoral models and to develop new ones. At present we are working on two sectoral models, for textiles and agriculture, and two industry cash flow models, for chemicals and machine tools, all of which are being used in the current industrial assessments. It seems probable that the present assessments will identify further industries where it might be both feasible and useful to construct such models.

35. All these developments may help in the difficult task of providing some contribution to macro-economic models from the sector level work. Two potential areas on which we hope we may be able to shed some light, for example, are the outlook for trade and the relationship between capital investment and increased labour productivity.

36. Finally, we shall need to develop further our technical capability in organizing and processing substantial flows of detailed industrial and economic information from many participants, and in communicating the results of the work to those who can use them. This may seem a somewhat pedestrian note on which to end, but it is really the heart of the matter.

Appendix A

List of industries covered by 1972–77 medium-term review

Chemicals	Mechanical engineering
Machine tools	Textiles
Motor manufacturing	Clothing
Iron and steel castings	Paper and board
Electronics	Agriculture
Electrical engineering	Food manufacturing

8: Report of the Discussion

Purpose

Five main purposes of medium-term models were discussed: the purpose of assisting in decisions on public expenditure; the purpose of assisting in the control of the medium-term development of the economy as a whole; the purpose of accelerating the growth-rate; the purpose of improving the flow of information to industry; and finally the purpose of predicting what was actually going to happen.

The one purpose which everyone accepted was the first of these—of assisting in decisions on public expenditure. This was a main objective of the Treasury and the Par models. Everyone agreed that medium-term public expenditure plans should be considered in relation to competing claims. This was not a negligible objective, since the public sector absorbs or transfers some half of the national product.

The comment was made that this concentration on public expenditure plans, rather than on broader plans for the whole economy, was perhaps becoming more general in Western countries. 'The Danish five-year projection, for example, is entirely a public expenditure projection, simply with a rough rate of growth added; this is partly because they are interested in the manpower demands for the growing social services. In Danish, Norwegian and Swedish plans, this is a very important point, and one worth examining for Britain as well. In Western Germany the macro-economic plan is essentially for the control of public expenditure. It has only been extended because the Government was pushed by Brussels to publish a plan which technically covered the whole economy. This of course will also happen to Britain.'

The second purpose—assisting in the medium-term control of the economy—is one of the purposes of the Stone model. It started off as a model to explore the requirements of certain rates of growth—it had then, as it were, one target and no instruments. 'It has been adapted to include other targets—such as full employment and the balance of payments—and also to include the effects of instruments. In this way the realism of the targets can be assessed by the realism of the instrument alterations which are required to meet them. So whereas originally there was one central view, now there is a "no policy change" view, and secondly a "target" view; targets do not have to be government targets, but they need to be explicitly stated. In the same way, the

179

instruments used to bring the target results about need to be given explicitly, since different combinations of policies have different effects on targets.' The Treasury model can also be used for other policy purposes, apart from simply examining the consequences of certain rates of growth of public expenditure. 'It can explore different policy assumptions; it can try simulations with different exogenous values and different parameter values. Targets can be imposed on the current balance, on output, or on prices.'

Some speakers doubted whether medium-term assessments were of much help here. 'Certainly in the end year of a medium-term assessment we should presume that we get a balance between public and private expenditure which does not lead to excess demand. However, demand policy in the intervening years is a short-term matter, and I do not see that medium-term assessments have any part to play. Even before the last round of incomes policy, I would have taken the view that any forecast of medium-term inflation, for example, was quite hopeless. Now we are in a new world; forecasting of prices seems to me quite clearly impossible. I doubt whether it is worth attempting to work out the possible medium-term effects of different anti-inflationary policies or adjustments. There are many ways of adjusting to inflation—and the actual outcome depends on how the various techniques are operated. We need a great deal of knowledge about the operation of these adjustments, and their time lags. We do not have this knowledge.' The same speaker was doubtful about detailed medium-term balance of payments assessments, with policy recommendations; the discussion of the balance of payments in the medium-term was extensive, and is reported separately (p. 188).

Could medium-term assessments assist in the policy of increasing the rate of growth of productive potential—the third purpose in the list? This proposition was heavily attacked. 'This purpose harks back to N.E.D.O. and to the National Plan. I am entirely sceptical about the value of medium-term assessments for this purpose—not only because these early attempts were unsuccessful. Two conditions are necessary for medium-term planning to be effective for this end. First, one needs to know what factors determine the growth of productive potential. Secondly, one needs to have instruments which affect those factors whose quantitative importance can be predicted. If these conditions exist, then medium-term planning of this kind is possible. It is because they do exist for short-term purposes that short-term forecasting is useful. However, in relation to economic growth, the conditions are not satisfied. We don't have instruments whose operation is understood and whose effect is quantifiable. Therefore quantitative planning on this basis is bogus, and any new round would also be bogus. Certainly one can have policies for a faster rate of growth; this is not the same as planning it, and these policies do not depend on a medium-term assessment. I should imagine that very few people now believe that it does any particular good to the growth rate to publish a set of consistent figures for the national product for five years ahead which show that in some sense a faster growth rate is possible. I should therefore be dismayed if we started on this again; in particular it might interfere with what I consider to be the important objective of medium-term assessments—the allocation of resources between the public and private sector. The N.E.D.O. 4 per cent growth rate did harm. It purported to be a technical operation which suggested firm conclusions, and it led to mistaken policies . . . I see an example of this danger in the publication of the 5 per cent case in the White Paper on Public Expenditure.[1] This is worse than useless. It shows a frivolous approach to medium-term assessment, and shows how far political and public relations purposes now tend to be dominant.'

There were defenders of indicative planning. The Stone group argued that there was no need to be wholly agnostic about the determinants of growth. Estimates can be made of the effect of certain instruments in producing increases in investment, and also of the relationships, industry by industry, between investment and productivity. This produces a situation in which the Government does have instruments which can influence investment and so influence the rate of growth. (The objection was made that the Stone model started with the assumption that productivity growth was generated by investment, and then in effect measured what the relationship must be, given that it was so generated.) It was also argued that the indicative planning experiment had not been tried properly in this country, because of the absence of a realistic idea of what was possible. With more realism, we might have had better experience. It was argued that it would be useful to bring together the official and the private planners. 'One can consider the economy as being composed of three sectors: the public sector; the planned private sector; and the non-planned private sector. It is the planned private sector which is the dynamic element in the economy, and is responsible for the growth in productivity and in investment. The non-planned private sector is essentially a satellite sector. If one were to include in the medium-term assessments the plans of the planned

[1] The reference is to Table 1.2 in *Public Expenditure to 1976–77*, Cmnd. 5178, H.M.S.O., 1973.

private sector, then the assessments are likely to be more accurate than they would otherwise be, for this sector also plans for three, five, or seven years ahead; and, as with the public sector, adjustments are marginal.' Some people doubted whether most firms' medium-term plans were as firm as this quotation suggested. Also, this consultation with the private planned sector was something which was supposed to have taken place during the period of planning; it was difficult to see any concrete results. One further point made was that indicative planning might have some value now. Government economists appeared to believe that productive potential had continued to rise on trend through the long period of increasing under-employment. This was widely doubted in industry; some industrialists do not think that a $3\frac{1}{2}$ per cent growth rate from 1972 to 1977 is easily within our capacity; there might therefore be a legitimate function for indicative planning, to persuade industry that at least this lower $3\frac{1}{2}$ per cent growth rate is possible.

The fourth purpose suggested was one of information—the medium-term assessment being seen as part of an information system jointly developed by the public and private sectors, so that the compatibility of their plans can be tested. This was one of the topics raised in the discussion of the N.E.D.O. medium-term assessment, which is reported in the next section.

The final purpose—of actually forecasting what was going to happen —was one suggested by some of the industrial economists present. 'I find a considerable gap between my requirements, in deciding about investment, and the matters which are being discussed at this Conference. My problem is to consider the forecasting implications of different policies, while most people here at this Conference seem to be considering the policy implications of different forecasts. My own concern is to get a sensible forecast on which I can base the investment decisions of my company; and in the context of the discussions we have had so far I am not very much further forward with this.' Others stressed the same point. 'Our point of view is that we want medium-term assessments in order to find out what is likely to happen, so that we can make our investment plans accordingly. What industry wants is forecasts.'

The Current N.E.D.O. Exercise

The discussion of the N.E.D.O. medium-term assessment also raised questions about purposes. An account was given of the objectives of the assessment:

'What we are doing at the moment is a partial and modest exercise of looking at the industries which the Council felt were likely to be affected by E.E.C. entry; we are now about three months away from completing our work on our medium-term assessment.[1] I should note that it is actually only in the textile industry that we have developed an input-output model to assist us in this assessment. We are essentially trying to test the feasibility of a $3\frac{1}{2}$ per cent and 5 per cent growth rate for particular industries. Our work has necessarily to be mainly qualitative. So what we are doing is different from what we did before: we are now considering the feasibility of certain growth rates at the industrial level only. However, we are still making use of our comparative advantage of tripartite consultation. In our various industry assessments, we are trying this time to include financial as well as other constraints, to decide whether or not there will be sufficient finance for the investment required, and whether the level of profitability is likely to be high enough. We hope to cover some of the macro-economic questions which have been raised at the Conference, such as the effect of investment grants or allowances, and the relationship between investment and productivity, at industry level.

'Our macro-economic assumptions were essentially derived from the Treasury medium-term model, though we recognize that the main purpose of this model now is for the control of public expenditure. In order to do the private sector properly, we probably need more information on the public expenditure side than the Treasury model gave us: for example, at the moment we have a single public expenditure figure for both rates of growth, which is hardly realistic.

'We certainly propose to develop the micro model side of our work, though there is a great deal to do, and given the number of people we have available it will take some time. We are also very interested in the development of input-output work in general; for our purposes, for discussions with industry, we need at least a 70×70 breakdown—one which is simply a breakdown into 30 or 35 sectors does not give us the degree of disaggregation which enables us to use the material realistically with industry. It is also important to be able to check the results of runs of an input-output model with the results of industry consultation.

'We have borrowed the Treasury's input-output model for use in our current assessment. One of the difficulties with the current exercise is

---

[1] N.E.D.O.'s report to the Council, entitled *Industrial Review to 1977*, was published in autumn 1973, and is available from Neddy Books, Millbank Tower, 21–41 Millbank, London SW1P 4QX, price £1.00.

that, since it only covers about one-third of the economy, we cannot explore all the linkages between industries. So essentially we are using the input-output model to provide figures for comparison with the results of our industrial inquiry, which should enable us to see whether there is a general bias in any particular direction. For the longer term future, we have the rather more ambitious idea of marrying consultation with the input-output exercise, by including in the input-output work changes in coefficients which are derived from our consultation.

'We have done something of this kind, in consulting industry about the relative prices which are incorporated in the Cambridge linear expenditure system; and in a number of instances they suggested changes in these relative prices which we have in fact incorporated. In the same way we have consulted industry about the consumers' expenditure pattern suggested by the Cambridge calculations, to see if they consider these projections realistic. We have also used the same kind of sources as the Stone model for the investment requirements for industries. So by this extension of the model to cover investment as well, we then have some investment figures which we can compare with those which we obtain by the process of industrial consultation.'

In discussion of the N.E.D.O. medium-term assessment, the following points were made:

(a) A question was asked about the effect of the medium-term assessment on industry: 'At what stage will anyone do anything different from what they would otherwise have done as a consequence of this work?' The answer was that, as a consequence of this process of consultation, firms' investment behaviour might be modified. Alternatively they might see the need for a structural change in their industry. Thus the wool industry's realization that there was not room in the long-term future for some thousand companies in this industry was at least partly a consequence of the N.E.D.O. study of that industry's long-term prospects. However, one should first envisage the N.E.D.O. work as providing an information system—in particular at the moment information about the possible consequences of joining the Common Market—and it is normal for better information to lead to changes in behaviour in a multiplicity of small ways. So information is the first objective. The E.E.C. point is an important one; in many of the diffuse industries the knowledge of E.E.C. consequences is scanty.

(b) Another objection was about medium-term assessments 'based on growth-rates of $3\frac{1}{2}$ and 5 per cent, both of which are figures drawn from the air; I can't see what you can tell people which is not likely to be misleading on the basis of those two figures'. The reply was that the main purpose of the exercise was to identify problems, some of which were relatively independent of the growth rate, and others of which were intensified with the higher growth rate assumption.

(c) A third problem raised was that 'the period 1972–77 will not be a period of steady growth; presumably up to 1975 there will be a great deal of absorption of the slack in the economy, and it will be then that the bottlenecks appear, and the question will arise of what growth rate can be sustained from 1975 to 1977. One really wants to know what the bottlenecks are at a full employment level; it is therefore misleading to start looking for the answers to this question at a time of under-employment. The $3\frac{1}{2}$ per cent growth figure from 1972 to 1977 will not explore the emergence of bottlenecks, since this is easily within the capacity of industry. Would it not be sensible to carry out this exercise on the assumption of full employment—because otherwise the real constraints which are likely to emerge when full employment is reached, such possibly as those on the balance of payments side, may not emerge? Surely one of the problems is to get industrialists to understand that the problems at a full employment level may be different from the problems at an under-employed level.'

Two points were made in reply. First, some industrialists do not agree that $3\frac{1}{2}$ per cent, 1972–77, is easily within our capacity, and will need to be persuaded about its feasibility. Secondly, the whole idea of productive potential at full employment is one that is foreign to the individual firm. The individual firm knows at any point how far it can increase its output from a given plant, by working additional hours and so on; the question 'What is your productive potential at full employment?' just has no meaning at all at the firm level. So it would be impossible to conduct an industry consultation on the basis of starting from a full employment situation.

(d) Two points were made on the possible use of N.E.D.O.'s 'comparative advantage' in its contacts with industry. First, it was useful that one did get discrepancies between the views of the future obtained from industry consultations and those obtained from input-output calculations. This could lead industries to question their own assessments, or to revisions of input-output coefficients, or both. Secondly, the work at N.E.D.O. should be seen as helping to improve our knowledge of supply-side relationships; it was a general criticism of medium-term assessment models that they are weak on the supply side.

Short-term and Medium-term Models: the Cycle and the Trend

The comment was made that the Treasury medium-term model was really very like their short-term model. Most equations seem to be about the same. So it raises the question whether it is worth having two models. Really all one needs to do is to invert the employment function to get output figures, and the short-term set of relationships would serve just as well in the medium-term. This point was, in effect, conceded: 'The main reasons for two models existing are historical ones: they grew up when there were two separate ministries. One of two things may happen: we may be able to put in more material on the determinants on the supply side in the medium-term model, and keep it separate; alternatively, if we don't discover useful supply side relationships, then the two models will probably be merged.'

There was a good deal of discussion of the cycle and the trend. One of the claims of the Par concept (p. 60) is that, with Par figures for the past as well as the future, the whole series was on the same basis, and therefore logically consistent. The Treasury group was urged to start with a trend year rather than an actual year. The Stone group disputed any logical inconsistency in having an actual figure for the initial year, and a trend figure for the terminal year of a medium-term projection. If there really was no basis for projecting the cycle, then a future 'trend' projection has the same standing as a past actual figure. If on the other hand there was some basis for assuming a cyclical movement in the future, then this should be incorporated into the medium-term projection.

The Problem of Productivity

Both the Par and the Treasury model make projections into the future of the trend of underlying productivity in the past. The Stone model has disaggregated relationships between investment and productivity for thirty-five industries. There were various comments on the Treasury and Par treatment of productivity. Both the Treasury and Par groups said that they had not been able to trace the effect of investment on productivity, and for this reason put a trend in instead. However, the Treasury did disaggregate the output-employment relationship between the public and private sectors of the economy—including the nationalized industries in the private sector.[1] This was because they thought that productivity in the public sector was likely to behave rather

[1] The description of the Treasury model on page 12 pre-dates this disaggregation.

differently from productivity in the private sector. It was suggested that the Baumol two-sector model had some relevance here; it has low and high productivity growth sectors, which can be considered to correspond with the private and public sectors. The consequence in the Baumol model is that an increasing proportion of resources is devoted to the low productivity growth sector, and this has as a consequence a diminishing rate of aggregate productivity growth.

One suggestion made was that, although it might not have been possible in the past data to discover good investment/productivity relationships, none the less it might be sensible to impose such a relationship in a medium-term model. It was noted that in the Treasury 5 per cent projection, the volume of private investment was higher than in the 3½ per cent projection.

There was some discussion of the past underlying productivity trend in the Treasury and Par models. It was explained that it was not part of the concept of Par productivity that it should be smooth; and that there were economic justifications for the dates at which changes in the underlying rate of growth were made. 'We tried to choose periods because we had some economic reason for thinking something different had happened. There is no strong commitment to particular years. We are really only making the proposition that the rise in productivity was slower in the first half of the sixties than in the second half, and that it has slowed down a little recently; the proposition is not more definite than that. The slowing down has been very small—3·3 to 3·1 per cent, nothing more.' It was noted that the breaks in the past productivity trend were different in the two models. The Par model had a change in 1965, and then again a smaller change in 1969. In the Treasury model, the productivity break came in 1963. This was explained as follows: 'The more ingenious you are with your econometrics, the greater the variety of possible answers. Lag patterns can vary from 6 months to 4 years. So in the end it is not so much the data determining the answers as the assumptions made about lag patterns. So it seemed more sensible to fall back on a simple-minded approach, and use the average of past experience over a reasonable number of years. That was the main reason for having the break earlier than 1965, which is too close to the present.'

There were some questions about the status of the 3½ per cent and 5 per cent projections incorporated in the Public Expenditure White Paper for 1971 to 1977. It was explained that—given a state of agnosticism about the future trend of underlying productivity—the purpose of the two projections was simply to demonstrate that there was sufficient room for the projected rise in public expenditure within a wide range of possible outcomes for the rise in output.

The Stone group pointed to the comparative advantage of their model, in that they could examine changes in the productivity trend industry by industry. They pointed out that a good deal of the change in underlying productivity had been in the service industries. Here, productivity had been rising between 1·4 and 1·7 per cent a year up to 1965; from 1965 to 1969, the rise was 3·1 per cent a year. In answer to questions about the effect of the selective employment tax, they said that in their model, in so far as this tax did have an effect on productivity, it would be mainly as a result of its effect on investment in the service industries. Since service industries make up some 40 per cent of the work force, this acceleration in productivity made a great deal of difference. One suggestion made was that the rise here was possibly largely in distribution, and closely connected with the rise of supermarkets; and this could be explained as much by the abolition of resale price maintenance as by the introduction of S.E.T. It was suggested that Britain might follow the American pattern, and we would discover ourselves faced with over-capacity, and consequently a loss of productivity increases. So service productivity might be following an S-shaped curve.

The Balance of Payments in Medium-term Assessments

The balance of payments discussion centred particularly on the Par balance of payments forecast; however some of it also applied to the Stone forecasts as well. A question was raised about the need for these forecasts, particularly for the first purpose of considering the resources available for public expenditure. 'For the balance of payments, there are some discernible medium-term trends, and some time lags about which we have some information. The Par model has a lot to say about this; indeed the balance of payments consequences are probably the main theme of their January report (p. 79). I have been somewhat impressed by their predictions. Certainly it is true that the balance of payments has to be in the resources table for the objective of considering the available resources for public expenditure. However, I am doubtful about the value of a full-scale attack on the medium-term balance of payments, with attempts at comprehensive figures. The uncertainties are so enormous that in my view it is not helpful. Indeed I have become increasingly sceptical of the value of short-term balance of payments forecasting, let alone medium-term forecasts. Simpler techniques would say all that one can possibly say about the balance of payments future: thus one can look roughly at the consequences of the continuation of certain trends. So I do not agree with the confident assertion made in the January report based on the Par model that none of the traditional methods will work to get the balance of payments right in the medium-term.' The same point was made in a comment which pointed to the very big difference between the Stone and Par balance of payments predictions for 1975—a difference much greater than the margin of error indicated for the Par figures.

In reply it was said that the medium-term balance of payments forecast was not central to the discussion of the resources available for public and private expenditure. 'Although we have got to forecast the necessary terms of trade for a Par balance of payments and for full employment, it should be noted that the resource requirement does not vary all that much. Even in our very pessimistic forecast of the change in the exchange rate needed to secure balance, nonetheless the deterioration in the terms of trade is only 4 per cent. On the actual prediction made in January 1972, the emphatic recommendations were entirely concerned with fiscal policy—which I confidently think is out of balance, and will necessarily result in serious balance of payments difficulties. The other proposition—that even if we fulfil the fiscal conditions, our balance of payments will still be unsatisfactory—this is not put forward emphatically. However, it is a possibility which should be taken seriously, with contingency planning.'

There were various criticisms of the structure of the Par balance of payments assessment. One was that the Par model is set up in such a way that it has to crash. 'Productivity does not make itself felt in any way on the balance of payments. Since exports are exogenously determined, and since imports are a function of output, then it inevitably follows that any acceleration in output or productivity must lead to a bigger gap between imports and exports. The balance of payments trap is built into the model. If productivity improves, the balance of payments gets worse. Yet one must confront this with the observation, in the field of international comparisons, that there is a strong correlation between productivity and the rate of growth of exports.' Another question raised was a possible asymmetry between the Par treatment of imports and exports. 'I note the strong time trend in imports of manufactures in the Par model of 16 per cent a year, which is essentially an extrapolation. This certainly incorporates considerable liberalization—a Kennedy round, and the effect from E.F.T.A. (which is small). It can now be assumed that there will be

Common Market effects to continue this trend; but it is noticeable that there is no such trend on the export side. The export projection is much more sensitive to price effects. There is a certain asymmetry here.' Another question raised was whether or not there should be capacity constraints on exports. It was pointed out that one Treasury equation had introduced a measure of the supply of export goods, reflecting the capacity for producing exportables, minus home demand. There is a case for saying that supply restrictions should be built in, and that in some cases demand relationships may be inappropriate. It may well be the supply constraints which are responsible for many of the lags in export relationships. However, other speakers said that in econometric work on exports they had not been able to find significant capacity constraints.

The Par group replied to the point on trade in manufactures by saying that there was really nothing surprising in the high figure given for future imports of manufactures. The puzzle is with exports. 'It really is not surprising if the rapid increase in imports of manufactures were to continue; the proportion of British manufactures which is imported is not high by international standards, and there is a great deal of liberalization and improved organization of international transport which will increase the figure. The puzzling trend is the figure for exports. All that we have done is to assume that the U.K. market share goes on declining as it has done in the past, except where unit costs become more favourable. It seems reasonable to assume this continuity; at least policy makers should consider the consequences of the possibility that these balance of payments forecasts are correct.'

One criticism on exchange-rates was addressed both to the Par and to the Stone models. 'We should consider carefully whether the balance of payments is as manipulable by the exchange rate as these models suggest. For the data and evidence are not provided in the description of the models themselves. We are giving the exchange rate a great deal more importance than it had ten years ago; I remain sceptical about the coefficients. A further point here is that the shifting of exchange rates means that one will have to consider this in terms of a new numeraire. The proposition that the exchange rate of sterling will come down to $1·60 as against the dollar is now fairly meaningless. One will have to begin to work in terms of movements as against some weighted index of the exchange rate against several other leading currencies'. On another point, the Par group explained that they concentrated all the effect of exchange-rate changes on the export side partly for convenience: they did not in fact take the view that a substantial devaluation of sterling would have no effect on imports at all.

Finally, a number of specific points were raised (not given in full detail here) about the actual figures in the Par treatment of the future balance of payments. For example, the treatment of the 'balancing item' in the balance of payments was questioned. This had been positive to the extent of almost £100 million a year on average over 1960–71; should it not be treated as unidentified receipts on current or long-term capital account, and therefore should not credit be taken for it in the future as well? Was the projected rapid rise in net long-term investment overseas correct—depending as it did on a sharp fall in inward oil investment? It was doubted whether in fact this flow of investment would fall. Should there not be a bigger improvement in net property income—even at 1963 prices? Was it in fact necessary for the target figure to be high enough to finance an increase in trade credit? The Par group replied that in fact the particular target figure choice was not in any way a property of the Par system. The various items in it were certainly defensible, but it was open to any critic simply to take another target—and in fact, in some subsequent work another target had been taken.[1]

The Par Concept

Various specific aspects of the Par model are discussed elsewhere. There was one general criticism of the comprehensibility of the whole system. 'I can see that the Par concept is a way of abstracting from the trade cycle, so that one can answer, for example, whether a tax change is likely to be viable in the long run. I can see the need to do this: but is there not a simpler method? The Par model means including a great number of dummy figures. It would be very difficult to get policy makers to think in these terms. Is there no simpler way of expressing the idea, with fewer artificial numbers? It also means that there are two sources of error; one's Par forecast may be right, and the adjustments to actuality wrong, or the Par forecast itself may be wrong.'

The reply was that the concept is surely not so difficult. 'The series for public expenditure is the observed series. So it is really like a full employment budget surplus, as modified by the terms of trade. It differs from the full employment budget surplus, in that it is doubly adjusted,

[1] In the London and Cambridge Economic Bulletin, *The Times Business News*, 8 January 1973, W. A. H. Godley and F. Cripps took a zero balance as a target.

not only to full employment but also to a zero balance of payments. I do not see that this amount of artifice is avoidable. But of course not all details need to be given.'

One commentator felt that the Par system was particularly useful for balance of payments analysis. 'It is similar to some work done in O.E.C.D. on a cyclically adjusted current balance of payments, to enable judgements to be made about exchange-rate policy. It is useful to have concepts of the balance of payments which are adjusted, for example, for the slow moving effects of exchange rates which are half way through the works.'

Disaggregation

One of the main things that marks off the Stone model from the other two is its degree of disaggregation (see page 126). However, the question was only discussed in general terms.

One question was whether or not disaggregation would be a help for the purpose which was put forward as the primary purpose of the Par and Treasury models—the assessment of the future course of public expenditure. Here, one frequent comment was that the composition of this expenditure surely made some difference; a given rise in public expenditure could take the form of increased investment in nationalized industries, or it could take the form of increased welfare expenditure. Surely the consequences for the rest of the economy of these two possibilities would be different.

It was also claimed that disaggregation made it possible for the Stone model to deal with many questions about changes in structure. 'For example, from their calculations the change to V.A.T. did lead to lower export prices, and consequently did have an important effect on the balance of payments. For a model to be able to deal with the effects of a high rate of inflation, it was necessary that it should include the various values of tax allowances which are fixed in money terms; otherwise it would not allow for fiscal drag. Then a model ought to have a theory about changes in the underlying growth rate. In the Stone model, this came about because of changes in the structure of output, and in investment in each industry. Here as elsewhere, the macro-variables are all calculated from industries and commodities.'

So in the Stone model it was possible—indeed in a sense necessary—to build in such things as the consequences of the discovery of North Sea oil, or trends in non-ferrous metal prices, or the investment plans of the British Steel Corporation; it was necessary, since the disaggregated model required specific series for oil imports, non-ferrous metal prices, and investment in the steel industry. Further, there is within the model some check that the consequences of these developments for other sectors are taken care of.

Of course an aggregate model can also include adjustments for specific effects: thus the Par model also took account of the consequences of the discovery of North Sea oil.

Directions of Development of the Three Models

It was suggested to the Par group that their definition of public expenditure—restricted to goods and services only—was too narrow; it was not appropriate if the final purpose was to decide as between public and privately financed consumption; on this the Treasury model was right. The total resources absorbed by all public expenditure should be included.

The Par group agreed with this point. 'However, I think it is inappropriate to extend it without incorporating the whole of the tax side, along with the transfers side. It is of no significance if family allowances go up and child allowances go down. So I want to incorporate the entire system of transfers, including transfers to the Government. The major advance is in the large area of public expenditure and tax planning. I would like to be able to say much more about the implications of public expenditure projections not just for consumption but also for taxation. In general I would like to build a model of public sector expenditure. At the moment the public sector is planned by default. The underlying system of information, as a basis for government decisions, does not exist—and there is no reason why it should not exist. If one takes just the simple question—how large a quantity of resources is going to be pre-empted by population changes? —this is a question that obviously can be answered; but is not answered at the moment. Then the whole of the assessment of the other side of public expenditure—that is, not what it costs, but what we get from the money—still awaits extensive development.'

'I do not believe that we can improve our system by much more econometrics or disaggregation; we do the general exercise now pretty much as well as we shall ever be able to. There are exceptions to this generalization in statistics of productive potential (including the influence on this of the structure of demand) and various aspects of international trade and payments. But the major areas where big returns are obtainable, if we want to control the future, is the area to which I have already referred—the public sector, both on the expenditure and the tax side.'

A second point on public expenditure assessment was put specifically to the Treasury. 'The presentation tends to be that the forecast of public expenditure is taken, and personal consumption is a residual. Would it not be possible and indeed useful to start at the other end: to take tax projections, and to constrain public expenditure to the resources likely to be available: that is to adjust public expenditure to whatever you regard as the Par borrowing requirement?'

The reply was as follows: 'I agree that in the presentation consumption appears as a residual. However, it should not be assumed that that is the end of the story. It is true the Treasury adds up estimates, and calculates the consequences for consumption; but it does go on to say, in effect, if you don't like the consequences of this for consumption or taxation, then you will have to cut expenditure. I agree, however, that this comes at the end of the process rather than at the beginning; and that it would be a very different exercise if the process began with a decision on the resources which would be available, and then this was divided out.'

For both the Treasury and the Stone model, it was suggested that the future course of development was to make them year-by-year rather than target year models. This followed partly from points made elsewhere in the discussion—that the path taken to the target year influences the figures that turn up in that year; and that once a year-by-year model is constructed, it should be easier to test the forecasts against actual figures.

Estimation Procedures

All three groups came under criticism from some econometricians present. 'All three groups use inconsistent estimation methods at some point. Most of the equations of the Treasury model are estimated by ordinary least squares, as are key behavioural relations in the Stone model (of course this comment does not apply to the input-output tables), while the Par model explicitly places itself "beyond the pale of conventional econometric analysis". It is well-known that O.L.S. estimates of an equation containing endogenous variables among the "explanatory" variables are biased and inconsistent, as are standard errors and other conventional summary measures—perhaps the Treasury appreciates this, for no such statistics are presented for any of their estimated equations. In consequence it is hard to know how much credibility to give to estimated elasticities, equilibrium multipliers, and other medium-term effects, never mind estimated short-run reactions. Computer programmes for consistent estimators which also deal with time series problems are available, and it is unfortunate that they are not more widely used.'

The 'Par' estimation procedures were defended as follows: 'Estimating problems are subsidiary. Par's estimating procedures are governed by three principles: to produce answers which are verifiable, so that one knows if one is wrong or right. In answer to the objection that our estimating methods are inappropriate, appropriate methods are those which produce the best answers; the judgement of the appropriateness of the method is by the verifiability of the results.'

This was not accepted without question. 'The proposition that the appropriate method is one which gets the "best" answers is insufficient. There is a well established body of statistical theory which accepts a specific definition of best and which sets out the methods required to produce the best answers; these methods are perfectly well known. Economists tend to assume that their problem is always that precise economic relationships are not known, and that in practice all their difficulties are the result of mis-specification. Nevertheless, in searching for the correct specification I would prefer to use a method which would leave no substantial biases if I did hit on the right specification and which would give me a better chance of finding that specification; O.L.S. is not such a method.

'In estimation relatively little attention appears to be paid to dynamic effects, and the range of adjustment patterns considered is often very restricted. While it is natural that economists should concentrate on getting the right variables into the equation to the neglect of timing considerations, where guidance from economic theory is virtually non-existent, statisticians have developed methods of analysis of time series which systematically explore dynamic relationships, and perhaps these might usefully be employed by model-builders.

'In the papers presented, standard errors are noticeably absent, and there is no indication of reliability. While "Par" estimation procedures are claimed to produce answers which are verifiable, the authors of the Par paper assert that "estimates of the expected accuracy of conditional predictions outside the estimation period . . . are notoriously unreliable and this must be a result of the unreality of the underlying assumptions." A mis-specified model would certainly be expected to have a forecast error variance rather larger than the sample period error variance, and a structural change would have the same effect, although it might be considered as a special case of mis-specification. (Of course a structural change results directly the estimated model is used to alter the Government's economic policy-making.) However, other possible causes of misleading standard errors relate to the choice of estimation method and so are avoidable. Thus, ordinary least squares methods provide a downward-biased estimate of the true error variance when applied to an equation containing jointly dependent variables on the right-hand side and/or auto-correlated errors. Pre-testing of equations or "data-mining" is perhaps slightly more difficult to avoid, but this also has the effect of under-estimating the standard error of forecast. Finally, even perfect econometric methods cannot prevent confidence intervals for forecast expected values from fanning out rapidly when an equation is used to predict far beyond its sample experience. A statement of the likely range of error would be useful to readers and also might be a cautionary tale for the model builders themselves.'

A specific criticism was addressed to the Appendix to the Par paper, on assessing the accuracy and reliability of the Par system. 'We are asked to choose between two models, but there appears to be an error in the argument. Model 1 is used to predict for a new period, outside the original observations, and does so very well; for convenience of exposition let us suppose it does so without error. We are told that the model is then re-estimated incorporating that new period; and we are asked to imagine that the model now surprisingly yields a rather large residual in relation to that period (suggesting that it is not as good a model as was thought, and therefore no better than some other model previously rejected). But none of this is possible. If the prediction for the new period was accurate, the inclusion of that period will not alter the previous estimates of the model's parameters (the reason is that, under usual estimation procedures, the original estimates were those that yielded a minimum sum of squares of residuals, and the addition of new observations—with zero error—has not altered that sum of squares: hence the parameter-estimates do not change). Consequently, a large residual cannot appear. Perhaps there is some other way of justifying the argument in the text, but I have not been able to find one.'

Finally, one other econometric criticism was levelled at the Par model. 'Several of the variables in the model showed a strong trend, which had been represented by a linear or exponential function of time. In these cases the deviations from trend had then been used to estimate structural relations by ordinary least squares.[1]

[1] The authors comment that in fact the coefficients were imposed.

'One can imagine a big model of this kind which has been functioning for some time without being subjected to any random shocks. Then the movement of the endogenous variables will be determined by the movement of the exogenous variables, and if the latter exhibit smooth trends, then so will the former. If the trends are removed, we are left with nothing at all! If random shocks were admitted, then only these would be left at the end of the detrending operation, and they would provide relatively little information about the underlying relationships. Likewise, a closed dynamic model in which the greatest root of the characteristic equation is just greater than one will exhibit exponential growth, and if we now take out trends then the influence of this dominant latent root is removed. It is not clear that different explanations are necessary for the different components of interrelated series, and by throwing away the slowly-changing or low frequency component, which generally dominates, valuable information about the relations between series will be lost.'

Part III

Industry Models

The final part of the book gives the papers presented on two industrial models. One was prepared under the auspices of N.E.D.O. for the textile industry, and the paper was jointly presented by Mrs. Miles and Mr. Bramson. The second was prepared at the Department of Trade and Industry and presented by Mr. Hutber. The discussion of these industry models follows.

The original idea of including a discussion of industry models was to examine in particular the connections between them and the macro-economic models of the economy. In fact, this was not the focal point of the discussion; the main interest was in the specific characteristics of the models themselves. The general impression left was that there was considerable potential for the further development of industrial model-building; there were fewer questions about the use and purpose of these models than there were for the macro-economic models of the whole economy.

9: An Input-Output Model of the U.K. Textile Industry[1]

M. J. Bramson and Caroline Miles

Background and Objectives

1. The construction by the National Economic Development Office of an input-output model for the textile industry is a logical step forward in the Office's work on textile industry questions. It has been carried out under the general supervision of the Joint Textile Committee (J.T.C.), an *ad hoc* body established by N.E.D.O. in 1969 to investigate the medium-term prospects for the clothing, textile and man-made fibre industries. Readers unfamiliar with the N.E.D.O. framework and the organizational structure of the textile and related industries may find a brief account of the origins of the J.T.C. helpful. Others are invited to skip the next paragraph.

2. The J.T.C. was set up in 1969, following the National Economic Development Council's invitation to the Economic Development Committees (the 'Little Neddies') to undertake an assessment of their industries' prospects in the medium-term, up to 1972, in the light of the Government's Green Paper *The Task Ahead*. At that time there were three E.D.C.s concerned with the clothing and textile industries: for Clothing, Hosiery and Knitwear, and Wool Textiles. They all agreed to a proposal to set up a joint committee to handle the assessment work, and the Textile Council (representing the Lancashire sector) and the British Man-Made Fibres Federation also agreed to participate. Representatives of management and unions from these five bodies, along with government officials, made up the original J.T.C. Its Report on the Economic Assessment to 1972 was published in October 1970. In mid-1972 the J.T.C. was re-convened to work on a new N.E.D.O. medium-term review, which was to span the period 1971–77. Two of the original corporate members, the Hosiery and Knitwear

[1] The completion of this project would not have been possible without the help and advice of many people. We would especially like to thank our co-workers at N.E.D.O., Caroline Brierley and Arati Baksi; our consultants Richard Lecomber, John Eaton and Diana Isserlis; staff of the Shirley Institute and the members of the J.T.C. and its technical advisory group.

E.D.C. and the Textile Council, no longer existed, but both sectors continued to be represented through their trade associations and unions, and the carpet industry was also separately represented.

3.   From the start, the J.T.C. decided to aim at a 'pan-textile' assessment of the fibre, textile and clothing industries. Although the significance of the rapid spread of man-made fibres into almost all the traditional sectors, and the consequent blurring of the boundaries between them, was becoming increasingly recognized, no comprehensive analysis of the interdependence of the different parts of the industry had been attempted. In order to demonstrate the extent of this interdependence the Office produced a flow chart for the year 1968. This chart showed the inter-sectoral flows between some thirty sectors, from raw materials to end-products such as clothing, carpets, household textiles, etc., and also showed imports, exports and flows to and from other industries. The flows were recorded in lbs. weight throughout, except for end-uses where only value figures were available.

4.   Data for the flow chart were built up from many different sources, including official and trade association statistics, consultants' reports, and, most importantly, estimates provided by companies and individuals. Considerable interest was shown in the original chart for 1968 and the Office therefore decided to revise and update the chart, incorporating data for 1969 and 1970. A display version incorporating the three years' data was published in 1972.[1] Since the later versions became increasingly complex we have chosen to reproduce here for illustrative purposes the original chart. (Pages 204–5.)

5.   Some of those who had worked on the flow chart from the beginning had always envisaged that, as well as being a useful display and educational tool, it might form the basis for the construction of a model that could be used to calculate the effects on the industry of changes in the pattern of demand, including the pattern of foreign trade, of shifts in the relative attractions of different fibres and processes (i.e. their 'competitiveness'), and of technological developments of all kinds. Experimental work on model construction began towards the end of 1971, and by mid-1972 was sufficiently advanced for the Office to be able to recommend its use by the J.T.C. for the 1971–77 medium-term review.

6.   The objective of the model is to provide a mechanism for the calculation of the impact of the various changes listed above on the

[1] *Flow Chart of the U.K. Textile Industry, 1968–70.* Obtainable from N.E.D.O. Publications Department, Millbank Tower, Millbank, London SW1P 4QX. Price: £1.25 (by post £1.50).

demand for the products of the 'intermediate' or processing sectors of the textile industry, measured in volume (weight) terms. A short description of the main features of the model is given in the next section of this paper, which concludes with brief comments on some of the detailed aspects of developing and running the model.

A Description of the Model

7. The main concept of the model is simply to take an assumed set of home and export demands for the final products of the industry, and to work backwards through the processing sectors, maintaining specified ratios ('technical coefficients') between the various inputs to each sub-sector. This basic idea is complicated by a number of additional features, including:

(a) imports of intermediate and final products;
(b) stock changes;
(c) re-use of waste and by-products within the industry or by other industries;
(d) process losses.

8. It has been possible to develop a mathematical structure to handle all these special features,[1] but certain data problems remain, and these are discussed later in the paper. The model has been programmed in FORTRAN and operates on a C.D.C. 6500 computer. Operation is mainly in a remote time-sharing conversational mode to permit rapid data checking and correction, but card-reading and line-printing facilities at the computer centre are used when large amounts of input or output are required.

9. An obvious way of constructing a detailed input-output model for a particular industry would be by expansion of the relevant rows and columns of a *national* input-output model. It was decided not to do this, but to construct an independent model, for three reasons:

(a) a reasonably up-to-date national model was not available at the time;
(b) national models can only be updated from quinquennial census data, whereas the N.E.D.O. model uses data available annually;
(c) a national model would impose additional requirements for projection of final demands and technical coefficients for the non-textile sectors.

---

[1] The Office intends to publish a paper on the mathematics of the model in due course.

Flow chart of the U.K. textile industry, 1968

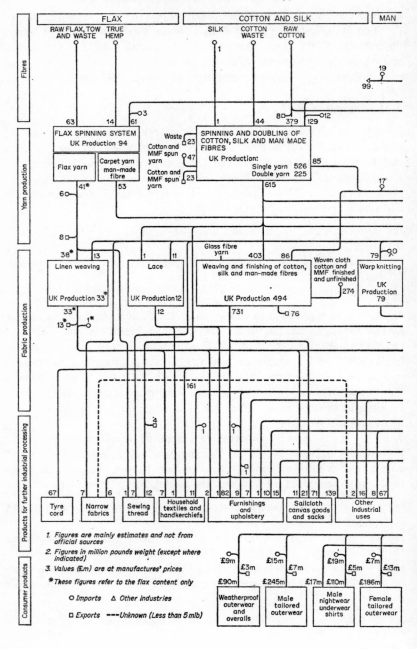

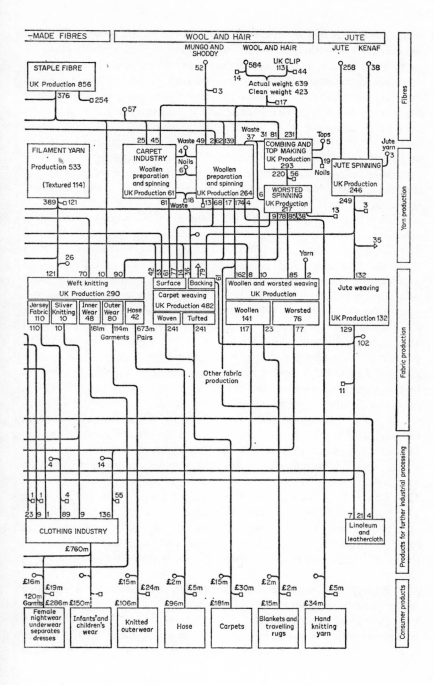

10. The layout of the various matrices in the model differs somewhat in appearance from that found in national models since it contains quite large 'final demand' and 'primary input' matrices in addition to the main square matrix for the manufacturing sectors. The final demand matrix covers all flows from the industry to outside sectors, including exports, stock changes (see paragraph 19) and sales to other industries as well as home sales of final textile products. The primary input matrix covers inputs to the industry from outside, including home and imported raw materials, man-made fibres, and inputs from other industries. (This method of dealing with the relationship to other industries was chosen instead of maintaining an 'other industry' sector in the main square matrix, because the homogeneity of output of 'other industry' implied by the latter method would have led to error.)

11. There has been considerable further disaggregation of sectors since the flow chart was prepared, mainly because of differences in input ratios. For example, cotton and man-made fibre spinning and doubling has been disaggregated into yarn for tyre cord, carpets, knitting and 'other' (largely cotton and man-made fibre weaving), since the proportions of cotton, staple fibre and filament fibre consumed are markedly different for each of these end-users. A full list of the primary, intermediate (i.e. processing) and final demand sectors is given in Appendix A, and it will be seen from this list that in addition to disaggregating existing sectors it has been necessary to add three new flows: polypropylene (mainly in its use as a substitute for jute in carpet backing); plastics and foam backing materials (also used in carpets); and staple for non-woven carpets. These additional flows are necessary in order to establish the input-output balances in weight terms, and to eliminate differences which might otherwise wrongly be ascribed to stock changes.

12. *Import* flows can be handled within the model in several ways. For each commodity they can be specified as absolute quantities, or as a proportion of total domestic demand for the commodity, or in relation to the individual output levels of each user sector. Moreover, the three methods can be mixed, with some flows being specified in each way.

13. *Exports* are exogenous to the model, and have to be specified independently as absolute quantities.

14. *Re-cycled waste products* are important (up to 10 per cent, and sometimes more) for certain sectors. With assistance from the Shirley Institute, estimates of re-cycled waste have been prepared as a basis

for calculating coefficients, as have estimates of irrecoverable *process losses*, which also have to be taken account of in establishing input-output balances.

Using the Model

15. A model of this type provides a method of determining sectoral outputs which is rather different from conventional methods. The latter generally consist of individual market studies for each manufacturing sector of an industry: by contrast, an input-output model concentrates on the *purchasing* behaviour of each sector, exogenous information on the demand side being required only for the end-products of the industry. To run the model, therefore, information is required on changes in technical coefficients, and on final demands including exports. The concluding section of this paper is mainly concerned with problems arising in preparing this information.

Projecting technical coefficients

16. The model team was unusually fortunate in having available the Shirley Institute's Delphi study[1] giving forecasts of types of fabric formation and patterns of fibre consumption by the U.K. industry in 1980. Some difficult problems were encountered in matching Shirley and N.E.D.O. base year data, and in taking account of the Shirley respondents' views of the net future trade position, about which the study is unclear. However, with the aid of further technical advice from institutions and companies in the industry it proved possible to construct a set of coefficients for 1980, from which coefficients for 1977 were obtained by interpolation.

Projecting final demand

17. For the 1971–77 medium-term review, the Office has used alternative illustrative average annual rates of growth of G.D.P. over the period 1972–77 of 3½ per cent and 5 per cent, together with appropriate values of other macro-economic variables, and in collaboration with Cambridge University Department of Applied Economics, it has prepared corresponding sets of projections of 1977 relative prices and consumers' expenditure.

18. The end product sectors used in the model (see Appendix A and the table below) are more detailed than the consumers' expenditure

---

[1] *The U.K. Textile Industry in 1980.* A technological forecast made using a modification of the Delphi technique. The Shirley Institute, Manchester M20 8RX, 1972. Price: £40.

categories. Most of them can, however, be linked to consumers' expenditure or to G.D.P. The following table shows the methods used to derive future demand for end products:

Product	Method used
1 Tyre cord	Independent[a]
2 Narrow fabrics	$\frac{2}{3}$ clothing; $\frac{1}{3}$ G.D.P.
3 Sewing thread	$\frac{3}{5}$ clothing; $\frac{1}{5}$ consumer expenditure; $\frac{1}{5}$ independent[a]
4 Household textiles	% of household textiles and hardware[b]
5 Furnishings and upholstery	$\frac{4}{5}$ household textiles and hardware:[b] $\frac{1}{5}$ as % of G.D.P.
6 Canvas goods and sacks	% of G.D.P.
7 Apparel (made-up clothing)	% of clothing[c]
8 and 9 Knitted garments and hose	% of clothing[c]
10, 11, 12 and 13 Carpets	Independent[a]
14 Blankets	Independent[a]
15 Hand-knitting yarns	Independent[a]
16 Lino and leathercloth	% of G.D.P.
17 Other industrial uses	G.D.P.

Notes (a) 'Independent' means that the forecast has been prepared independently of the consumers' expenditure projections, in consultation with industry sources.

(b) 'Household textiles and hardware' is the breakdown given in the consumers' expenditure projections. The two components and the totals have moved closely together in the past.

(c) These items together constitute 'clothing' in the consumers' expenditure projections.

Stocks

19. We have adopted the standard treatment of stocks in input-output models, which is to regard an increase in the stock of a commodity, whether in the hands of suppliers or of users, as part of the final demand on the suppliers of the commodity. When calculating technical coefficients from past data, the inputs and outputs are, in principle, first converted for stock change in order to give the true inputs to, and outputs from, each manufacturing process. In practice, however, the data are, for most sectors, insufficiently detailed for this purpose. It was at first thought that one could assume that the residual differences between inputs and outputs were due to stock changes. However the accumulated errors from all sources also appear in these

residuals, and these appear larger than the feasible stock changes. It has therefore been thought more important to adjust the data in order to eliminate or minimize these residuals, using the assumption that cumulative stock changes over the three base years were relatively small. Clearly, this is an area where better statistical information will be required for future studies.

Cyclical fluctuations

20.   As is well known, the textile industry is subject to marked cyclical fluctuations with the added complication that the periodicity is not the same in all sectors of the industry. In practice, these fluctuations are apparent in input-output models through stock changes. For analysis of past data, corrections as outlined above should be made. For forward projection, the method will depend on whether path or trend projections are required. For a path projection it would be necessary to supply, exogenously, the detailed cyclical pattern of future stock changes for each commodity. For a trend projection, as required for the present study, only the trend change in stocks need be supplied, and for most sectors there is no evidence to support making this other than zero.

Conclusion

21.   We believe that the input-output model affords the best chance of developing an objective pan-textile approach to medium-term forecasting of output and inter-sectoral flows. It has the merit of making explicit all the assumptions on which it is based, including those on technological changes, changes in the competitiveness of fibres and processes, and changes in the pattern of final demand and overseas trade. There are inevitable data problems, but it should be borne in mind that other methods of forecasting for this industry would have to make use of the same data sources.

22.   The model clearly has further development potential, including, in addition to regular up-dating, such areas as forming links to national input-output models, and the inclusion of cyclical factors.

Appendix

SECTORS IN THE MODEL

End products
   Tyre cord
   Narrow fabrics

Sewing thread
Household textiles
Furnishings and upholstery
Sailcloth, canvas, sacks, etc.
Apparel (made-up clothing)
Knitted innerwear
Knitted outerwear
Hose
Tufted carpets
Woven carpets
Non-woven carpets
Blankets and rugs
Hand-knitting yarn
Lino and leathercloth
Other industries
Exports
Stock change and discrepancy

Textile processes
Flax spinning for carpets
Flax spinning, other
Cotton and man-made fibre spinning for carpets
Cotton and man-made fibre spinning for knitting
Cotton and man-made fibre spinning for tyre cord
Cotton and man-made fibre spinning, other
Wool scouring
Wool topmaking for knitting
Wool topmaking for export
Wool topmaking, other
Carpet yarn spinning
Wool spinning for carpets
Wool spinning, other
Worsted spinning for knitting
Worsted spinning, other
Jute spinning
Linen weaving
Lace making
Cotton and man-made fibre weaving for tyre cord
Cotton and man-made fibre weaving for clothing
Cotton and man-made fibre weaving, other
Warp knitting

Weft knitting, jersey fabric
Weft knitting, sliver
Weft knitting, innerwear
Weft knitting, outerwear
Weft knitting, hose
Carpet manufacture, tufted
Carpet manufacture, woven
Carpet manufacture, non-woven
Woollen weaving
Worsted weaving
Jute weaving
Clothing industry

Primary inputs
Raw flax
True hemp
Silk
Cotton waste
Raw cotton
Man-made fibre staple, synthetic
Man-made fibre staple, cellulosic
Man-made fibre filament, synthetic
Man-made fibre filament, cellulosic
Mungo and shoddy
Wool and hair
Jute
Kenaf
Wool waste
Polypropylene
Non-textile inputs

10: The D.T.I. Energy Model

F. W. Hutber

I. Introduction

1.   The Energy Model Group was formed in 1967 by the Ministry of Power (now part of the Department of Trade and Industry). It now constitutes a branch of one of the six Economics and Statistics divisions of the Department of Trade and Industry and this branch is concerned with Energy and Steel statistics. On energy matters the division services the four main policy divisions concerned with coal, oil, gas and electricity as well as advising the Atomic Energy division and the Fuel and Nationalized Industry Policy divisions. With the addition of one further division, Energy Technology division, it can be seen that a total of eight full divisions are responsible in various ways for advising the Minister for Industry on energy policy decisions.

2.   The problem of co-ordinating the work of such a large group poses problems, not least of which is that of ensuring that the effect of decisions in one sector on the other sectors is realized and accounted for. It was in this climate of interacting sectors that the idea of the Energy Model was conceived. The scale of the area being modelled is large, covering 13 per cent of total domestic expenditure and 8 per cent of gross domestic fixed capital formation, and is second only in size to the modelling of the national economy by the Treasury. Further, since the model is expected to contribute to individual decisions in each sector, the modelling system has to operate at the micro- as well as the macro-level of analysis. Whether this can be achieved within a unified system of modelling must be judged from the results reported below.

II. Objectives

3.   The long-term aim of the Model Group is to produce a computable model of the U.K. energy economy that balances supply and demand by fuel in each market in time. By time we mean future time and we expect the model to resolve the system for current problems or problems a single year ahead, in the medium-term (from now to five or ten years

212

ahead) as well as the long-term (from now to thirty years ahead). A single modelling system may not be found to perform all these functions efficiently so that if different structures are specified for the different time-scales then the results from them must be compatible in the broad sense that one result may be interpreted in terms of others.

4. A statement of the objectives should not be passed without identifying the needs that they are intended to satisfy. One of these has already been mentioned—co-ordination of fuel industry policy. Another is the reconciliation of the investment proposals of the energy industries—making sure that the sum of the parts does not exceed the anticipated total investment in energy and determining where any adjustment is needed. The re-alignment of national and corporate interest is required from time to time when perhaps some national economic or social development makes it necessary to modify the commercial judgement of one particular industry. This can sometimes be achieved indirectly by the manipulation of some regulator such as a tax, thus conserving the freedom of commercial judgement of the industries concerned. At other times, due to the lack of a suitable regulator, direct intervention can be justified in the national interest. The effect of such variation may be demonstrated with a suitable model structure by modifying the basis of the data set used and/or objective function to suit the specific need and then evaluating an optimal solution obtained by the use of one data set in terms of another data set.

III. Structure of the Model

5. For the purposes of the supply side of the energy sector it is regarded as comprising four main industries—coal, petroleum, electricity and gas—which either individually or in combination take primary energy in the form of coal, oil, natural gas, nuclear fuel, hydro power, etc. and sell it to final consumers in the form of the fuel products that they require. The flow of fuels from their primary sources direct or through the secondary processing industries to the final consumers is illustrated in Figure 1. There the outer ring represents the primary fuels, the next ring the conversion to products in the required form and the inner circle the final consumers. Costs can be regarded as building up in the same directions as fuel products move, whilst expenditures flow in the opposite direction.

6. The current experimental version of the integrated model of the energy economy consists basically of five sub-models, namely a demand

sub-model and four supply models, one for each of the main fuel industries. Demand for energy depends mainly on relationships outside the energy sector such as growth of the national economy, industrial production and consumers' expenditure. The share for each fuel depends principally on the price asked, and this in turn depends on the cost of

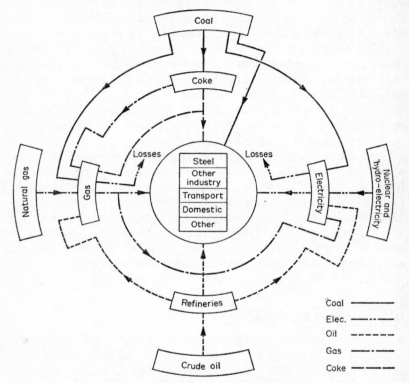

Fig. 1. Structure of the energy sector.

supply and is affected by the scale of protection for indigenous fuels in the form of taxes, subsidies and import controls.

7. The supply sub-models calculate the unit costs of meeting the demand in terms of the capital expenditure, operating costs and manpower required. To do this, they are provided with general information as to the prices of materials, the level of wage rates and the costs and performance of various factors of production that might be used to meet the demand. It will be seen that the operation of the energy model is in the form of the closed loop illustrated in Figure 2 and the

interchange of information between the demand and supply sub-models is the essential feature of the balancing process so that either the sub-models have to be used simultaneously or sequentially in iterative fashion to obtain a solution.

8. Our approach has been to build the model in sections (the sub-models) each with its own project group enabling the work to proceed

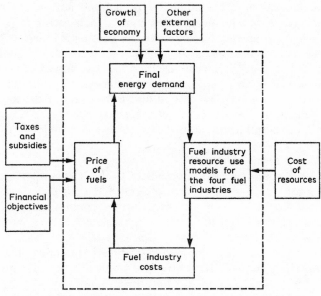

Fig. 2. Diagram of the energy sector model.

on a broad front and using a sixth project group to develop the control and integration side of the model work as a whole. The gas, electricity and coal supply models have been developed in considerable detail. The oil model is still in a rudimentary state and is used with simplified models of the other industries in the integration experiments. The form of development adopted has a number of advantages:

(i) it enables the overall time-scale for construction to be shortened;
(ii) it induces expertise in the project group in one of the fuel industries as well as in the modelling techniques used;
(iii) whatever the outcome of the integrated energy model research we have created with the detailed sub-models a worthwhile analytical capacity for the individual industries concerned.

M T—H

IIIA. The demand sub-model

9. The demand sub-model is the main link with the national economic variables which are exogenous to the energy model. It is a regression type model and a technical description is given in the Appendix. The original concept of the demand model was one in which an assumed growth in the national economy as a whole could be interpreted by means of a set of activity indicators into total energy demands in each sector of the economy. This unified approach has not proved satisfactory and currently total energy demand in each sector is projected individually by the method found to be best suited to the historic behaviour and the data available, which is not consistently good. This 'bottom up' approach is then checked against forecasts using the macro-indicators such as G.D.P. for consistency before arriving at the final values to be used. The second and third parts of the model are the determination of desired market shares and the lagged relationship between desired and actual market shares.

IIIB. The gas supply sub-model

10. The gas supply industry consists of twelve virtually autonomous Area Boards.[1] In 1971 nearly 90 per cent of the gas sold was natural gas, mainly from the North Sea, entering the country through only a few terminals. The production side of the industry is represented by a single geographical area or point model.

11. The modelling technique used is linear programming. The model considers mainly the activities of the Gas Council such as the purchase, transmission and storage of gas and goes as far as the bulk supply points to Area Boards. The distribution costs are taken into account by adding a cost per therm to the other supply costs. The industry has major choices that it can make, for instance in building more pipeline, storage facilities or capital-intensive gas plant to meet the winter peak. The cost of each individual activity (such as building a plant, running it, buying gas from the North Sea producers or elsewhere) is known or assumed, as are the quantitative relationships between the constraints on these activities.

12. More detailed local distribution and service activities of the Area Boards are represented by a separate regression type model. These activities are characterized by a large number of individual investment decisions, each one leading to an expenditure on a much smaller scale than any in the production model described above, although they add

---

[1] From the end of 1972, the Area Boards' responsibilities have been combined in the Gas Corporation.

up in total to two-thirds of the total cost of supply. The local distribution expenditures are related to appropriate levels of activity in the industry (such as annual demand, peak demand, and the number of consumers) as well as the available data will allow. These costs are not as clearly defined or as easily estimated as those in the bulk production model.

IIIC. The electricity supply sub-model

13. The Electricity Supply Industry consists of twelve Area Boards which supply consumer service and distribute electricity purchased in bulk from the Central Electricity Generating Board (C.E.G.B.). Our model represents the C.E.G.B. and covers the generating of electricity in England and Wales. It is basically a linear programming model and there are two versions of it, one modelling investment decisions, the other modelling the detailed operation of the system in a single year. The essential difference is to be found in the type of problem it is intended to resolve. Investment decisions are essentially long time-scale decisions involving plant lives of thirty years or more, so that some detail on the system definition can be sacrificed for detail in the time dimension. Thus the investment model is a single geographical area or point model seeing in the time dimension one coal supply area and a crude grouping of power stations by fuel type, efficiency, etc., whereas the operations model (called the Electricity, Coal, Transport or E.C.T. model) sees fifteen coal supply areas, a larger number of power station groups which allows for grouping by geographical location, and a transportation matrix to connect them.

The two models interact in such a way that a system description has to be determined before the E.C.T. model can be used and this may be generated by the investment model. Conversely, the E.C.T. model can be thought of as producing cross-section data for the investment model provided that they work in dimensions essentially orthogonal to one another.

IIID. The coal supply sub-model

14. The coal supply model is a straightforward data processing programme which unbundles the latest available cost structure of the National Coal Board (N.C.B.) and then reassembles the data for a future year with new projected productivity values obtained exogenously. This type of programme is conditioned by the contraction of the industry in that the dependent parameters are the productivity and the latest tranche of output due for closure. This type of analysis is done

for each area, fifteen in all, to produce supply tranches for the E.C.T. model. The electricity-generating industry currently accounts for over 50 per cent of the total consumption of coal so that the view is taken that electricity generation takes all marginal coal. Other markets of domestic and coking coals are taken as prior demands on the industry to be met first before general purpose coal is made available to the electricity industry.

IIIE. The oil supply sub-model

15. The oil model has not yet been developed to the same extent as the sub-models previously described for the following reasons. The previous three sections describe supply models for fuels which are indigenous to the U.K. and the national fuel policy as such determines the framework within which the industries operate. For oil, the supply is determined by international markets and by the price of crude oil ruling in them at the time. Until recently, the combination of crude oil price and charter rates kept the landed price of crude oil steady enough for us to employ a simple 'tap' supply model in which it is assumed that unlimited quantities of oil are available at the ruling market price. Changes in the international oil scene although controlled by renegotiable agreements between participants at regular five-year intervals make longer-term estimates of oil prices more uncertain and the tap model less credible so that an improved representation of oil supply is now necessary. Until the new model is available, the results from our energy sub-models are therefore very dependent on the quality of the advice on the oil price and quantity available fed to it exogenously.

IV. Integration

16. Given the sectoral basis of the models, our first approach to integration was a modular one. A system was designed to run the various sub-models in turn starting with the demand module and transferring information on prices and quantities between them after each sub-model had been run. At the end of a complete pass through all the sub-models, the price generated by the gas model, for example, will be different from the price assumed by the demand model, when it was run. An additional control module was devised to choose a new price which would try to reconcile the difference on the next pass. Similarly, the other supply sub-models have generated prices which will need to be reconciled with the demand model. The combined effect

of these will require an alteration to the market shares in the demand model. A complex multidimensional search problem is thus created.

17. There are two major problems with this method of integration:

(a) will it converge?
(b) the expense of running it to convergence.

No guarantee can be given that the technique described will reach a solution which will satisfy the demand and supply models jointly. It would appear plausible, given the inbuilt sluggishness in the response of demand to price changes, that such a solution would exist but this is not certain. On cost, a large number of what may be very expensive iterations could be required before a satisfactory solution is obtained.

18. A pilot study of this area was undertaken with very simplified supply models which shed light on both these problems. The main objective of the study was to examine properties of various convergence strategies which attempted to select improved values for the prices. Even with simplified supply models, the system took over ten iterations to converge to anything approaching a compatible set of quantities and prices and was found to be an expensive system to run. With more representative supply models, the system may take even longer to settle down.

19. At about this time, a new system for building L.P. models (the matrix generator generator) became available which encouraged the team involved to look at the possibility of producing an integrated fuel sector model within the framework of a single L.P. The difficulty in achieving this centred mainly on the problem of formulating the demand model in L.P. terms. The first approach was to tranche the demand curves and give each tranche a fixed preference for the four fuels. This approach has many difficulties, not least the problem of developing a price *difference* tranche structure for a price *ratio* model. Attempts to resolve this problem led to a parameterized separable programme in which a parameter in the model is adjusted until an equilibrium is reached. However, if the demand model could be expressed in price difference terms as opposed to price ratio terms, the parameterization would be unnecessary. The full development of this latter model has not been completed.

20. Linear programming has the disadvantage that the models are relatively complex, they are expensive to run and the results can be difficult to explain. A simpler approach is the econometric or projective type of model in which the optimizing power of L.P. is abandoned during the course of the iterative run.

21. The supply equations used must reflect the resource allocations that are to be made but these may be computed externally to the integrated run by means of a survey of the possibilities so that the cost, quantity, time space can be represented by a small number of parameters. This approach would be valid for problems that involved the normal market price mechanism, even with regulators, provided they operated across the board as is usually the case, but clearly distortions caused by differential subsidies on tranches of supply could not be represented without carrying out a special survey. It seems likely that such a macro-econometric model would require a special set of 'interpretative' runs on an L.P. model to generate the precise implications of the macro-model solution.

V. Conclusions

22. There is little doubt that the construction of an integrated model of the energy economy is feasible. The component sub-models have been developed to the point of being used separately by policy makers on analytical work in aid of policy decisions. Our experiments on modular integration though successful in achieving convergence lead us to believe that at the level of complexity of the developed sub-models the cost of execution is too high for it to be used widely. The integrated L.P. has emerged as a result of finding this out and about a further man-year's work is required before we know whether the resolution of the simplified structure is adequate for policy determination. We propose to press on with the development of an econometric type macro-model as this holds out the hope of dealing with the major technical obstacle — size — and therefore the cost of operation.

Appendix
TECHNICAL DESCRIPTION OF THE DEMAND SUB-MODEL

The total final demand for energy to final users is broken down into nine sectors:

> Domestic
> Iron and Steel
> Other Industry
> Public Administration
> Miscellaneous and Agriculture

> Transport—Rail
> Transport—Road
> Transport—Water
> Transport—Air

Demands for primary fuels to be converted to secondary forms of energy are not considered.

Choice of Model. The form of model used has been largely dictated by the following considerations about the nature of the problem:

1. The determinants of the behaviour of fuel consumers are not known. The method used to investigate them is basically an empirical one. It is assumed that at least part of this behaviour of consumers will give some useful information about the nature of the processes involved and that this information can be applied directly or extrapolated for useful application in the future.
2. It is further assumed that the systematic aspects of consumer behaviour can be described by a mathematical model and that this model can be chosen on the basis of its capacity to represent those features believed to be important in the field.

The form adopted for the model has been further influenced by the nature of available data. All relevant historical data available on a consistent basis is highly aggregated although it is disaggregated as far as the principal sectors of the fuel economy—Domestic, Industry, Commercial, Public Administration, Transport. Differences between these markets as regards fuel purchasing behaviour are expected but they are thought to be differences of degree rather than of the underlying mechanism. To represent this, the structure consists of models of identical form for each sector but with parameters varying between sectors. For technical reasons the Transport sector and the Iron and Steel industry cannot be represented satisfactorily by the selected model form.

Although the estimation of models of the type used is based on consistent time series data, reliable estimation of any parameters by alternative means will tend to improve the remaining estimates [1]. The possibility of such alternative estimation using census data such as that obtained by the Family Expenditure Survey has been examined and the initial indications are promising although results from this approach have not yet been adopted.

The Model. The model is in three parts.

Initially, the total energy demand within a sector, E, is expressed as a function of an activity indicator, A, for the sector, the average price of fuel, P, calculated as a weighted average and the temperature, T. In addition, any time trend in the total energy series is estimated by the use of a trend variable, t, whose value increases by 0 in each successive time period. t is also used as a suffix to indicate the time period to which any particular observation on any variable relates. The form used for the total energy demand equation is then

$$E_t = a_0 A_t^{a_1} P_t^{a_2} T_t^{a_3} e^{a_4 t} \qquad (1)$$

which is preferred to the linear alternative

$$E_t = b_0 + b_1 A_t + b_2 P_t + b_3 T_t + b_4 t \qquad (2)$$

partly on intuitive grounds and partly because empirical investigation suggests that it tends to perform better. (The a_i and b_i are constants varying only between the sectors. e is a known constant$=2\cdot7183$.) The second part of the model examines the unrestrained or ideal choice of fuel for given total energy. This is distinguished from the actual choice of fuel and represents the choice which consumers would make if they were able to adjust their purchasing behaviour immediately, without the lag imposed in practice by considerations of buying and installing equipment. The model form suggests that the quantity of any fuel, q_i^*, which would be purchased is determined essentially by the price of the fuel, p_i, with reference to a price response factor, θ, which is assumed the same for all fuels.

$$q_{it}^* = A_i p_{it}^{-\theta} \qquad (3)$$

The constant A_i represents the effect of non-price factors. The importance of certain of these to the work done with the model and the possible opportunity for improving explanation in terms of measurable variables has suggested removal from this term of economic activity for the sector measured by a suitable indicator, I_t, and any time trend present in q_i^*. The A_i continues to represent the effects of advertising, taste, convenience and other factors and equation (3) becomes

$$q_{it}^* = A_t P_{it}^{-\theta} I_t^{b_i} c_i^t \qquad (4)$$

with the responses to activity and time assumed to be fuel specific.

Changes in q_{it}^* will be constrained by changes both in total energy demand and in demands for other fuels. These effects are incorporated by transforming the relationship (4) to that determining the corresponding market share.

If total ideal demand is Q_t, then

$$Q_t = \sum_{\text{all } i} q_{it}{}^*$$

and $r^*_{it} = \dfrac{q_{it}{}^*}{Q_t}$ where $r_{it}{}^*$ is the ideal share of fuel i at time t.

Equation (4) then becomes

$$r_{it}{}^* = \frac{A_i p_{it}^{-\theta} I_{ik}^{b_i} c_i^t}{\sum\limits_{\text{all } j} A_j p_{jt}^{-\theta} I_i^{b_j} c_j^t} \tag{5}$$

Ideal shares are not observable and their behaviour must be deduced from that of actual shares. To do this the third part of the model is brought into use with actual shares, r_i, in time periods t and $t-1$ assumed related by

$$r_{it} = (r_{it-1})^\sigma (r_{it}{}^*)^{1-\sigma} \tag{6}$$

which implies that purchasing behaviour is adjusted towards the ideal share but at a rate determined by the parameter ϕ which allows for the fact that only a certain proportion of consumers will change their fuel-using equipment in any one year. An alternative mechanism which has been experimented with is

$$r_{it} = \phi r_{it-1} + (1-\phi) r_{it}{}^* \tag{7}$$

but this has been found generally less useful than (6). In the remainder of the discussion (6) and (7) are referred to as Model 2 and Model 1 respectively.

ϕ is assumed to be the same for each fuel and

$$\sum_{\text{all } i} r_{it}{}^* = \sum_{\text{all } i} r_{it-1} = \sum_{\text{all } i} r_{it} = 1$$

Units. Use of market shares means that fuel demand data must be prepared in terms of common units and those used are useful therms, calculated from consumptions measured in original units by use of thermal contents and efficiencies. The thermal contents are physical constants but efficiency factors depend upon assumptions about the population of fuel-using appliances in each sector and the conditions under which they work. A future application of the model will be improvement of the approximate efficiencies used at present.

Regression. The technique used for the analyses is multiple linear regression. This is described extensively in numerous sources, e.g. [2], [3], and is not explained here.

Linearization. The use of multiple regression requires linearization of the model functions and addition of a stochastic term to the specified relationship to allow for non-systematic variations in the dependent variables. In the case of relation (1) this can be done directly by assuming a multiplicative stochastic effect and expressing the relation as a linear structure in logarithms. If the stochastic term is represented by u, then (1) becomes

$$E_t = a_0 A_t^{a_1} P_t^{a_2} T_t^{a_3} e^{a_4 t} u_t \tag{8}$$

and in logarithms this becomes

$$\log E_t = \log a_0 + a_1 \log A_t + a_2 \log P_t + a_3 \log T_t + a_4 t + \log u_t \tag{9}$$

In following the same procedure for equation (6), r_{it}^* must be removed since it is not measurable. This is done by substituting equation (5), giving

$$\log r_{it} = \phi \log r_{it-1} + (1-\phi) \log \left[\frac{A_i p_{it}^{-\theta} I_t^{b_i} c_i^t}{\sum\limits_{\text{all } j} A_j p_{ji}^{-\theta} I_t^{b_j}] c_j^t} \right] \tag{10}$$

which is not linear in the logarithms of the observed variables. To overcome this relation (11) is constructed as a log ratio of the shares of any two fuels in the form

$$\log \left[\frac{r_{it}}{r_{kt}} \right] = \phi \log \left[\frac{r_{it-1}}{r_{kt-1}} \right] + (1-\phi) \log \left[\frac{A_i}{A_k} \right] - \theta (1-\phi) \log \left[\frac{p_{it}}{p_{kt}} \right]$$
$$+ (b_i - b_k)(1-\phi) \log I_t + (1-\phi) \log \left[\frac{c_i}{c_k} \right] t \tag{11}$$

and a stochastic term added to this.

Such a transformation cannot be made directly in the case of relation (7) and the equivalent reformation of this used is

$$\log \left[\frac{r_{it} - \phi r_{it-1}}{r_{kt} - \phi r_{kt-1}} \right] = \log \left[\frac{A_i}{A_k} \right] - \theta \log \left[\frac{p_{it}}{p_{kt}} \right]$$
$$+ (b_i - b_k) \log I_t + \log \left[\frac{c_i}{c_k} \right] t \tag{12}$$

in which one unknown parameter (ϕ) appears on the left-hand side. In estimating this relation regressions are carried out for each of a number of ϕ values and the 'best' value of ϕ and the other coefficients deduced from a consideration of the various statistical measures.

Estimation. Consideration of relations (11) and (12) shows that for any number of fuels there will be only a limited number of ratios from which valid information can be derived. For the four fuels examined in our studies, only three ratios will yield independent results. Further, if as assumed, the parameters ϕ and θ are the same for all fuels, their values should be obtained more efficiently by pooling the data for all three ratios in the estimation of these quantities. For estimation by regression special variables must be constructed to allow for the fuel-specific responses to the other variables.

References

1. DURBIN, J.   A Note on Regression when there is Extraneous Information about one of the Variables, *J.A.S.A.*, **48**, 1953, pp. 799–808.
2. JOHNSTON, J.   *Econometric Methods*, New York, McGraw-Hill, 1963.
3. DRAPER, N. R. and SMITH, H.   *Applied Regression Analysis*, New York, Wiley, 1967.

11: Report of the Discussion

The Textile Industry Model

'The model we are presenting here is being used to assist the N.E.D.O. textile committee in answering questions posed by the medium-term assessment.

'Like other committees, we are given the general growth rates, and the total figure for private consumption: that is, alternative figures for private sector demand are our starting point. We are also supplied with certain supporting assumptions—a world trade assumption, and something on how the UK's competitiveness might be sustained. These assumptions may not be wholly satisfactory; but they do not in our view prevent us from getting somewhere in consideration of the textile industries' future. We then form views of the rates of growth for different areas of the textile home market. This, as the paper shows, was done in a variety of ways. One point of interest is that the direct links to clothing consumption are really quite limited; there are large numbers of other areas of consumption, where we have had to use other relationships.

'We then form a view about the likely development of export demand, allowing for entry to the E.E.C.; we also take a view about imports; and from these views, we draw out our set of U.K. output figures. I say "form a view" deliberately; the use that one can make of historical data for some of these sectors is limited. For example, on imports, the most significant factor is the likely international control regime for trade in textiles. We therefore have to make some assumptions about what will be decided in G.A.T.T., and about what will happen to the Common Market's attempt to get some common policy on textiles.

'Why develop a model? I think the flow chart may help to explain this: we are trying to understand a group of industries with a very complex set of inter-relationships. It would be very crude, for example, to make an estimate of the output of fabrics woven from cotton and man-made fibres just by relationship to clothing. Output also goes to five other industries, apart from exports. We really could not allow for this without a model.

'The model is only just beginning to be used; and there is a long period of development ahead. We want to use it to give us calculations about output, and also the resources required on the labour side. We

226

do know something about employment and productivity in the various sectors, so we can do something about labour requirements.

'We expect to be able to come to some useful supply side conclusions, pointing to some areas of excess supply, because of the lags of adjustment of output to demand, and other areas of shortage.'

It was explained that the decision to construct a model working in physical units, and independent of any national input-output model, was taken largely on grounds of data availability, and to avoid the need for detailed work on non-textile sectors. However the use of physical units brought its own problems, in connection with stock changes, process losses, etc.

In the discussion of the textile model, the following points were raised:

(a) It was interesting that the input-output analysis could be conducted in weights (though surely the weights used should have been kilograms rather than pounds). Were there other industries for which this approach could be used? It was suggested that it might be possible with the chemicals industry; and it was pointed out that it was possible to have a model in which different units are used in different cells—for example an input-output model of the car industry which gives the square yards of upholstery fabric used per car.

(b) More ambitious uses were suggested for an input-output analysis of this kind. 'Could one use it for an optimizing process? What would we need, and how would we get it? Essentially, we would need to build up information on comparative advantages. For the various cells, it should be possible to get added values from the Census of Production; and possibly also to attach manpower figures to these cells. Then it would be interesting to analyse imports in terms of the manpower required by corresponding British production. Some of the cells are very large; how far would it be possible to break them down into more detailed qualities or specifications—though it would not be possible to do this from the Census? So I am envisaging a study which might give greater detail on types of cloth and yarns, and would add average values for production and imports. This should make an optimizing study possible, establishing in which sections of textiles British industry has a comparative advantage.'

(c) There was some discussion of the problem of changing technical coefficients. This could follow from the very big movements which have occurred in the relative prices of raw materials; from changes in techniques of production; and from amalgamations in industry. The authors commented:

'We have certainly thought about this. The purpose of the Delphi study (see page 207) was to study changes in the coefficients. The Delphi study which we used was conducted two years ago, and in consulting industry we find that the coefficients suggested there are already felt to be out of date; and we have agreed to change some of them. There has to be a constant updating exercise here. This is one of our comparative advantages—that we have continuous contact with industry, where a number of people are expressing substantial interest in our model.

'Certainly there are large areas of uncertainty. In using the model, we can do sensitivity analysis, running the model with alternative parameters. The Delphi studies produced results in the form of a distribution of opinions; we can use these as well.

'We have taken account of the emergence of big companies in our assumptions about exports, in that there is now an increasing number of firms which require to export to maintain their scale of production.'

(d) It was suggested that in industry studies of this kind, it should be possible to find out more about some of the macro-economic questions discussed—the effect of investment incentives, and the connection between investment and productivity. Here perhaps the N.E.D.O. model of the chemical industry was more relevant, since it is a financial model; it has balance sheets, profit and loss accounts, and cash flows.

The D.T.I. Energy Model

'It is perhaps misleading to say that this is an industry paper; energy covers four major industries, whose output enters into every S.I.C. order. So it is more like a microcosm of the economy as a whole.

'Our sub-model of demand for energy is an econometric type model, using econometric type relationships derived from the recent past. This always includes the danger that there may be some "dormant" event which we shall overlook. Thus if we had made this model ten years ago, we should have been wholly wrong on gas. We build up a picture of the total demand for energy by relating it to G.D.P., to manufacturing production, and to consumers' expenditure. But we also build the picture up from the bottom, using our knowledge of the investment intentions of energy intensive industries: and the "bottom-up" method may not necessarily agree with the "top-down" method. We then break down the demand for energy between the different industries, based on our expectations of prices.

'The industries with which we are dealing are loosely coupled; but they are very much independent of each other, and have their own plans. Our job in the D.T.I. is to reconcile their plans with some overall view of the demand for energy; to protect social policies; and to avoid investment waste.

'Our model is basically the same model for the short term, the medium term, and the long term. It stretches over thirty years for a consideration of investment; with the same structure, but with different data, it will produce figures for the coal burn and oil burn next year.

'For any optimizing process, the concept of multiple goals is false; any optimizing procedure must have one objective. If you have more than one objective, then you must have a known relationship between them. One of our problems which illustrates this is the problem of dealing with social questions, such as how many miners will be put out of work, on certain assumptions about coal production? We cope with this through shadow prices for mining labour. We consider we have made great progress with resource costing; we can look at alternative futures on an accounting basis, and on a resource-costing basis, and consider policies to bring about a coincidence of the two.

'One general rule about modelling is that ninety per cent of the effort is required for ideas. The mechanics are not the problem; techniques can always be found. It is the ideas which matter. What the future is like for macro-models, I do not know; but for micro-models, the future is bright. They are proving very useful, and there is plenty of scope for development. One of the difficulties of these models is that the country's economic data collection is geared to a Keynesian world, of macro-economic intervention. For our world, we need more disaggregation. With the shift to the use of computers, it should be possible to adjust to this new world.

'Our long-term scale for forecasting is very difficult, because we have not got techniques for assessing long-term effects. For example I am not satisfied with the test discount rate; it is not satisfactory for problems of gas or oil depletion. The D.T.I. energy model is essentially a group of models, of loosely connected systems. We have tried experiments in integrating the model, but have discontinued these in order to concentrate on the individual sub-models. When you have a certain degree of decoupling between systems, you can look at one system on its own and only at a certain stage look at the connections with other decoupled systems.'

In discussion of the energy model, the following points were made:

(a) There was support for the proposition that the economic data system was essentially constructed for Keynesian macro-economic intervention; consequently the material was lacking for experimentation with more disaggregated models. The C.S.O. was beginning to provide more figures on a commodity flow basis; these should help further advances.

(b) On resource costing, it was made clear that the main adjustment was to construct a shadow price of mining labour in each of the coal fields; this was calculated by comparing the values of output of the men in employment in the mines with the value of output which they would be likely to produce if the mines were closed. This amounted to a 25 to 30 per cent discount for the regions where there are few alternative employment opportunities. There was a foreign exchange premium for imports. Open-cast mining was treated separately.

(c) For any optimization, it was noted that the D.T.I. were working with a limited degree of control over only three of the four energy industries. This limited the possibilities. Optimization necessarily means control; it always means that some group has to give way in the interest of the whole, and it is not possible to make them do so without controls.

Appendix A

1. PRODUCTIVITY IN THE PAR ECONOMY

G. D. N. Worswick

The Par economy can best be defined by a quotation from the C.E.P.G. paper above (page 73).

'The Par estimates describe the economy as it could have been in the past, or would be in the future, if demand were adjusted to maintain a steady level of unemployment (a level of 2½ per cent has been used in this study) and if U.K. producers were always sufficiently competitive to ensure a viable balance of payments and reserve position.'

It is clear, from the way in which the C.E.P.G. model is set up, that there is no feedback from the requirement of balance of payments equilibrium to the level or rate of growth of productivity, either directly, or indirectly through the level of productive investment. In the account of the variables given in Sources and Definitions to Table 1 in the Statistical Appendix, from which Par productivity is derived, there is no reference whatever to the balance of payments. In other words, the balance of payments requirement tells us how much of total output is available for consumption (public and private) and 'non-productive' investment, but does not influence total output itself. Thus dynamic theories of the Beckerman/Lamfalussy type which generate faster growth through a virtuous circle set in motion by an initial devaluation, are excluded. This is not intended as a criticism of the model, but merely to emphasize that so far as productivity is concerned, the balance of payments aspect of the Par concept is not essentially involved, and that consequently if we are interested in productivity, the study of a Par closed economy is perfectly adequate.

The Par values of output and employment, and hence of productivity, are derived from the observed values of output, employment and unemployment, with the aid of three coefficients—the elasticity of output with respect to adjusted unemployment, the elasticity of productivity with respect to adjusted unemployment, and a coefficient used in getting from actual to adjusted employment and unemployment. The two elasticity coefficients are not constant, but both decline at uniform (? linear) rates from 1960 to the average of 1972/76. (It is not clear whether the lower figure is reached in 1972 and remains constant through 1972/76 or whether the lower figure is the average for that four-year period and that the coefficient continues to decline from year to year.)

231

In the 1973 papers there is no explicit economic justification of any of the equations used or of the values of the coefficients chosen, although it is possible in a number of instances to make plausible guesses why these forms or values were chosen.

Par productivity P^* is the end product of a sequence of arithmetical calculations, and its values are recorded in the penultimate column of Table 1 of the Statistical Appendix, from which one can derive the annual percentage rates of change. If we derive these percentages we get the following results (which are also reported in the main text). The annual rate of increase is virtually constant for the first five years from 1960 to 1965 at 2·8 per cent per annum. Then between 1965 and 1966 the increase steps up to 3·3 per cent, at which level it remains again virtually constant for the next four years until 1969. At this point it steps down again to around 3·1 per cent, where it stays until 1972. No economic explanation is offered for this curious sequence, but it is clear that the authors attach importance to it, for they project Par productivity over the next four or five years to increase at only 3 per cent.

The sequence is very odd for two quite different reasons. First, productivity in this model is a somewhat shadowy concept. There is no production function: investment as such makes no appearance. One would expect, therefore, that productivity rise would be assumed to come, like manna from heaven, from technical progress, let us say, and that in the absence of any empirical evidence we would expect the postulation of a steadily increasing or decreasing annual rate of change. Par productivity, like *natura*, '*non facit saltum*'. However, the figures for Par productivity do show two sharp steps: one up, between 1965 and 1966, and a smaller one down between 1969 and 1970.

The first oddity, then, is the mere existence of sharp breaks in a rate of change which one would expect *a priori* to change smoothly, if at all. The second oddity is the dating of the actual jump. Nowadays there are two principal hypotheses about productivity in the UK, each of which attracts a number of adherents. The first is that in the late 1950s underlying productivity was rising at around 2 per cent a year, but that since then there has been a fairly steady, though not necessarily absolutely uniform, acceleration to a present rate of something over 3 per cent. One implication of this view is that the slow acceleration might continue so that in the early 1980s the underlying rate might have risen to nearer 4 per cent. The second view is that there have been two steps upward in the level of productivity, one just after 1966 and the second around 1971, with otherwise steady annual increases. These two hypotheses, of course, are not mutually exclusive. As regards the first jump, there is agreement that if it occurred, it did so after 1966, and different explanations have been offered. Reddaway has offered S.E.T. and the ending of R.P.M. for part of the service sector; others have suggested the effects of the previous investment boom or the shake-out of labour. In any case it is quite clear that there were sharp breaks in a number of time series, occurring after the 'July measures' of 1966. Whatever the truth of the existence of a jump, and whatever the explanation of it if it does exist, no one, so far as I am aware, has talked about a jump between 1965 and 1966.[1] As regards the more recent step-up, those who hold this view would be inclined to say that we shall have to wait until 1974 before we can see whether there is anything in it. But again, I know of no-one except C.E.P.G. who has put forward the idea of a step-*down*, still less offered any explanation of it. It is my suspicion that the C.E.P.G. jumps are purely accidental, the arithmetical consequences of the short cuts used to reach the Par economy estimates. They have no economic significance and certainly ought not to form the basis of any projections.

The formula used for 'adjusted' employment and unemployment
The trouble seems to originate with the formula used to 'adjust' actual employment and unemployment, namely:

$$E'_t = \lambda E_{t+1} + (1 - \lambda)E_t \tag{1}$$
$$U'_t = \lambda U_{t+1} + (1 - \lambda)U_t \tag{2}$$

where $\lambda = 0.625$

The text does not explain why this procedure is followed, but the problem is a familar one, and we can make a guess as to the reasons for it, and ask C.E.P.G. for confirmation. The notion is that if, following a period in which output has been steady for some while, there is a rise in demand and output to a new and higher level, some time must elapse before employment, and hence unemployment, are fully adjusted to the new level of output. When output rises employers will, of course, seek additional workers, but they will not be wholly successful at once, but will (somehow) nevertheless secure the additional output from the partially increased labour force. In any one year, therefore, when output is rising, actual employment will fall short of 'desired' or 'adjusted' employment, where the latter is the number of employees which would be employed to produce the given output were there sufficient time to acquire the optimal number. When output

[1] Mr. McLean's paper has a jump in 1963.

is not merely rising but accelerating there will be a tendency for actual to lag further behind desired employment. On the other hand, when the rise in output is slowing down, the gap between them will narrow. Similar reasoning can be used with respect to unemployment. The formula chosen and quoted above has the desired properties if, instead of changes in the rate of expansion of output, we start with changes in the rate of expansion of employment.

Now consider a special case and examine the performance of the equation (1) when employment is rising uniformly according to the equation $E_t = a + bt$. It follows that $E'_t = E_t + b\lambda$; that is to say, the curve of desired or adjusted employment is a straight line shifted by amount

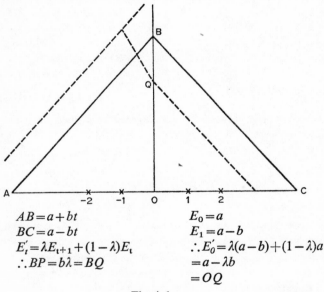

$$AB = a + bt \qquad\qquad E_0 = a$$
$$BC = a - bt \qquad\qquad E_1 = a - b$$
$$E'_t = \lambda E_{t+1} + (1-\lambda)E_t \qquad \therefore E'_0 = \lambda(a-b) + (1-\lambda)a$$
$$\therefore BP = b\lambda = BQ \qquad\qquad = a - \lambda b$$
$$= OQ$$

Fig. A.1

$b\lambda$ above the E_t line. If, on the other hand, E_t was falling along a straight line, then adjusted employment would lie below the actual employment by the same absolute amount. The question arises, in the case illustrated in the diagram (Fig. A.1), what happens if rising employment reaches a peak and is immediately followed by falling employment at the same rate. This presupposes, incidentally, that output must have reached a peak some time before. We can, of course, work out from the formula what the value of the adjusted employment in year zero would be. It gives: $E'_0 = a - b\lambda$.

Thus in one year adjusted employment has moved smartly from being above the actual employment to being below it. This gives a break in the Par productivity curve. Now essentially the notion of the desired employment is that if, after a period of rise, a particular level of output were held for some while, actual employment will gradually adjust asymptotically to the desired level. If, however, in the course of this adjustment output began to fall, it would not be reasonable to expect employers to neglect this fact and go on adjusting to the old level of output when they were already aware that it would not be sustained. Much here turns on the actual length of the lags built into the original relationship between output and employment, which had been disguised in the reduced form relating actual to desired or adjusted employment. To put the point in a somewhat different way, corresponding to any level of output there should be a unique level of adjusted employment.

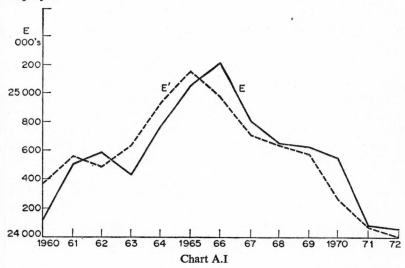

Chart A.I

So long as actual employment is moving in one direction, either faster or slower, adjusted employment will also move on a wiggly curve, getting sometimes nearer and sometimes farther away, but it will not have a break. However, if the actual employment changes direction, then the adjusted curve has a sharp break. This does not, I suspect, correspond to anything real, but merely reflects the fact that the formula is inappropriate for a turning-point.

The remaining question is whether the example illustrated in the diagram is realistic. A glance at the Chart of actual and adjusted employment taken from the C.E.P.G. paper shows it to be a very good first approximation to what happened between 1963 and 1968. Consequently I suspect that the step-up in productivity rates between 1965 and 1966, and the somewhat smaller step-down in productivity rates between 1969 and 1970, are purely arithmetical, originating from the sharpness of the turns in the actual employment curve.

2. A REPLY

T. F. Cripps

In the analysis of Par productivity growth, we make use of two employment variables, defined as follows:

E_t actual employment in March of year t

E'_t desired employment corresponding to output in year t

We assume that these two variables are related by a general formula of the form.

$$E'_t = \lambda E_{t+1} + (1 - \lambda)E_t$$

and we have thus far adopted the value $\lambda = 0.625$.

In his note, Worswick suggests that this model is not satisfactory because it implies that actual employment may continue to rise after a peak in desired employment even when desired employment has fallen below actual employment, and similarly at a lower turning point actual employment may continue to fall after desired employment has risen above actual employment.

The arguments used to support his contention contain a misunderstanding of the definitions of the two variables. In his graphs and discussion he assumes that for any t the values of E_t and E'_t indicate actual and desired employment at the same points in time. But in fact E_t is defined as actual employment in *March* of year t. E'_t is defined as desired employment corresponding to output in year t, and is therefore to be taken as an average of levels of desired employment which may lag behind output and are centred on some point after the middle of the year.

Since neither variable contains information about the pattern of employment (actual or desired) within years, it is not possible to infer directly from our model any proposition about turning points and cross-overs at which actual and desired employment are equal, without making some further assumptions. Worswick's discussion implies the view that actual employment reaches turning points at points of time when desired employment becomes equal to actual employment. This seems a reasonable contention. To explore the point he has raised further, we shall make the assumptions that over a three-year period around turning points the pattern of changes in employment can be represented by a quadratic function of time and that there is a fixed lag between output and desired employment. These assumptions enable us to discover the conditions under which our model can be consistent with the hypothesis that turning points in actual employment occur when desired employment becomes equal to actual employment.

Let x be a continuous measure of time taking an integer value $x=t$ at the beginning of year t. We assume that actual employment, e, and desired employment, e', can be represented by the quadratics

$$e = a + bx + cx^2$$
$$e' = a' + b'x + c'x^2$$

The turning point in actual employment occurs when

$$x = -b/2c$$

Let E_t denote actual employment at a point δ after the beginning of year t (in our analysis, δ was approximately $\frac{1}{4}$).

$$E_t = a + b(t+\delta) + c(t+\delta)^2$$
$$= (a + b\delta + c\delta^2) + (b + 2\delta c)t + ct^2$$

Suppose the lag in adjustment of desired employment to output is μ. Then desired employment corresponding to output in year t is

$$E'_t = \int_{t+\mu}^{t+\mu+1} (a' + b'x + c'x^2)dx$$
$$= (a' + \{\tfrac{1}{2}+\mu\}b' + \{\tfrac{1}{3}+\mu+\mu^2\}c') + (b' + \{1+2\mu\}c')t + c't^2$$

The model $E'_t = \lambda E_{t+1} + (1-\lambda)E_t$

then determines a', b' and c' as functions of a, b, c, λ and μ. Equating coefficients of powers of t,

$$a' + \{\tfrac{1}{2}+\mu\}b' + \{\tfrac{1}{3}+\mu+\mu^2\}c'$$
$$= \lambda(a + \{1+\delta\}b + \{1+\delta\}^2c) + (1-\lambda)(a+b\delta+c\delta^2)$$
$$= (a+b\delta+c\delta^2) + \lambda(b + \{1+2\delta\}c)$$
$$b' + \{1+2\mu\}c' = \lambda(b + 2\{1+\delta\}c) + (1-\lambda)(b+2\delta c)$$
$$= (b+2\delta c) + 2\lambda c$$
$$c' = c$$

Substituting back

$$b' = b - (1+2\mu-2\delta)c + 2\lambda c$$
$$a' = a - (\tfrac{1}{2}+\mu-\delta)b + (\{\tfrac{1}{2}+\mu-\delta\}^2 - \tfrac{1}{12})c + \lambda(b + 2\{\delta-\mu\}c)$$

The condition for actual and desired employment to be equal at the turning point $x = -b/2c$ is

$$a - a' - (b - b')b/2c + (c - c')b^2/4c^2 = 0$$
$$\text{or } \tfrac{1}{2}(1 + 2\mu - 2\delta)b - \lambda b$$
$$(\tfrac{1}{2} + \mu - \delta)b - (\{\tfrac{1}{2} + \mu - \delta\}^2 - \tfrac{1}{12})c - \lambda(b + 2\{\delta - \mu\}c)$$
$$\text{or } 2\{\delta - \mu\}c\lambda = \tfrac{1}{12}\{\tfrac{1}{2} + \mu - \delta\}^2)c$$

$$\text{or } \lambda = \tfrac{1}{2}(1 + \mu - \delta) + \frac{1}{12(\mu - \delta)}$$

When $\delta = \tfrac{1}{4}$ we obtain the following correspondence between μ and λ:

μ	λ
0	0·042
$\frac{1}{12}$	−0·083
$\frac{2}{12}$	−0·542
$\frac{3}{12}$	±0·000
$\frac{4}{12}$	1·542
$\frac{5}{12}$	1·083
$\frac{6}{12}$	0·958
$\frac{7}{12}$	0·917
$\frac{8}{12}$	0·908
$\frac{9}{12}$	0·917

If desired employment is to lead, rather than follow, actual employment, a further condition must be satisfied. For an upper turning point in e we should have $c < 0$.

At the turning point e' should cut e from above:

$$\frac{de'}{dx} = 2c' - \left(\frac{-b}{2c}\right) + b' = b' - b < 0$$

For this condition to be satisfied with $c < 0$,

$$(1 + 2\mu - 2\delta) > 2\lambda$$

$$\text{or } \mu - \delta > \frac{1}{12(\mu - \lambda)}$$

This requires either $\quad \mu < \delta - \sqrt{\tfrac{1}{12}}$

or $\quad\quad\quad\quad \mu > \delta + \sqrt{\tfrac{1}{12}}$

In the example with $\delta = \tfrac{1}{4}$ we must therefore have $\mu > 0·54$ approximately. The only satisfactory values of λ in our mode would therefore be those at the bottom of the table, all greater than 0·9, and implying very long lags in the adjustment of desired employment to output.

Needless to say, the value of λ used in our analysis of Par productivity ($\lambda=0\cdot625$) was not chosen with all these considerations in mind. The above suggests that in order to obtain reasonable estimates without assuming too large a value of μ we should do better to use a zero or negative value for δ. But of course functional forms other than the quadratic need to be considered and allowance must be made for the unsystematic element in the apparent timing of peaks and troughs due to chance fluctuations or special factors. Finally one needs to take some account of the form of the implied adjustment process relating e to e'.

Accepting in the light of the above that the values which we have used for δ ($0\cdot21$) and λ ($0\cdot625$) are not very satisfactory, how much would our results be affected by the use of more appropriate values? We have examined the effect on E' and U' of changing to the values $\delta=-\cdot04$ and $\lambda=0\cdot9$ which are consistent with a lag of between four and six months in the adjustment of desired employment to output.

It is found that U', and consequently the estimates of Par G.D.P., are hardly altered at all. The estimates of E' are shifted up by about 50,000 throughout the period 1962–69 (this happens because we do not use a seasonally adjusted figure for E), and the pattern of changes in E' is scarcely altered. For 1960–62 we now find a smoother path for E' which would imply a less smooth path for Par productivity. In 1969–71 we now find a substantially greater fall in E' which would be sufficient to remove the slight fall in Par productivity growth found previously, but for the fact that 1971 is the only year in which U' is now substantially higher than before, implying a smaller increase in Par G.D.P. in 1970–71. Of course the main evidence for a reduction in Par productivity growth compared with 1965–69 is the substantial fall in U' in 1971–72 which implies a much slower growth of Par G.D.P. since 1969 than we had previously expected.

Appendix B

PARTICIPANTS IN CONFERENCE ON MEDIUM-TERM ASSESSMENTS, APRIL 1973

Professor M. J. Artis, University College of Swansea.

T. S. Barker, Department of Applied Economics, Cambridge.

J. Beath, Department of Applied Economics, Cambridge.

J. A. Bispham, National Institute of Economic and Social Research.

F. T. Blackaby, National Institute of Economic and Social Research.

T. A. Boley, Electricity Council.

M. J. Bramson, National Economic Development Office.

S. Brittan, *The Financial Times*.

Dr. W. R. Buckland, Economist Intelligence Unit.

A. P. Budd, H.M. Treasury.

R. Bull, University of Birmingham.

T. Burns, London Graduate Business School.

Miss Frances Cairncross, *The Observer*.

W. Callaghan, T.U.C.

P. T. Cast, Shell-Mex.

T. F. Cripps, Department of Applied Economics, Cambridge.

R. G. Davis, I.C.I.

J. C. R. Dow, Bank of England.

G. C. Fane, National Institute of Economic and Social Research.

Dermot Glyn, C.B.I.

W. A. H. Godley, Department of Applied Economics, Cambridge.

Professor W. M. Gorman, London School of Economics.

Miss Barbara Holford, Bowater Corporation.

S. F. Hampson, National Economic Development Office.

A. Harris, *The Guardian*.

J. R. S. Homan, National Economic Development Office.

Professor Sir Bryan Hopkin, University College, Cardiff.

R. Husain, National Economic Development Office.

F. W. Hutber, Department of Trade and Industry.

John Hutton, University of York.

D. C. Inkster, Ford Motor Company.

D. Jaques, Courtaulds.

M. A. King, Department of Applied Economics, Cambridge.

R. D. Knott, Hawker Siddeley Group.

A. Lindley, Richard Costain.

J. R. Lomax, H.M. Treasury.

Miss J. Magyari, National Economic Development Office.

R. L. Major, National Institute of Economic and Social Research.

M. Marks, Unilever.

Mrs Caroline Miles, National Economic Development Office.

Tudor Miles, British Steel Corporation.

John Morley, Department of Employment.

P. Mottershead, National Institute of Economic and Social Research.

A. A. McLean, H.M. Treasury.

O. Nankivell, Central Statistical Office.

Miss Nadia O'Reilly, British Gas Corporation.

M. Panic, National Economic Development Office.

M. H. Peseran, Department of Applied Economics, Cambridge.

A. W. A. Peterson, Department of Applied Economics, Cambridge.

S. J. Prais, National Institute of Economic and Social Research.

P. W. Robinson, H.M. Treasury.

C. R. Ross, Cabinet Office.

A. D. Roy, Department of Trade and Industry.

T. M. Rybczynski, Lazard Brothers.

C. T. Saunders, Centre for Contemporary European Studies, University of Sussex.

J. R. Shepherd, H.M. Treasury.

R. Smail, Turner and Newall.

C. T. Taylor, Department of Applied Economics, Cambridge.

A. R. Thatcher, Department of Employment.

K. F. Wallis, London School of Economics.

K. Westaby, British Railways Board.

A. Winters, Department of Applied Economics, Cambridge.

V. H. Woodward, Department of Applied Economics, Cambridge.

G. D. N. Worswick, National Institute of Economic and Social Research.

Index